WEATHER
IN THE WEST

OVERLEAF: *A world of weather as seen by the Apollo 16 astronauts ten thousand miles in space. Though much of the West is clear, cloudiness over the central Rockies portends the birth of a cyclonic storm like the swirling mass pushing into the northeastern states.*

Radiation fog was formed during the night near a tundra lake at the foot of Mount McKinley. It persists because the morning air is still cool in low-lying areas. Higher up, the summit and icy slopes catching the morning sun can be seen through stratus clouds.

JOSEF MUENCH

NATIONAL AERONAUTICS AND SPACE ADMINISTRATION (NASA)

CONTENTS

ACKNOWLEDGMENTS

In the two years I have been involved with this book, I have received information, suggestions, critiques, and encouragement from many people, some friends and acquaintances, some I have never met. To all of them, including those not mentioned here, I am grateful. As consultants, Dr. Margaret Le Mone and Dr. Walter Dabberdt were not only generous in sharing their meteorological know-how but most tolerant of the demands of a tight publishing schedule. I am also indebted to Professor Alistair Fraser of Pennsylvania State University, who offered advice on meteorological optics, and to Dr. John T. Anderson, physicist, who gave technical assistance closer to home. Thanks are due also to Virginia Bonnici and the staff of the Physics Library at Stanford University for their consideration and watchfulness on my behalf whenever a new weather book appeared on the shelves. Among the others who deserve mention are George Pfeiffer III, who suggested the topic and encouraged the work even when progress was slow; Patricia Kollings, who supplied a considerable patience along with her excellent editorial scrutiny; Ed Holm, who gathered photographs from far and wide; and Dannelle Pfeiffer, whose pleasing design and artistic execution of technical ideas have added much to the book. Finally, I thank Fred and Beulah Roda for first showing me what lay west of the mid-continent.

B. R. A.

The editors wish to express appreciation to Henry Lansford, information officer for the National Center for Atmospheric Research, for his counsel at various stages in the preparation of the book; also to Ed Weigel, information officer for the National Weather Service; William West, of the Office of Public Information for the National Oceanic and Atmospheric Administration; and the many others who provided information and photographs.

Material from the following works has been excerpted with permission of the copyright holders: Edward Abbey, *Desert Solitaire* (McGraw-Hill, 1968), reprinted by permission of Harold Matson Co., Inc.; Bernard DeVoto, *Across the Wide Missouri* (Houghton Mifflin, 1947); Robert Frost, "Two Tramps in Mud Time," from *Complete Poems* (Henry Holt, 1949), reprinted by permission of Holt, Rinehart & Winston; F. K. Hare, *The Restless Atmosphere* (Hutchinson & Company, London, 1968); Jacquetta Hawkes, *Man and the Sun* (Random House, 1962); David C. Holmes, *Weather Made Clear* (Sterling Publishing Co., 1965); E. R. Jackman and R. A. Long, *The Oregon Desert* (Caxton Printers, 1964). Also portions of "So Long It's Been Good to Know Yuh" ("Dusty Old Dust"), words and music by Woody Guthrie, TRO—©1940 (renewed 1968), 1950 & 1951, Folkways Music Publishers, Inc., used by permission. Information in the "Guide for Amateur Forecasters" was adapted from material in the Swift Weather Forecaster, Swift Instuments, Inc., San Jose, California.

Varieties of Western Climate

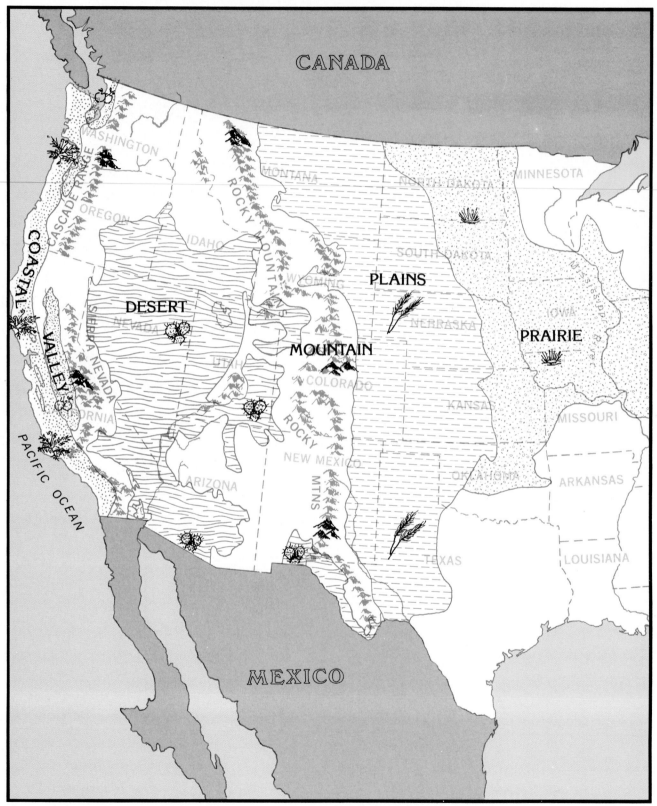

MARY RANDLETT

SPECIAL CONSULTANTS

Walter Dabberdt, Ph.D.
Senior Research Meteorologist
Stanford Research Institute

Margaret LeMone, Ph.D.
Research Meteorologist
National Center for Atmospheric Research (NCAR)

Library of Congress Cataloging in Publication Data

Anderson, Bette Roda, 1945–
  Weather in the West: From the Midcontinent to the Pacific

  (Great West series)
  Includes index.
  1. The West—Climate. 2. Weather. I. Title.

QC984.W38A5   551.6′9′78   73–90799
ISBN 0-910118-48-5
ISBN 0-910118-61-2 de luxe

FIRST EDITION

WEATHER IN THE WEST

From the Midcontinent to the Pacific

by Bette Roda Anderson

GREAT WEST SERIES

AMERICAN WEST PUBLISHING COMPANY
PALO ALTO—CALIFORNIA

Winter snows provide valuable water in semiarid regions like this ranch country near Silver Lake, Oregon.

These stately Arizona yuccas are a living confirmation of nature's adaptability to desert climates.

OVERLEAF: *Wind, a source of energy from weather, has pumped water for more than a century in the West.*

The temperate rain forest—a climate unique to the Olympic Peninsula of Washington. Though short on sunlight, the forest floor is long on available moisture, which exceeds 100 inches annually.

Part 1
EVERYONE'S FAVORITE SUBJECT

It is impossible to determine when weather first became part of daily conversation, for that origin is known only in lore. Concerns about the weather have flourished through time, of course, partly because weather — like life — never stands still.

CHAPTER 1

THE WESTERN ELEMENTS

The many climates of the West ❖ How western weather differs from eastern ❖ Climate and the western landscape ❖ How climate has influenced the history and development of the West

THE WEST HAS BEEN CALLED a land of contrasts, having the highest peaks in the contiguous United States and lowlands far below sea level, austere deserts in the Southwest and luxuriant rain forests along the Northwest coast. Three great mountain ranges—the Rockies, the Sierra Nevada, and the Cascades—divide the West into spectacular canyons, lush valleys, and broad, desolate basins. Beyond them vast stretches of semiarid flatlands known as the Great Plains roll away eastward until they meet the black-earth prairies of the Mississippi Valley.

Climate in the West, like its geography, offers many contrasts, providing all kinds of weather for all kinds of people. The western Olympic Peninsula is perennially wet, while coastal California, similarly located with respect to the ocean, has a dry summer–wet winter, or Mediterranean, climate. Death Valley has virtually no rain, but farther inland the Great Plains receive sufficient rain to provide much of the nation's grain. Although the Southwest is generally dry, the mountains of Arizona and New Mexico supply useful quantities of irrigation water from their winter snowfalls.

Climatic contrasts because of changing topography can also be great enough that sharp differences in vegetation result. In the space of a hundred miles, growth may range from cactus and sagebrush to grassy parks and open timber, or from dense mixed or coniferous forests to alpine pasture. Though the United States offers a rich variety of landscapes, only in the West do such diverse geography and life forms exist so closely together that

they are seen in panorama. And yet, so vast is this country that it may stretch unchanging for hundreds of miles—the Great Salt Lake Desert, the Great Basin, the wheatlands in western Kansas, the forests of the Northwest, or the north-south stretch of the Great Valley of California. It is a land of immensity, of superlatives, and its weather often tends toward extremes.

Climate is weather—the day-to-day state of the atmosphere—aggregated over a long period of time. It is more than an average or prevailing "normal" condition, and it considers extremes as well as means. The word *climate*, from the Greek, means "inclination," referring to the increasing equator-to-pole slope of the earth's surface with respect to the sun's incoming rays, which is partly responsible for the world's climatic zones—an indication that Greek scholars were aware of the sun as a significant influence over climate and weather.

The climates of the lower forty-eight states are more moderate than those of Canada or Mexico. Neither the expansive regions of arctic and subarctic cold, as in Canada, nor the wide extent of tropical forest and tropical desert of Mexico are found in the United States. However, as in Canada and to a lesser extent, Mexico, giant rotating air systems that carry weather across the country, called cyclones and anticyclones, bring invigorating changes in temperature, humidity, and wind.

The strong contrast in climate between the eastern and western halves of the continent has been a significant factor in the migration, settlement, and development of the West. East of the Rockies major climate zones tend

A path through California coastal redwoods, Sequoia sempervirens—*taller, younger, and more graceful than the inland sequoia. They thrive where fogs form and air is moist from the nearby sea.*

DAVID MUENCH

Crater Lake, Oregon. A balance between precipitation, evaporation, and seepage preserves the water at a nearly constant level. With greater annual precipitation the lake would overflow, cutting through its rim.

to run east and west, with the most pronounced differences evident between the extreme northern and southern parts of the country. There is a gradual transition from a land with bitter winters and a short, hectic growing season to one of mild winters or almost perpetual summer.

The West's dominant climatic regions, on the other hand, run north and south, paralleling the Pacific Coast and the major mountain ranges. Unlike the Appalachians, which are no longer high enough to cast a rain shadow, western mountains stand as formidable barriers to hinder, divert, or even block the flow of weather. The Cascades, Sierra Nevada, and Rockies all weaken the influence of warm, moist Pacific air as it moves eastward. The Rockies also block the westward advance of cold polar air as it sweeps south from the Arctic over the

heart of the continent. Thus western climate zones are more sharply defined than eastern, for they are locked in place by the mountains.

Since climate in the West depends so much on its distance from the ocean, it may be useful to consider the successive climate zones from west to east, starting at the shores of the Pacific.

The long, narrow coastal strip—from Vancouver to Los Angeles, and from tideline to the ridge of the coastal ranges—enjoys a "mesothermal" climate born of moist ocean air. In the north winters are mild and summers cool, tempered by the warm Kuroshiro (Japan) Current that flows along the coast as far south as Oregon.

Father south the marine climate gives way to a Mediterranean type with wet winters and hot, dry summers.

The broad valleys that lie between the coastal ranges and the higher mountains—the Cascades in the north and the Sierra in the south—share to some degree the climate of the neighboring coast. However, the ocean's influence is already being dulled by distance and the rain shadow of the coastal mountains; in the valleys rainfall is less abundant and seasonal temperatures are more extreme, trends that become more and more apparent as one moves into the heart of the continent.

Mountain climates, whether in the Sierra and Cascades or in the Rockies, have much in common, all being most influenced by the two factors of altitude and exposure. The clear, less dense air at high altitudes allows bright sunshine and sparkling night skies. This air has less ability to retain heat and radiates heat readily, so nights cool quickly. The earth's atmosphere is colder at higher altitudes, too, so generally lower average temperatures predominate.

Beyond the Sierra lie the vast arid stretches of the Great Basin and the Southwest deserts. Separated from the moisture sources of both the Pacific and the Gulf of Mexico by either distance or mountains or both, they receive only traces of rain. Often when it does come, it comes in sudden cloudbursts, creating flash floods that carry away the precious moisture before it can soak into the soil. Air humidity is, of course, very low in these regions, and summer temperatures are torrid.

The Great Plains share some of the arid features of the deserts to their south and west. They, too, lie in the rain shadow of a great mountain range, in this case the Rockies. However, they also lie in the path of cold polar air that moves south over the midcontinent in winter, and occasionally moist air moving north from the Gulf. Hence they are classified as semiarid, receiving enough annual moisture to support a rich cover of native shortgrass pastureland. The plains are thus a transition zone between the arid West and the humid East. As one travels eastward, they gradually blend into the rain-blessed long-grass prairies of the Midwest.

Together the Great Plains and prairies form one of the largest interior plains in the world. The climate is described as "continental," because it is influenced more by the characteristics of land than of water, lying as it does nearly two thousand miles from either ocean.

IT DOES NOT TAKE AN EXPERT to recognize the climatic differences that exist between the eastern and western United States, because the landscape shouts it out. It is as if the earth were molded according to separate plans, one bent on rounding and gentling the eastern hills, the other incising and roughening the western rock. Climate is so imprinted upon the shape and texture of the land as to prompt experts within the last decade to declare that climate and the erosion it causes are more influential than are mountain-building or human tampering in forming the planet we live on.

An early geomorphologist, G. K. Gilbert, studying the modeling effect of climate upon the face of the land, formulated this law: a landscape is steeper in a dry climate than in a wet one. The reason is simple—a humid landscape is deeply weathered chemically and decomposed in the presence of great quantities of both surface and ground water. The small rock fragments resulting from this deep wastage lie over the top of any bedrock, smoothing irregularities of the landscape by filling pockets and creeping down hillsides. On the other hand, in a dry climate the earth's surface is less active chemically. Mechanical decomposition, aided greatly by variations in temperature, dominates the action, and the coarse debris that is produced cannot lie on the slopes but slips, tumbles, and bounds downslope, and forms talus where it finally rests, leaving the high ramparts clear-cut and rocky bare.

Climate determines what the dominant erosional process will be. For instance, in arid regions running water will create arroyos, whereas wind will produce dunes and deflation basins (bowl-shaped, wind-carved landscapes); in semiarid regions such as the Great Plains, running water is the only dominant erosional process, and it forms long, low outwash plains and fan-shaped deposits. The landform is always distinctive to the individual climate. Sharp, lofty escarpments and meltwater channels gently fingering through the moraines are the imprint of our Ice Age glacial climates. In many places— Yosemite in California and Glacier in Montana—this is the most distinctive landform to meet the eye. Or it is seen curiously in association with the gentler relief produced by modern climatic conditions: rivers too small for their valleys and lake shorelines higher than their present beaches.

It has been estimated that two-thirds of North America

If the Utah climate had been wetter, Bryce Canyon might have been a valley between rounded hills; instead, millennia of heat, cold, and dryness have weathered out spires and pinnacles.

was covered by ice during the great glacial ages, and that the landforms left by the ice may long remain to remind us of their formative era. By one counting, it would take ten million years before the warm climate of today with its dominant erosive force, water, could erase the work of the Ice Ages. Before that new equilibrium between climate and landscape is reached, climate will undoubtedly have changed once more.

THE SUPPOSED AMERICAN PERSONALITY has been attributed to American climates. Science writer Robert Claiborne has speculated that the tempestuous American climate has imbued the settlers from Europe and their children with some of its violence, but concedes that the idea may be far-fetched because when the elements conspire against man, the adversity spurs cooperation, not antagonism. However, climates may contribute to the characteristic pragmatism, empiricism, and show-me attitude of Americans. "The European settlers on the North American frontier," Canadian climatologist F. K.

Hare has noted, "encountered not one climate but many, each with its special hazards."

Colonists learned early the trials of American weather. They discovered the violent terrors of occasional hurricanes, rainfall that was nearly twice the northwest European average, and a growing season shorter and hotter than they were used to. Spring frosts came later and autumn frosts earlier, and they had to estimate the dates of each on scanty information and no experience.

As settlers pushed across the Appalachians from the Atlantic Coast, they at first found little climatic change—summers only slightly hotter and winters slightly colder. But farther west, the rainfall diminished; the forest yielded to long grass, and then the long grass to shortgrass at the point where the humid Midwest prairies turn into the Great Plains. Indefinite and varying with fluctuations of rainfall, this division is of historical, climatological, and biological significance. It is also perhaps the only climatic region in the West not delineated by physical geography.

The grasslands were avoided by the pioneers because

of lack of timber. Instead they settled in the river valleys, where stands of trees lined the stream banks. Some trekked all the way across the arid plains to the forests of the Pacific Northwest, a land that seemed more like their homes back east and necessitated fewer changes in their life-style.

What was to prompt the rapid growth of the prairies was the need for cheap food by the industrial populations of eastern America and Canada. Rails were laid over the Appalachians and across the plains, and the great Iron Horse accelerated growth in the interior. The development of the self-regulating, windmill-driven water pump in 1854 allowed settlers to farm lands away from permanent rivers. And barbed wire, invented in the 1870s (and denounced by ranchers as the scourge of the West), made agriculture a bit easier by reducing interference from range cattle.

When they plowed the virgin sod, pioneers discovered that the soil was extremely fertile, perfect for wheat farming. Acreages were large with few trees, which could be cleared easily so farming could begin immediately. Wheat growing was both efficient and profitable. Practical experience, however, soon taught prairie farmers that in the more humid areas corn did even better than wheat, and wheat farming moved to the drier climate farther west.

On the western Great Plains, where soils resisted the raising of grain, shortgrass and bunchgrass were left to feed cattle or sheep. In the 1880s, as railroads pushed west to Cheyenne and, later, to Denver, these dry grasslands became an American cattle empire. In only a few years, however, the ranges became overdeveloped and overgrazed, and soil erosion began to plague the West. Prices at the stockyards fell as beef glutted the market, and many ranchers were forced to quit.

The last years of the decade brought heavy precipitation, and wheat farmers moved farther west to buy out the destitute ranchers, plow up the shortgrass, and sow wheat. The land was developed as though it was part of the more humid plains farther east. Exploitive farming practices, unmindful of conserving the soil, brought drastic ruin to thousands of farmers when the rainy years were followed by drought. The land, its natural, protective sod shredded by the plow, literally blew away in the dry winds of those years. Immigration stopped, and many of the settlers moved on to the Far West—California. In their exodus, entire towns were abandoned. The final resolution of the battle with climate on the Great Plains was the initiation, around 1900, of dry-farming techniques that took optimal advantage of seasonal rains and allowed grain farming to continue, combined with ranching.

The Mormons, one of the first groups to settle west of the Rockies, broke ground where the streams emerged from the Wasatch Mountains and earned for Utah the name "Cradle of American Irrigation." Water was diverted from City Creek to irrigate corn, potatoes, beans, and other crops. Making the Salt Lake region productive was one of the great accomplishments of western colonization, one that helped to open the intermontane plateaus to settlement and development.

The desolation of the Great Basin desert discouraged the first groups of California-bound immigrants almost as much as the mountains that flanked it. But they continued to stream westward, especially after the discovery of gold in California. As the placers played out, many of the forty-niners turned to farming in the California valleys, learning to cope with the unfamiliar pattern of dry summers and wet winters, and to apply the irrigation techniques employed by Spanish settlers before them.

Similarly, pioneers bound for the Pacific Northwest on the Oregon Trail encountered the arid lands of the Columbia Plateau and the Snake River Plain of southern Idaho. They could never have imagined how, in a little more than a century, irrigation has transformed those desolate wastelands into the highly productive agricultural areas we know today.

AND SO THE CLIMATE of the American West, with all its power, diversity, and extremes, has left its mark—on the land and on the people. The variety, the drama, the panoramic sweep of the western landscape are in many ways the product of the skies above it. And so, too, were the emigrants who came here to settle, braving a climate that often forced upon them the virtues of hard work, frugality, and innovativeness. If they cursed its rigors, they must also have blessed it for bringing forth the ample harvests, vast grazing lands, magnificent stands of timber, and power-charged rivers that have helped to make their children the most prosperous in the history of the world.

CHAPTER 2

LEGEND AND LORE

Weather wisdom of the ancients ❖ Folk forecasting tips from
Indians, seafarers, and others who lived close to the elements—
some as reliable as the official forecast, others purely myth

BECAUSE IT HAS SUCH AN EFFECT on man's activities—
even to determining his very survival—weather
has become richly dressed in lore, the origins of
which are often lost in antiquity.

In ancient China and Japan, Greece and Rome, indeed in all societies that wished to influence the weather, its control was placed in the hands of some venerable or clever member of the group who was believed to be in communication with the gods. Like the shamans of the Arctic or the Zuñi medicine men, they were charged with both prediction and manipulation of the elements. As they sought to understand weather phenomena, for their people's survival and preservation of their own status, they became keen observers of the skies and the world of plants and animals. They noted coincidences and repetitions, became aware of regularities, and hypothesized laws. Thus, though the pronouncements of these elders fell considerably short of the infallibility with which they were accepted by their audiences, they did become increasingly "scientific." Many bits of weather lore had their beginnings in such early predicting.

The weather wisdom of elders and medicine men of American Indian tribes was at times demonstrated by their subtle understanding of the limits of their weather-making powers. The Mandan tribes of the upper Missouri were among those with rainmaking rituals. In times of drought, the medicine men would gather at the medicine lodge and, sitting around its central fire for days, would smoke the medicine pipe and pray to the Great Spirit for rain. As they sat, young men of the village would volunteer to make it rain. Each in turn surmounted the wigwam at successive sunrises and, with bow and arrow in hand, asked, cajoled, threatened, or commanded the clouds to rain. The procedure never failed, for it was continued until rain fell. The fortunate youth who could claim to the tribesmen that it was his arrow that punctured the cloud and brought forth the rain became a medicine man. Those who once succeeded in bringing rain never risked it a second time, saying they would rather give someone else a chance!

Not all rituals worked. A certain clan of the Dakotas claimed the exclusive power and privilege of challenging thunder. To avert impending storms, they whooped and yelled, blew on ceremonial whistles, shot arrows and lances at the menace—all attempts at frightening it away. For one afternoon's attack, they brought their battery of magic to a hilltop from which they hoped to gain the advantage over approaching storm clouds. Almost as if in retaliation, lightning struck one of the warriors and killed him as he was in the act of threatening the clouds. Henceforth this clan concluded that no power of mortals could silence the thunder.

As religions became more sophisticated, the common man began to rely more upon his own observations. Of the weather proverbs still being handed down today, most have come from farmers, sailors, fishermen, and others who lived close to the elements. Often couched in catchy rhymes, these weather wisdoms were easily remembered and passed along orally from one generation to the next.

*This early forecaster believed he could predict weather by a tree frog in a jar of water;
the higher the frog ascended the ladder, the finer tomorrow's weather would be.*

Whoever wished to be a medicine man in the Mandan tribe might prove himself by bringing rain.

BY GEORGE CATLIN, SMITHSONIAN INSTITUTION

Men who took to the sea kept a particularly mindful eye on the weather—for good reason—and sound maxims became mixed with sheer superstition. In the days when sailing ships plied the coastal waters, it was believed that scratching the mizzenmast would beckon a fair wind. Whistling softly, too, would bring a breeze, but take care, for whistling too loud would bring a gale! Curiously, sailors in many parts of the world seem to have associated whistling with the wind.

Aside from the aches and pains brought on by cold or dampness ("A coming storm your shooting corns presage,/And aches will throb, your hollow tooth will rage"), human beings are meagerly endowed with instincts that will alert them to changes in the weather. But some animals, being closer to nature, are still responsive to changes in atmospheric conditions that presage changes in the weather. In its current state, however, our knowledge of animals' weather foresight is a mixture of empirical information and legend.

It is said that, preceding rain showers, animals "feel" bad weather looming ahead. Field mice run in and out of their holes with much commotion; dogs dig holes and eat grass; goats and rams butt one another; horses stretch out their necks and sniff the air; donkeys bray;

oxen and sheep gather together as if to seek shelter (an Apache myth), and pigs grunt and shuffle around. What is not said is that these same activities can actually happen any time.

It is understandable that an animal, living out in the elements, will be restless if it expects a storm. But meteorologists question whether the particular behavior exhibited by animals hours before a storm has anything to do with the weather change, for then the storm may be hundreds of miles distant. For animals to sense the coming change, they would have to be within the air that comes just before the new weather, something that happens only minutes before the storm strikes. And even if there may be subtle early warnings—a gradual change in wind direction, in humidity of the air, in the electrostatic charge of the air, in atmospheric pressure (animals are probably insensitive to this)—these "warning" signals may be false prophets with no storm behind them. Thus, if animal behavior is correlated with weather change, meteorologists consider it a coincidence.

There is a whole flock of weather maxims based on the habits of birds, probably because of their great migrations, which are even now not fully understood. "When birds of long flight hang about home, expect a storm," says one proverb. It is true that some species— Capistrano's famous swallows, for instance—are amazingly punctual, completing their migrations on practically the same date every year. By expert reckoning, the occasional delays of a few days in either direction are caused by local weather conditions en route—a downpour, a blizzard, a tornado—or more particularly the supply of food, but not by long-range meteorological conditions.

Other claims of bird prognostications are equally fantastic, such as: "Gulls will soar aloft and, circling around, utter shrill cries before a storm"; "Loud and long singing of robins denotes rain"; "If sea fowls retire to the shore or marshes, a storm is approaching"; or "When chimney swallows circle and call, they speak of rain" (Zuñi).

Swallows flying low are supposed to foretell rain, and flying high, fair weather. On first consideration, this might seem founded in fact. The birds fly high to find insects in air currents rising over heated ground on sunny days, and they fly low on cloudy days before a storm, when there is insufficient sunshine to create strong up-

A doubtful prophet: the ground hog's seeing his shadow has little to do with the coming of spring.

Thor, the god of storm and thunder, wielded a hammer against demons but treated man with benevolence.

drafts. However, the observer on the ground can be fooled on those occasions when the strong air currents that carry the swallows aloft ultimately result in rain and thunderstorms.

In their watery environments fish would seem insulated from weather's influence, and indeed biologists who have looked for correlations between fish catches and the weather have found none. Nevertheless, many fishermen still believe that their quarry refuses to take a lure before a storm, preferring to stay just under the surface ready to snap at the many insects skimming the water's surface. Falling atmospheric pressure, by lowering the oxygen content of the water, may encourage fish to rise, but what keeps them from taking the bait is not clear.

Plants, like animals, respond to the gentle tug of weather and its changes because their life cycle—budding, leafing, flowering, fruiting—depends upon atmospheric conditions. Photoperiodism, which describes when a plant flowers in terms of varying length of the night, is never the same between flower types. Thus lilies open at Easter, and poinsettias at Christmas; crocuses bloom in spring, petunias in summer, and asters in fall, each to its season and photo period. If weather takes no dramatic

turns, farmers can predict harvest dates from the growth condition of a crop. Some people believe that when the onion grows thick skins, winter will be hard. Actually thick- or thin-skinned onions grow in direct relation to the amount of heat and dryness they endure during the growth period, not because of weather still to come.

Folklore predicts that rain is in the offing when daisies and milkweed close up. Similarly, the leaves of the artichoke and the scales of the pine cone are said to open in dry weather and close in damp. Plants are indeed sensitive to their immediate microclimates, and species such as these do respond to increased humidity by closing in on themselves. However, they are not very dependable rainy weather indicators, since humidity often becomes heavy without a sign of precipitation.

No proverb based on weather observation has ever been infallible, but there are two maxims that come close to being indisputably true: "All signs fail in dry weather," and "In wet weather it rains without half trying." The first explains that, for rain to fall during a drought, weather-making activity has to be inordinately vigorous; the second rejoins the nearly saturated air needs little impetus to start a downpour. As both sayings imply, weather goes in spells, with one type reigning until it is overtaken. In a sense these proverbs succeed for the same reason as the Indians who harassed the clouds until it rained.

Sometimes the appearance of the sky barely hints at the weather just ahead, and sometimes it's a sure clue, but the visible signals of change loom large in weather wisdoms. For instance, the size, shape, and color of the clouds depend upon the humidity, temperature, and motion of the air. Big, puffy cumulus clouds that billow high overhead on a summer's day are an assurance of fine weather ahead, since such clouds do not hold enough moisture to produce much rain or snow. Thus: "The higher the clouds [cumulus], the finer the weather." High and veil-like cirrus clouds carry news of a coming storm: "Trace in the sky the painter's brush, / The winds around you soon will rush." In mountain country after the peaks disappear, the legends say, watch out: "When Breedon Hill puts on his hat, / Ye men of the vale beware of that." More universally, "When the clouds are upon the hills, / They'll come down by the mills."

SINCE BIBLICAL TIMES, morning and evening sky colors have been used to forecast the weather. Jesus said to the Pharisees and Sadducees, "When it is evening you say, It will be fair weather, for the sky is red. And in the morning, It will be stormy today, for the sky is red and has a gloomy and threatening look." What validity sky colors have as predictors relies on the generally eastward movement of weather systems. A red (or golden) sky at night presages clear weather, because it tells of dust particles in dry air—a combination indicating that the air temperature has not fallen below the point at which moisture, condensing onto the dust, forms rain. A leaden evening sky reveals that the dust particles have become loaded with moisture, favoring rain. A red sky at morning happens when the dry weather is to the east and a storm may be moving in from the west. If the evening sky is red, the dry weather is approaching. Thus, in the proverb: "Sky red in the morning / Is a sailor's sure warning; / Sky red at night / Is the sailor's delight."

A related saying looks to the rainbow rather than the rising or setting sun: "Rainbow at night [evening], shepherd's delight; / Rainbow in morning, shepherds take warning." In the temperate zones, where the prevailing wind is from the west, nearly all showers move

from west to east. Since the rainbow always appears on the opposite side of the observer from the sun, it predicts fair weather when seen at sunset, for it is forming on the rear of the storm, and foul weather at sunrise, for then the storm is in the west and drawing near.

The signs of approaching rain are numerous, but there are few weather wisdoms telling of the rain itself. One— "Rain long foretold, long last; / Short notice, soon past" —is fairly reliable. The gradual accumulation of clouds over a day or two marks a widespread storm bringing several hours of rain. But the hurried gathering and lowering of clouds denotes a local storm that will quickly pass.

Many proverbs foretell rain and other bad weather from the appearance of solar and lunar halos and coronas. As they are common to certain types of clouds that precede a storm, they are usually well-founded sayings. "The moon with a circle brings water in her beak" and "When the sun is in his house, it will rain soon" (Zuñi)— both refer to the halo phenomenon, an arc or circle of relatively large diameter produced by refraction of light and commonly seen in veils of cirrus clouds, emissaries of stormy weather (see chapter 9). The number of stars seen within a halo about the moon is said to be the number of days before the next storm. Although its accuracy may be questioned, this belief is based on fact, since a distant storm will have thin, high cloudiness through which many stars are likely to shine, and the clouds from a storm close at hand may obscure all but the moon.

The corona, a small, colored ring around the sun or the moon, is caused by diffraction—the bending of light at the boundary of an object, in this case water droplets. It gives its message in another way: the larger the droplets, the smaller the corona, and the closer the storm. An enlarging corona implies evaporation of water droplets and clearing skies.

The moon creates a slight tidal pull on the earth, but it does not have the active influence on the atmosphere that many weather proverbs would imply. However, its appearance does depend on the clear or cloudy state of the earth's atmosphere, so the moon has become a sometimes credible weather prophet. "Clear moon, / Frost soon" and "Moonlit nights have the heaviest frosts" are two ways of saying that on the clearest nights, those when the moon is most easily seen, the cooling of the earth by radiation is at its greatest and thus most

Bulging-cheeked cherubs have traditionally symbolized the winds, particularly on mariners' charts, suggesting that their origins are divine. In ancient times some people thought instead that winds arose in caves.

likely to condense moisture in the form of dew or frost.

One of the more weather-related moon sayings is "Sharp horns do threaten windy weather." In clear air otherwise imperceptible temperature differences in the earth's atmosphere may cause a fuzzy outline of the moon. But when the air is mixed, as by high elevation winds, the moon's horns are sharp. As the proverb states, one then expects the upper level winds to dip down to the earth's surface.

EVERY WIND HAS ITS WEATHER," as Francis Bacon put it. Indeed, wind directions are responsible for most local weather signs. The south wind brings warmth, the north wind cold; the east wind in the middle latitudes signals the approach of a storm, and the west wind shows that the storm has passed to the east. According to Texas and Southwest proverbs, when the wind shifts and is blowing strongly during a drought, you can expect rain. Also in Texas, when brisk winds from the south continue for a day or more, one can expect a "norther" (see chapter 14); and when, during a storm, the wind shifts from east to west, clearing weather will follow soon.

Even as technological advances continue to improve the accuracy of scientific weather prediction, weather wisdoms are likely to remain the source of tomorrow's weather information for a great many people. The more reliable ones can serve as a useful bridge between the weatherman's general forecast and the individual's local weather, which they best describe.

CHAPTER 3

CYCLES OF CHANGE

The familiar rhythms of day and night, summer and winter ❖
Long-term cycles, measured in millions of years ❖
Microclimates—sometimes sharp differences within a small space

CHANGE IS THE ESSENCE OF WEATHER. It is also the raison d'être for weathermen, weather prognostication, and weather in the news. If atmospheric conditions stood still, man's interest in the weather might never have developed. The year's gamut of weather may have days that are rainy or clear, hot or cold or comfortable, windy or still, dry or humid, or marked by blizzards, drought, tornadoes, hail, or other excesses of nature. Collectively, the progeny of the atmosphere bring limitless variety.

Weather is the specific condition of temperature, humidity, wind, atmospheric pressure, and precipitation in a given place at a given time, and is in a constant state of change. *Climate*, on the other hand, describes the typical state of these variables over long periods and often for a wider geographic area; because climate is compounded of averages, the differences that create change tend to disappear. Of course, climate does change. But whereas sweeping changes in the weather can occur in minutes, similar fluctuations in climate take tens of thousands of years. Even minor climatic changes are rarely detectable in a single life span.

Statistics on average weather of a locality belie its daily changes and tell one little about the true atmospheric character of the place. The annual temperature of Havre, Montana, for example, is a brisk 42° F. Since most plants require temperatures in excess of about 43° F. for growth, the region's plentiful grasslands would seem to defy nature. The explanation lies in the wide seasonal variations that include summer highs in the eighties to offset subzero winter lows. The average also does not indicate temperature extremes of —50° F. in winter and 100° F. in summer, or freezing temperatures as late as May or as early as September. Though the average monthly precipitation is about one inch, some months may have two, while others have only one-half. Three "average" months' rain can fall in a single day. That will-o'-the-wisp weather is contemptuous of averages.

Weather is both rhythmic and random. Its daily and annual cycles, though distinctive in themselves, are to some degree predictable. But they have superimposed on them an uncertainty by which each day and each year differs from the preceding one. The eleven-year sunspot cycle further influences the weather in a general way, but its gradual effect is almost obscured by the daily and seasonal flux.

Randomness pervades the weather picture. Where, when, and whether a thunderstorm brings rain is a matter of chance. Weathermen can predict only its probability in a particular area, not all of the specifics. How much snow a storm will drop, the date of the winter's first cold wave, the path of the next cyclone to swing out of the Gulf of Alaska, and a plethora of other details of atmospheric motion can only be described in terms of probability. So it is also with most local weather events. Weather forecasts can be very reliable, but their accuracy depends on the amount of detail and the length of time covered in the forecast. The passing of each day's weather establishes unique atmospheric conditions that provide the following day with completely original weather.

Climate, like weather, changes. Less than 100,000 years ago, rivers of ice like this one in the Alaska Range snaked through the Cascades, Rockies, and Sierra Nevada.

A moment in the daily cycle: sunset. The high clouds may indicate an approaching storm, one of many reasons why weather of the day to come will differ from that of the day past.

Weather is created in an atmosphere that follows the laws of physics; man simply has not yet found the way to solve all of nature's equations. Given the number, diversity, and immensity of the phenomena that go into the making of weather at any moment at any place, however, meteorologists have come to understand weather processes surprisingly well. With the help of increasingly sophisticated instruments for measuring the important variables, such as atmospheric pressure, humidity, and temperature, and with giant computers to digest the resulting mass of data, they are steadily improving the accuracy of their predictions.

Each twenty-four hours, as the earth makes one complete rotation about its axis, a myriad of weather changes come full circle. The most prominent is the progression from the warmth of the day to the chill of the night, quite clearly related to the position of the sun in the sky. Every morning pronounced local winds blow up valleys and mountain slopes, and sweep onshore from the Pacific; after evening falls, they reverse—again, slavishly subject to the presence or absence of solar heat.

The regularity of the daily cycle may be interrupted by storms, whose winds and temperatures are determined by other influences. In warm months, thunderstorms may participate in daily weather of many inland areas. Morning sunlight heats the ground, churning the atmosphere almost like a pot of boiling water, and carrying surface air high into the cooler reaches of the atmosphere, where its moisture condenses into thunderheads. Rain may be expected to fall by afternoon or evening, cooling the land; the chance of a thunderstorm usually diminishes before dawn renews the cycle.

Noticeable, but small, weather changes abound in the course of a day. A cloud-cast shadow cools the ground, promoting breezes and local coastal fog. Heated ground releases whirling dust devils and columns of rising warm air crowned with puffy cumulus clouds. Moisture from an afternoon shower may foster fog under clearing night skies. The changes are local, but their diversity is universal.

Annual weather cycles, like daily cycles, are caused by

KEITH GUNNAR

A record of the annual cycle: bands of winter snow and summer dust alternating in glacial ice.

Colorado—atmospheric conditions are inadequate for the growth of another for a long period of time; then it may be substantially more than seven days before another cyclone passes. Come summer, cyclonic storms are less pervasive, and locally spawned daily thundershowers become more frequent.

All of the weather variations discussed so far are changes over time. There are also changes over space. A good example is the variation between microclimates—small regions whose climates differ from their surroundings because of highly local factors. Beside a highway in the desert, for example, a lush riparian growth may flourish, watered by runoff or rainfall from the nearby pavement, while only a few feet away is the decidedly different community of the creosote-bush plain. Deserts are good places to observe these small climate worlds, because where vegetation is so sparse, variations are easy to see. From a hill overlooking the sweep of desert terrain, the eye can follow the course of a wash by the tree growth along it, the plant life responding to a distinctly cooler, moister zone in the canyon.

Microclimates are established whenever a wall is built to keep wind off a house, whenever a tree is planted to provide shade. All living things are aware of the climatological nuance. A lizard on a rock slab in the sun is perfectly content to soak up the heat of the day. A soft-bodied invertebrate would die there but can hide its vulnerability under a few nearby leaves, thus surviving. Just a few feet under the surface, burrowing animals find a cool, moist hideout in which they can be oblivious to summer and winter, night and day.

In deserts temperature changes dramatically with increasing height above the surface of the land. At dawn ground temperature is at its lowest point of the day, perhaps 85° F., while just five feet above the ground temperatures are five degrees warmer. In effect, there is a ground-level temperature inversion. By eight o'clock in the morning, conditions are reversed; the surface is hotter than the air one foot above it. By noon the temperature at ground level hits its peak, now perhaps twenty degrees warmer than the air, or about 125° F. Air temperature continues to rise, hitting its peak about three in the afternoon; meanwhile surface temperature has been steadily dropping. By eight in the evening the surface is again cooler than the air and the ground-level inversion is reestablished.

a periodic variation in the amount of sunshine reaching the earth's surface, and its effects are global. The world's moving weather systems bring each geographical region its seasonal weather; where and how they are spawned are at the command of the seasonal cycle. When people say that the weather is "seasonal," they mean that it is average for the time of year. Just as averages tell little about the actual daily weather, however, they also present an inadequate picture of weather in any given season. The dates of arrival of the first seasonal weather are variable. Although it is the position of the earth in relation to the sun that programs seasons, many modifying factors, including complicated interactions between weather systems, intervene and render accurate predictions difficult. (Seasons are described in more detail in chapter 8.)

Winter weather in the West is dominated by the erratic behavior of cyclonic storms, which on an average, seem to move through a given place once every four to seven days. Sometimes, however, after a cyclone has left its zone of formation—such as the lee of the Rockies in

*Life zones reflect how climate changes with altitude. On the east side of the Sierra Nevada,
sagebrush desert gives way to forest in the cooler, rainier climate of higher elevations.*

Plants and animals living on the ground and in the shallow life layer of air near it are thus severely stressed by temperature fluctuations that can be as much as forty degrees in a single day. Elsewhere this amount of change might be experienced only in an entire year of climatic variation. Plants and animals respond to these local, as opposed to prevailing, climate conditions. Thus, the great range of microclimates within a given climate makes possible a wide variety of vegetation, as well as a diverse community of animal life.

A gardener becomes aware of inherent microclimates on his patch of ground. He knows that loose, dry soil warms up during the day but rapidly gives up its acquired heat at night. Firm, unturned soil warms less but retains its heat at night. Germination of seeds proceeds well in the warmth of tilled soil, but after sundown the seedlings could better use the warmth of a firm soil. The condition is similar to the larger world relationships that exist between the continent and the sea: the land, like open soil, warms quickly and cools rapidly; the sea, like

TEMPERATURES OF THE PAST

YEARS AGO	ERA	PERIOD	EPOCH	AVERAGE TEMPERATURE, °F., FOR THE NORTHERN LATITUDES
				20° 30° 40° 50° 60°
15,000–	Cenozoic	Quaternary	Recent	
			Pleistocene (Ice Age)	
3,000,000–			Pliocene	
13,000,000–		Tertiary	Miocene	
25,000,000–			Oligocene	
36,000,000–			Eocene	
58,000,000–			Paleocene	
63,000,000–	Mesozoic	Cretaceous		
135,000,000–		Jurassic		
180,000,000–		Triassic		
230,000,000–	Paleozoic	Permian		
280,000,000–		Pennsylvanian		
310,000,000–		Mississippian		
340,000,000–		Devonian		
400,000,000–		Silurian		
430,000,000–		Ordovician		
500,000,000–		Cambrian		
570,000,000–		Precambrian		

Average temperature (north of 40° N latitude) has varied through geologic time and presently is at one of its cooler extremes. A time scale that emphasizes recent eras shows that in the last 3 million years the earth has been an average of twenty degrees cooler than in most of its known history.

After the work of C. E. P. Brooks, as expressed by John Oliver

Drought may have driven the ancient Anasazi from their cliffside homes in Arizona's Canyon de Chelly.

compact or very damp soil, is slow to warm and to cool. Because the sensitivity of vegetation to inhospitable climate is a fine indicator of both unseasonal and abnormal conditions, it appears that vegetation provides as good a record of recent climate change as any measure available.

M AN HAS NEVER KNOWN a "normal" climate in his geologically brief existence on earth. Having lived only in the climatic violence of a diminishing ice age, he has not experienced the long times of genial climatic uniformity that geologists call normal, though such conditions have prevailed during most of the existence of the earth.

Geologists know that past climates were different from today's because of the fossil record written in the rocks. Coal beds found in the Antarctic show that tropical and semitropical plants and animals once flourished in polar regions. Layers of glacial debris, representing four advances of glacial ice in the most recent glacial episode, have been found in the Pacific Northwest. Large lakes

once existed throughout the arid Great Basin and other parts of the West. Tree rings present strong evidence for climatic shifts in the last two thousand years. Archeological data suggest that there was a drought about A.D. 1300, which drove cliff dwellers from Mesa Verde, Colorado. Climatic change has been significant in the past, is a part of the present, and probably will continue in the future.

During most of geologic time, the climate has been milder than it is today. Precipitation was generally lighter, and less of it fell as snow or hail; storms were less frequent; the summer and winter seasons were more nearly alike; and the contrasts between seacoasts and continental interior, and between high and low latitudes were not so marked.

Geologists have demonstrated that cycles on the order of millions of years have influenced the earth's weather. For the most part temperatures in each cycle were higher than they are now. Four widely separated glacial episodes interrupted these warm periods, with glacial ice advancing from the polar zones into the temperate latitudes. In the last glacial advance, there were four

This map shows the maximum extent of glaciers during the Ice Age. Subarctic chill, today found only north of the Canadian border, once reached all the way to the Gulf of California. As the ice receded, the western United States warmed to its present temperate climate. (Isolated mountain glaciers in the Rockies, Cascades, and Sierra, which did not adjoin the great ice sheet, are not shown here.)

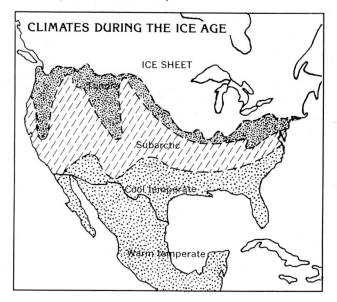

CLIMATES DURING THE ICE AGE

ICE SHEET

Subarctic

Cool temperate

Warm temperate

separate waves of ice, the last of which shrank away from northern North America and Europe about ten thousand years ago. The earth has not yet recovered from this ice age, some climatologists believe, and present climates are actually a part of the worldwide period of temporary glacial retreat.

The succession of past climates was not haphazard but followed an ordered sequence, as one can see from the approximate times of the great glaciations. The first of the four major ice ages cannot be dated precisely, but one estimate places its beginning between 700 and 800 million years ago. Subsequent glaciations began over 570 million years ago, just before Cambrian time; 280 million years ago, the end of the Carboniferous period; and recently, in the Quaternary, three million years ago. So, there appears to be a glaciation cycle about 250 million years long. Between these times of glacial stress, worldwide climate was generally genial. Two noteworthy but relatively minor exceptions occurred— one in Silurian time, the other from the Cretaceous to the early Eocene times—producing local valley glaciers and sometimes piedmont ice. Their presence suggests that superimposed on the long cycle is a shorter cycle of glaciation.

The balance between normal and glacial climates is extremely delicate. A prolonged drop in average polar temperatures to only five degrees below the freezing point of ocean water could cause growth in polar ice, which in turn, because the ice itself promotes further cooling, might eventually result in a drop of fifty degrees in polar winter temperatures and a return of glacial climates. On the other hand, a two-degree rise in present world temperatures would be enough to clear ice from the polar seas, raising the surface of the oceans and causing widespread coastal flooding. Such temperature changes, however, are not so trivial as they may seem. For one thing, to change the average temperature of the world ocean (all 317 million cubic miles of it) would require an exchange of tremendous amounts of heat energy. Furthermore, these new temperatures would need to be sustained many years to nudge world climate one way or the other.

Yet, difficult though the process is, earth is unique among planets of the solar system in that it *has* experienced climatic fluctuations both cold and warm. Only the earth has the combined features of extensive

oceans of water and polar temperatures not far below freezing. The change of state between liquid and solid makes world climatic fluctuations possible. A swing from having a polar ice cap to not having one would spell a change from glacial to "normal" climates for the entire earth. Without an ice cap the surface of the oceans would grow, and their moderating marine influence would grow with them. If, however, the polar ice cap were to increase in size, cold polar temperatures would predominate. In fact, ice resembles the land surface, and with its spread the continents effectively increase both their area and their influence on the weather.

The reasons advanced for climatic change are many, but all are hypothetical. There are two kinds of theories, those that relate such changes to extraterrestrial sources and those that connect them with happenings on the earth. However, it seems evident that from the retreat of the glaciers ten thousand years ago to the present, climatic variations could not have been caused by changes in the relative positions of the earth and the sun, or of poles, land masses, and oceans, for these differ little now from then.

*Extinct arctic-dwelling woolly mammoths
roamed the United States during the Ice Ages.*

CAVES

Nowhere on the face of the earth is the weather unchanging. But below the surface, in caves, are worlds without seasons, where temperature changes only one or two degrees. It is dark, the air may have over 90 percent humidity, there is usually no wind beyond a slight draft—and warmth, cold, rain, and drought have no meaning. Neither does time. If a cave ages, it may collapse and be destroyed by the simple agent of running water. But a dry cave, like Carlsbad, pictured here, may survive thousands of years.

Totally cave-dwelling animals live in sharp contrast to their surface relatives. They have no breeding season and no daily routine. Many are sightless and colorless; in the dark such attributes are unimportant to species survival. As if to compensate, many develop touch organs. Insects, for example, may have long, sensitive legs instead of wings. There is no need to hurry, for in the typically 40° to 60° F. temperatures, life is slow and therefore long.

Many cave animals could not go back to the surface except by the path they took to the cave—long evolution. Taking them from their nether world would be fatal, for most would expire at the first breath of change.

JOSEF MUENCH

One of the first extraterrestrial sources suspected (in the 1920s) of perpetrating climatic change was the sun. A warming sun would be capable of producing increased evaporation at the Equator, where such an effect would be strongest and most easily noted. The temperature contrast between Equator and poles would be heightened, and mid-latitude storms would be more intense. Cloudiness and precipitation there and in the polar zones would increase, and the clouds, by shading the earth, would keep polar temperatures low. If they remained low, snow and ice would accumulate, and another ice age would be forthcoming. So far as can be determined, however, the heat from the sun has been constant throughout time.

The amount of energy reaching the earth's surface, however, has varied. After the 1883 eruption of the volcano Krakatoa in the Pacific, the reflectivity (*albedo*) of the earth's atmosphere increased suddenly because the normal amount of solar energy could not penetrate the new layer of dust in the stratosphere. Less heat reached the earth's surface, and mean temperatures echoed this reduction until after the turn of the century. Some scientists have believed glacial periods of the past followed volcanic activity and mountain building, because of the additional sun-screening dust in the atmosphere. More recently, concern is being voiced that dust from modern industrialized civilizations may be having a similar effect. Increased atmospheric haze from air pollution—including condensation trails from stratospheric aircraft—acts as a sun shade, reflecting light back into space.

With many competing theories to explain climatic change, the subject continues to be one of sharp controversy among scientists. Regardless of the theories, evidence of climatic change in the last two thousand years suggests that it tends to be gradual rather than cataclysmic, and there is reason to expect that any changes in the future will provide ample time for man to adapt.

Part 2
THE WEATHER MACHINE

*Of all the ingredients that combine to make weather, sun
is the sultan, the only energy source powerful enough
to cause the endless variety of our skies. Nearly
everything relates eventually to it: clouds, winds,
precipitation patterns around the globe — everything except the
seasons; they ebb and flow because of a simple accident
of nature that the earth is tilted first toward then
away from the sun.*

CHAPTER 4

THE OMNIPOTENT SUN

The power plant of the weather machine—source of heat and light
❖ The Dust Bowl ❖ Sunspots and their effect on weather ❖
The atmospheric screens that hold the sun's power in check

I N TWENTIETH-CENTURY CITIES—heated by petroleum, lit by electricity, fed from supermarket shelves—it is easy to take the sun for granted. But farmers and others who still live close to nature know, as simpler societies have known for thousands of years, that the sun more than any other factor determines the quality of life on earth. Indeed, it determines whether there is life at all. It lights; it warms; it carries water from ocean reservoirs to the thirsty land; it shares its vast energy, through photosynthesis, with all living things. It is our clock and our calendar, the arbiter of day and night, summer and winter. And it does all these things with a moderation and regularity that turn its potentially devastating power into man's greatest boon. An eloquent way to appreciate the value of the sun is to imagine the earth without it.

Nonetheless, there are times when even wise men are understandably tempted to curse this, their greatest friend. Such a day was July 9, 1860. Throughout the heart of the Great Plains, corn, wheat, cattle, and people baked under a fiery sun. The editor of the Lawrence, Kansas, *Republican* reported: "During the past week the weather has been hotter than we have ever known it before in Kansas. Last Monday . . . was a terrible day. The wind blew a gale from the south, and was as hot as though directly from the mouth of a blazing furnace. Thermometers exposed to it in the shade ran up to 115° F." Inferno-like temperatures scorched Topeka, Leavenworth, Kansas City, Wichita. The official highs will never be known, for it was not until the 1880s that formal U.S. weather records were established.

Some forty-one years after that Kansas "Hot Blast," in 1901, another long, hot summer came to the Great Plains. During the month of July, Kansas registered ninety-degree or higher temperatures every day, with 100° F. or above for nine consecutive days and an official peak of 112° F. at Phillipsburg, Kansas.

An even longer and more disastrous cycle of drought and heat enveloped the Great Plains in the 1930s. Millions of acres of America's heartland became a vast waste referred to all too accurately as the "dust bowl." As farms became worthless, desperate men gathered together their families and a few belongings, and started on a migration to other places—most of them to that hoped-for Garden of Eden, California. John Steinbeck wrote of these emigrants in *The Grapes of Wrath*, and folk singer Woody Guthrie recalled the effect on his own hard-pressed people:

A dust storm hit and it hit like thunder,
It dusted us over, it dusted us under,
It blocked out the traffic, it blocked out the sun,
And straight for home all the people did run singing:
So long, it's been good to know you. . . .

It is likely that farmers trapped by such unrelenting drought stood in the middle of their parched fields and scanned the horizon in search of the storm that would block the sun, settle the dust, and bring life to their crops. But nature was not the sole villain in the dust bowl—indeed perhaps only the catalyst. Man's massive

Without the sun there would be no light, no heat, and no clouds to bring rain; lacking these, the earth would be devoid of life.

Unrelenting heat and too little rain were the direct causes of Dust Bowl scenes such as this in South Dakota,
but particles emitted by the sun may have contributed to the shift to a drier climate.

annual plow-ups of the earth, his determination to extract more from the land than it could offer, his stubborn belief in the convenient fiction that "rain follows the plow"—all combined with natural weather changes to turn what had been rich and fertile soil into an unproductive wasteland.

No other single factor affects the earth's weather as much as the sun. In the short days of winter, the sun's oblique rays graze American latitudes delivering about one-third the radiation received in the longer days of summer, when the sun's rays approach the vertical. The sun's annual ritual is constant, its position in the sky repeating the same pattern each year. If the sun alone determined weather, it too would repeat its pattern each year. But this is far from so. Winters can range from mild to extremely cold, and summers from cool to excessively hot. Though the sun's simple seasonal cycle dominates the earth's weather, there must obviously be other factors as well.

To explain the periodic droughts that plague the Great Plains, Walter Orr Roberts, formerly director of the National Center for Atmospheric Research and more recently president emeritus of the University Corporation for Atmospheric Research, has been a major proponent of the theory that events on the surface of the sun may have been one of the factors that brought on the dust bowl years. Scientists know that the sun emits "streams of particles of its own substance," as well as light and heat. Some of the particles, sometimes called *corpuscles*, bombard the earth's atmosphere, creating the spectacular aurora borealis, or northern lights, and causing magnetic storms, disturbances in the earth's magnetic field. "Geomagnetic records show," Roberts says, "that the dust bowl period of the 1930s was a period of magnetic storms causing blackouts in radio communication and noise on telephone cables." When there is great solar activity, which astronomers can detect by dark spots on the surface of the sun, billions of corpuscles flare out from the sunspot areas.

The earliest recording of sunspots was by the Chinese,

GRANT HEILMAN

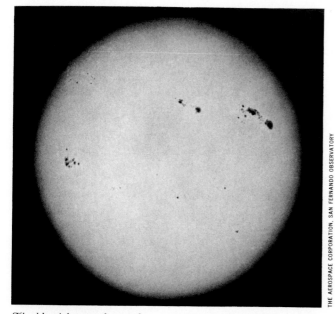

The blemishes on the sun here are sunspots, dark only by comparison to their surroundings. Scientists believe sunspots to be part of "solar weather," much as thunderstorms are part of earth weather.

who thought they were birds flying over the sun. Galileo, who was the first man to observe this phenomenon through a telescope, surmised that clouds were hovering over the solar atmosphere. It is now known that sunspots are calm, relatively cool islands in the solar atmosphere. During periods of extremely intense activity, they extend as much as 25,000 miles in diameter and can be seen with the naked eye (which must be protected by a solar filter). Viewed this way, sunspots appear to be dark holes in the sun; but when observed through a telescope, they reveal more intricate detail, looking to one astronomer like "rice grains floating in a bowl of soup."

Evidence does exist to show a relationship between sunspots and weather over long periods of time, thanks in large part to research performed early in this century by the late Andrew E. Douglass, an astronomer at the University of Arizona. Professor Douglass began with the known fact that the annual rings in the cross section of a tree trunk form a substantially accurate record of the weather during its years of growth. A thick or wide ring indicates good growing conditions, probably copious rainfall and warm temperatures, while a series of thin or narrow rings can be evidence of an extensive period of meager precipitation.

Douglass avoided drawing conclusions from a group of

trees growing in a single area, since adverse conditions other than weather might have existed. Therefore he collected cross sections of numerous varieties of trees, including ponderosa pine from Arizona, Douglas fir from Oregon, sequoia from California, and other conifers from throughout the world. Wherever possible, he used specimens from living trees, whose growth rings he could relate to weather records during the lifetime of the tree. With the cooperation of the American Museum of Natural History and the National Geographic Society, Douglass also obtained preserved timbers and charcoal remnants at archeological sites in New Mexico, Utah, Colorado, Arizona, and Wyoming. From the tree rings of a petrified sequoia in Yellowstone National Park, he inferred that sunspot cycles existed fifty million years ago.

After making extensive studies of tree growth and rainfall—and taking into account other variables—Douglass verified that weather followed a pattern directly related to an eleven-year sunspot cycle. Whereas Roberts believes that drought is correlated with high sunspot activity, Douglass found that drought conditions existed during periods of a quiescent sun. Current speculation is that sunspots do not directly cause drought years or wet years, but instead cause a shift in weather patterns such

Width variations of growth rings in this tree sample provide clues to past weather patterns.

The McMath Solar Telescope, a modern temple to the sun at Kitt Peak National Observatory in Arizona, is the world's largest telescope designed specifically to observe the sun.

that raininess or drought temporarily predominate in some areas.

By 1929 Douglass had not only verified that a relationship exists between the sun and weather, but he had also been able to pinpoint, by the analysis of wood samples, the dates when nearly forty prehistoric southwestern communities had flourished. Largely through his efforts, southwestern archeology is the most precisely dated in the world.

The Douglass exhibit in the Arizona State Museum at Tucson includes a photograph showing a continuous record of tree rings, pieced together from individual cross sections of trees. Gathered by this remarkable dendrochronologist over half a century, they date all the way back to A.D. 11.

UNTIL THE DAWN OF THE ATOMIC AGE in the early 1940s, man had virtually no knowledge of the means by which the sun sustained itself in a state of perpetual combustion. The English journalist and author G. K. Chesterton marveled that man could live fearlessly with a light in the sky so bright that it might blind him if he

In the viewing room of the McMath Solar Telescope, astronomers study the sun's 33-inch image.

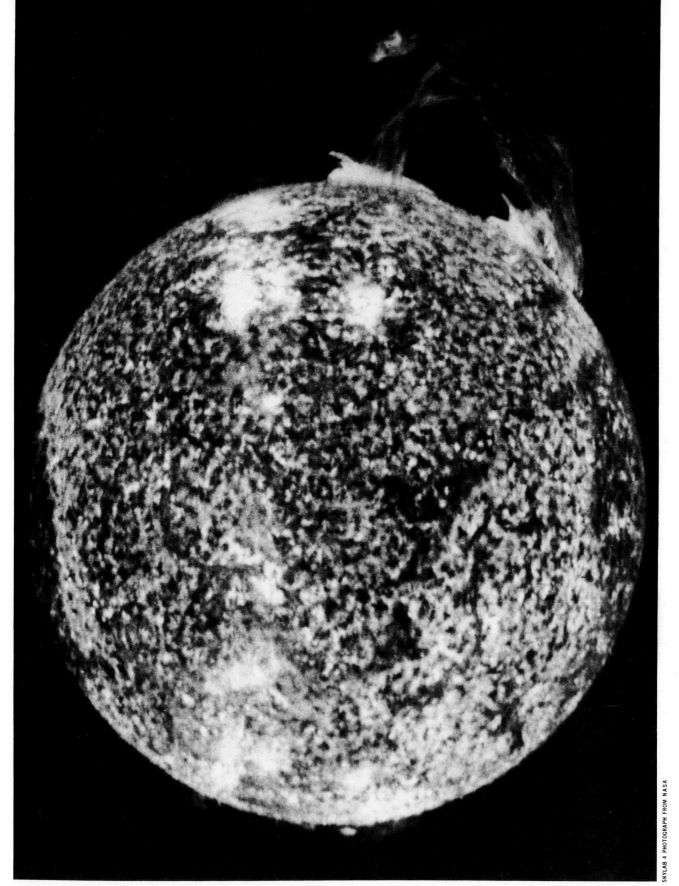

The sun as photographed by a camera sensitive to ultraviolet light. The arch, a corpuscle-spewing solar flare, has its feet in sunspots and its crown 200,000 miles above the sun's surface.

looked directly at it for more than a few seconds.

Scientists, in their quest for an understanding of the power of nuclear energy, discovered hydrogen to be the "fuel" of the sun and helium to be the "ash" produced by this massive atomic furnace. The burning of hydrogen to produce helium creates fantastically high temperatures and releases energy in tremendous quantity. Arthur C. Clarke, noted scientist and science fiction writer, explains the process as atomic rather than chemical, taking place at temperatures of millions rather than thousands of degrees. "The sun's interior, in fact, is far too hot for fire as we know it to exist."

"Today," he adds, "thanks to the patient detective work of generations of scientists, we have not only learned the secret of the sun but in the achievement of nuclear fusion we have ignited its fires on earth."

Solar astronomers focus on the sun from such platforms as Kitt Peak National Observatory in Tucson, Sacramento Peak Observatory near Alamogordo, New Mexico, and the Big Bear Solar Observatory in California. They do not study the "splendid silent sun" of Walt Whitman but a tumultuous, white-hot ball of gas, far more dense at its core than steel, which consumes eight billion pounds of its own substance every second yet has remained in existence for billions of years and will for billions more.

From the dawn of mankind tens of thousands of years ago until the last few centuries, man did not relate the myriad pinpoints of light in the night sky—the stars—to the brilliant orb in the heavens that dispelled the darkness. Today, it is known that the only difference between the stars and our sun is distance, the sun being a mere 93 million miles away as compared to 25 trillion miles for the next nearest star.

The amount of energy radiated by the sun staggers the imagination and is difficult to reduce to figures readily understandable. It has been estimated that its energy is equal to 70,000 horsepower for each square yard of solar surface; or expressed another way, the light from each square inch of the sun's surface has the intensity of 300,000 candles. Fortunately, our planet receives but one two-billionth of the sun's total output. The rest escapes into interstellar space, imparting ever-dwindling warmth and light to the remote planets.

That portion of the sun's energy directed toward the earth buffets the ozone layer, an invisible wall of re-

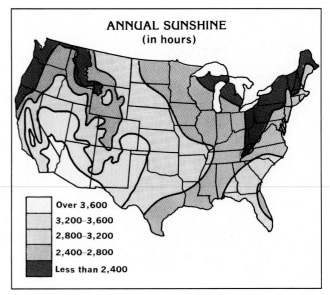

ANNUAL SUNSHINE
(in hours)

Over 3,600
3,200–3,600
2,800–3,200
2,400–2,800
Less than 2,400

The West receives the lion's share of the sunshine that falls on the nation each year. The sunniest spot: Yuma.

sistance six to thirty miles above the planet's surface. Ozone, a molecule consisting of three atoms of oxygen bonded together, is but one of the sunscreens in earth's atmosphere, blocking out primarily the far ultraviolet light. The ordinary two-atom molecule of oxygen blocks out red and infrared rays. Closer to earth, carbon dioxide and less abundant compounds, water vapor, dust, and the man-produced discharges of smoke and smog screen out more of the sun's energy. Ultimately, on a clear day, no more than 70 percent, and usually less, of the sunlight destined for earth ever reaches the surface.

Some of the sunlight depleted in transit through the atmospheric layer warms the upper atmosphere. Some is reflected back into space, but the blue rays filter downward to become the skylight, creating the illusion that light comes not only from the sun, but from all of the air that surrounds us.

FROM THE BEGINNING OF RECORDED TIME, the sun has been an object of mystery, a symbol either of goodness or of evil, an awesome fiery god, sometimes worshiped and sometimes feared.

The sun first appeared in legend as a minor hero in Stone Age hunters' tales, achieving by the Bronze Age the elevated status of deity, worshiped with ritual, prayer,

An Indian mother presents her child to the rising sun that he may be blessed by the Sun Father.

and sacrifice by the early people of Egypt, Persia, Mesopotamia, and India, and by the Indian tribes of North and South America. Yet he was a peculiarly predictable god, not capricious like others in the pantheon. How could the sun—the Sun Father in American Indian legend—have been reduced to such a state of obedience and servility? Sun Father, wise men would tell the tribal young, was originally erratic, sometimes hurrying across the blue heavens, sometimes dawdling. He would draw too near the earth, or he would wander too far away, and sometimes he would not be seen at all. According to the Utes, he was finally conquered and made the subject of man's will; other mythologies concluded, similarly, that the sun was caught in a trap, beaten into submission, and required as a kind of penance to perform his duties with absolute regularity.

This fearsome sphere, though it challenged man to turn away his eyes or suffer eternal blindness, nevertheless sent his warm rays to germinate the seed and was therefore, considered masculine in Indian myths. The earth, which gave birth to new plants each year, was—and still is—considered feminine.

According to an Apache folktale of creation, there was at first only Darkness, Water, Cyclone, and the gods, who had the materials to make a world. "They made the world first, the earth, the underworld, and they made the sky. They made the earth in the form of a living woman and called her Mother. They made the sky in the form of a man and called him Father. He faces downward, and the woman faces up."

Tribes of the Northwest Coast deified the raven, which found the sun and placed it in the heavens to give comfort to man. A legend of the Pomo Indians of California credits the crow with hanging the solar light in the sky. In Yuma tradition the great god was Tuchaipa, who created the world and the moon, and seeing that there was not enough light, added the sun. The range of mythological tales is wide, and their embellishments are as limitless as the imaginations of the tellers. Some of the myths deal with that frightening possibility, the disappearance of the sun, probably inspired by solar eclipses, volcanic eruptions, or heavy storm clouds that temporarily obscured its light.

The sun was a particularly important god to the Pueblo agriculturalists of the Southwest. They called him Oshatsh, and he was a shield between man and the brighter light of the Great Spirit, maker of the universe. A source of illumination, happiness, and fertility, Oshatsh was the god who guided the irrigation and ditching of the Pueblo lands, signaling the time to start with the morning sunrise. The war chief of the village would interpret Oshatsh's signs and proceed to make his daily offering of corn meal, plant his prayer sticks, and chant this song of supplication:

> Now this day, my Sun Father,
> Now that you have come out standing
> To your sacred place.
>
> That from which we draw the water of life
> Prayer meal—
> Here I give unto you.
>
> Your long life,
> Your old age,
> Your waters,
> Your seeds,
> Your riches,
> Your power,
> Your strong spirit,
> Of all these, to me may you grant.

This simple prayer asked no more of the sun than that it fulfill its destiny. For more than three billion years, it has been so arranged.

CHAPTER 5

THE RAIN MAKERS

Types of clouds—recognizing them and reading their weather forecast ❖ How clouds are formed ❖ How they are affected by topography ❖ Clouds as precursors of frontal storms

IMAGINE A WORLD WITHOUT CLOUDS—nothing but clear, blue sky from horizon to horizon, 365 days a year. What a monotonous world it would be, bereft of the imagery of billowing castles, dragons, and winged steeds, deprived of the drama of motion and shadow, innocent of the expectancy and foreboding that cloud changes arouse in the human spirit.

But clouds are far more than an aesthetic and emotional adjunct to man's psyche. They are one of the key components of the earth's intricate weather-making machine.

There is always some invisible, gaseous water vapor in the air—commonly called humidity. The chief suppliers of vapor are vegetation, bodies of water such as rivers and lakes, and rain itself. Air currents carry the vapor upward to high levels, where the atmospheric pressure is lower. (The pressure of air is 29.92 inches of mercury at sea level, but only 17.57 inches at fourteen thousand feet —the summit height of many of the West's highest mountains.) Air expands, and in doing so, it also becomes colder. In a simple process this cooling condenses some of the water vapor into the visible droplets that form the billowy mass of a cloud.

Condensing vapors are not alone in the upper atmosphere, for they join already suspended particles such as microscopic dust from the land or salt crystallized from sea spray. Other particles, electrically charged ions too small to be distinguished in a microscope, are present, too. Whatever the size or origin, meteorologists term the foreign bodies "condensation nuclei." By acting as

growth seeds, they help to form water droplets from condensing water vapor.

From such humble beginnings great clouds grow. Like snowflakes, no two are ever alike, although within a given classification similarities do exist. Born of water vapor in the restless atmosphere, clouds are the vagabonds of the sky. In the nineteenth century, a Victorian meteorologist made two voyages around the world to prove that the same basic clouds are found everywhere. He concluded that his hypothesis was valid, though he observed that some regions have one cloud type more frequently than others. This difference can be seen between areas of the West; stratus clouds, for example, are very common on the Pacific Coast, while cumulus are more likely to be found in the Southwest desert regions.

An English pharmacist-meteorologist, Luke Howard gave cloud watchers their first useful classification system in 1803. He classified in a technical way, using Latin, but he did so with a layman's appreciation for the pictures made by clouds. He used *cumulus*, meaning "heap," to refer to a puffed-up cloud; *stratus*, meaning "layer," for a sheetlike cloud; *cirrus*, meaning a "curl," for a cloud that is wispy; and *nimbus*, meaning "violent rain," for rain clouds. Howard considered these to be the four basic cloud forms.

Most of the others could be described by combinations of the original terms or by joining one of them to another pictorial word. For example, *cirrocumulus* refers to dappled high clouds; *cirrostratus*, to high, sheetlike clouds; and *cumulonimbus* to the thundercloud. Howard's sys-

Cumulus clouds. Their flat bases mark the level where invisible water vapor becomes fine water droplets. Forecast: a slight chance of showers. (Canyonlands National Monument, Utah)

*A cumulonimbus with its typical vertical development and anvil top
—the parent of thunderstorms, hail, and cloudburst.*

tem, being simple and yet expandable, remains today as the standard method of classification by meteorologists throughout the world.

Cloud types are primarily determined by the degree of vertical air motion, which, in turn, responds to differing conditions on earth. If a cloud forms in the absence of vertical motion, it usually lies near the ground and is called fog. A thermal, an air mass rising from a sun-warmed patch of ground, usually will create a cumulus cloud in the upper air. Lens-shaped clouds with very smooth outlines, called wave clouds, are formed where air rises as it flows over the ridges of mountains. Extensive layer, or stratus, clouds are associated with slow but prolonged ascents of air; these are the type of clouds found in cyclonic depressions, fronts, and other bad-weather systems.

Clouds generally are found within certain ranges of elevation, but with these qualifications: they float higher over arid country than over moist landscapes; they tend to remain at higher altitudes in summer than in winter; and they are higher over the equator than over the poles. Also, cloud heights vary somewhat with the elevation of the land, increasing over mountains such as the Rockies.

Lying at lower levels of the atmosphere, with their bases less than 6,500 feet above the ground, are the cumulus clouds—those billowing beauties that punctuate blue skies throughout the American West. Individual cumuli have dramatic vertical development—castlelike tops and an endless parade of animalistic shapes. When widely spaced and quiescent, they are fair-weather clouds. When they become so abundant that they leave little space for the sun to shine through, however, they are called, collectively, stratocumulus and portend stormy weather.

A more threatening form of the cumulus is the cumulonimbus, or thunderhead, developed from the overzealous growth of a peace-loving cumulus, and containing violent ingredients such as tempest winds, heavy rain, pelting hail, or lightning. This gigantic monster may sometimes be the harbinger of fierce hail or a tornado. Airline pilots veer far off course to avoid a cumulonimbus, for air currents within the cloud create updrafts and downdrafts with speeds up to two hundred miles per hour. The huge top may soar as high as twelve

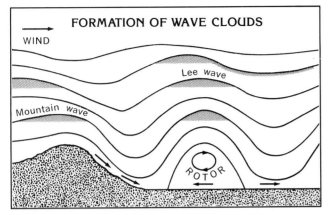

FORMATION OF WAVE CLOUDS

WIND

Lee wave

Mountain wave

ROTOR

Mountain and lee wave clouds are due to the wave pattern established downwind in the air flowing over mountains—a pattern like ripples over rocks in a stream. Clouds form in the ascending, cooling part of the wave and evaporate in the descending, warming part. When air between cloud-forming layers is too dry to form clouds, wave clouds appear to be stacked one above another like a pile of plates. Higher-level clouds will contain ice crystals that evaporate slowly, and consequently they continue downwind in a wavy, overcast layer. Below the wave crests a "rotor" cloud may form.

miles, reaching the base of the stratosphere, which clouds do not normally penetrate. High altitude winds spread out the cumulonimbus, reshaping it into the huge anvil on which the mythic Jove was said to forge his weapons.

In the middle level (between 6,500 and 20,000 feet), clouds are prefixed *alto. Altocumulus* are white cloudlets and clumps, sometimes rolled out in parallel bands, sometimes constituents of a spotty mackerel sky. *Altostratus* are translucent, milky sheets of cloud that often appear fibrous or striated.

The highest common, natural, clouds are the cirrus, floating 20,000 to 30,000 feet or more above the landscape. Cirrus are the most delicate of clouds, composed of tiny snowflakes and fine ice crystals, blown by strong winds, and combed into a sheer gossamer. The bottom surface is often untrimmed and ragged, where the ice crystals are falling, evaporating, and then rising back up into the cloud as vapor. There, within the cloud's frigid interior, where cold has been measured at —65° F., the moisture sublimes again into more ice crystals.

Lenticular clouds, when stacked into "piles of plates," might be mistaken for hovering spacecraft, but their smooth form is indeed earthly, caused by undulating waves in the air above and downwind of mountains.

DAVID MUENCH

TYPES OF CLOUDS

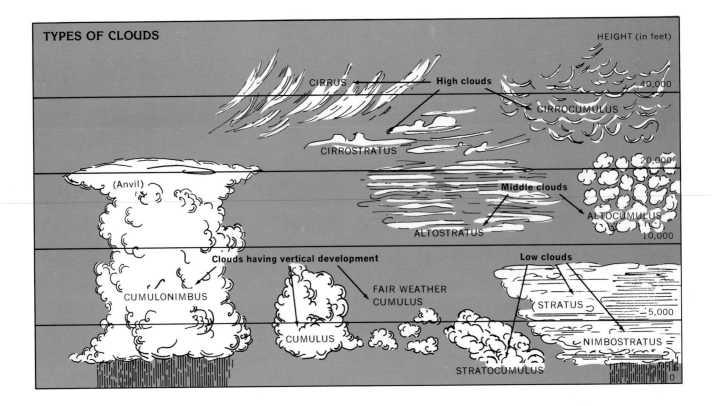

HEIGHT (in feet)

CIRRUS — High clouds

CIRROCUMULUS

40,000

CIRROSTRATUS

20,000

(Anvil)

Middle clouds

ALTOCUMULUS

ALTOSTRATUS

10,000

Clouds having vertical development

Low clouds

CUMULONIMBUS

FAIR WEATHER CUMULUS

STRATUS

5,000

CUMULUS

NIMBOSTRATUS

STRATOCUMULUS

0

HUMIDITY AND DEW POINT

All air contains water vapor, and from it come clouds, rain, and a degree of one's personal comfort. How much water vapor the air can hold depends on temperature, approximately doubling for each twenty-degree (F.) increase. Even on a hot, humid day, there is less than one ounce of water in each cubic yard of air; in freezing weather there is only one-tenth as much.

The weight of water vapor in a given volume of air is called the *absolute humidity*. When water vapor in the air is expressed as a percentage of the capacity of the air to hold it, at a given temperature, it is called *relative humidity*.

When the temperature of the air changes, its relative humidity changes, because the capacity of the air to hold water varies greatly with temperature while the absolute humidity does not. Thus when the temperature drops, relative humidity increases. When the air is cold enough, the relative humidity reaches 100 percent, and when further cooled, water must come out of the air as, for example, fog, dew, or frost. The temperature at which the relative humidity attains 100 percent is called the *dew point*.

Another high altitude cloud is the veillike and layered *cirrostratus*, which sometimes refracts sunlight and forms a halo around the sun. Less frequently observed are *cirrocumulus* clouds—puffs of cumuli flying in packs, another source of a mackerel sky. Weather verses use them as predictors:

> Mare's tails and mackerel sky,
> Not long wet, nor not long dry.
> Mackerel scales and mare's tails
> Make lofty ships carry low sails.

These two predictions, based on the observations of the ages, are usually accurate, for lacy cirrus clouds are usually a part of a storm system. Their long streamers sweep over the horizon as emissaries, warning of rain or snow as much as two days in advance.

WITH THE ADVENT OF RADIO and television weathermen, such terms as *cold front* and *warm front* have become household words, but they are not always understood. A front is the boundary where air masses having

FORMATION OF A CUMULUS CLOUD

Air Motion →

Condensation Level

1

2

3

4

5

6

A cumulus cloud forms over a heated area of the earth. There air warms, bulges upward, and breaks free as an invisible, churning bubble that will cool as it rises. When it reaches the ''condensation level''—the point at which its temperature has decreased to the dew point—a puffy, flat-based cloud suddenly appears. Generally it is a fair-weather cloud and, if it continues to rise, will mix with surrounding air and slowly dissipate. The cloud base will be higher in dry weather.

Cirrus clouds, distinctively wispy and windswept, are masses of ice crystals at high altitudes.

Patchy altostratus clouds, composed of water droplets, occur in middle levels of the atmosphere.

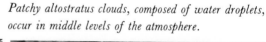

JOSEF MUENCH

GRANT HEILMAN

substantially different temperatures or moisture content meet, a condition that frequently produces stormy weather. There are three basic types of fronts, depending on the temperature of the incoming air mass: a warm front occurs when warmer air replaces colder air; a cold front, when colder air replaces warmer air; and an occluded front, when warm air is overtaken and forced aloft between two bodies of cold air. If the front does not move, it is termed a stationary front.

Because the life of a warm front is a common sequence, well defined above the Great Plains, the East, and the Pacific Coast (where occluded fronts may also be seen), it is used here to illustrate how anyone can predict weather by knowing the cloud types to look for.

The warm front storm, common in the West, is announced well in advance by cirrus clouds that appear in the sky as much as two days before passage of the storm center. If the wind is blowing the cirrus wisps from the southwest or the west, and the sky is blue around them, fair weather will normally continue for twenty-four hours or more. By the time the sky is blanketed with translucent cirrostratus clouds, rain or snow will soon follow.

The scenario of a warm front storm runs something like this: Within a few hours after the sky is coated, lower clouds begin to replace the higher ones. Altostratus form below 20,000 feet, turning the sky dull and white. When more than 60 percent of the sky is thus opaque with clouds, there is what flyers call a "ceiling."

Within twenty-four hours the darkened underside of the low clouds may begin roiling, and ragged, wind-battered *fractostratus* (from the Latin meaning "broken layer") may initiate the first rain or snowfall. The passing of the warm front is marked by low stratus or nimbostratus clouds, just preceding the front's leading edge. Any precipitation that falls will be steady and may continue for hours or even days.

A shift in wind, a rising temperature, and a clearing sky announce that the warm front is passing, another weather cycle completed. Often it will be followed by a cold front and a return to rainy conditions; but sometimes the next day will be clear, and cumulus clouds will begin forming, as if to emphasize that fair weather is at hand.

With the passage of a front—warm, cold, or occluded—weather does not come to a halt, of course; it is a continuing process, minute to minute and year to year.

There are some complications in forecasting weather

Much of the West's precipitation is triggered by mountains. As air is forced up over a range, the rising causes it to cool and release rain or snow on the windward slopes. Beyond the summit the air contains little moisture and a "rain shadow" results. In this cross section of central California, Parkfield, Coalinga, and Visalia lie in the rain shadow of the Coast Range. On ascending the loftier Sierra Nevada, the air has more moisture wrung from it, so that Giant Forest on the high slopes receives substantial annual precipitation while Independence, in the arid Owens Valley, lies in a rain shadow.

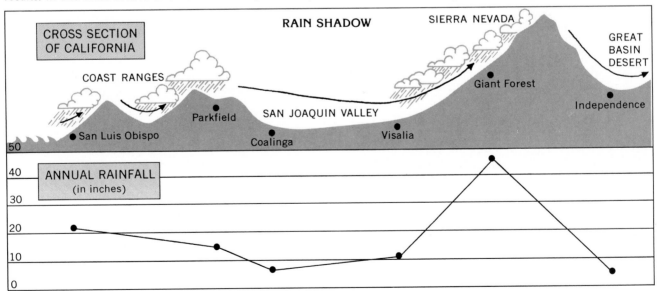

from the clouds; big, fluffy cumulus can be rain clouds ("When clouds appear like rocks and towers, / The earth's refreshed by frequent showers"), so also may rain occur with the stratocumulus cloud, and snow with the winter altostratus. But by knowing the normal sequence of the clouds—cirrus–stratus–nimbus–cumulus, in the case of a warm front—one has a good start in learning to predict tomorrow's weather today.

In 1964 a freak storm hit the Pacific Northwest coast during the Christmas season. Warm, windy, and wet, it was a storm type that forms over tropical seas and rarely invades the West Coast. On December 24, eight inches of rain fell along Oregon's shoreline; the next day a rain-swollen Willamette River, twelve feet above flood stage, was lapping the top of the seawall at Portland.

As the torrential rains continued, forty-five bridges were washed out, leaving dozens of communities without food or medical supplies. Flooding knocked out railroads and highways, including U.S. 101, where sections of the road were inundated, leaving hundreds of motorists stranded. The air force joined with private pilots to organize airlifts to isolated towns. The storm reached as far east and south as Yosemite Valley, where it flooded

When total annual precipitation is plotted on a map, it is easy to see the great diversity in the West and its prevailing dryness compared to the more humid East. Because snow and rainfall vary with elevation, mountainous regions stand out as high points much as they would on a contour map of the country.

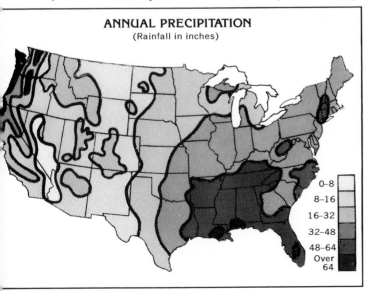

ANNUAL PRECIPITATION
(Rainfall in inches)

0–8
8–16
16–32
32–48
48–64
Over 64

In early 1969 unexpected winds blew a storm from Hawaii across the mesquite-covered slopes of the San Gabriel and Santa Monica mountains and into Southern California. It hovered over Los Angeles for nine days and left in its wake more than ten inches of rain. The ensuing floods and mud slides destroyed dozens of homes and claimed the lives of ninety-five people, among them a group of campers caught in a flash flood. Southern California was declared a disaster area.

To further foil the amateur forecaster, there are times when the rain released by a mother cloud never reaches the earth. Rain streamers, called *virga*, fall toward the earth and then hang in midair, their frayed ends held above a layer of dry air, which is absorbing all the moisture. The elements of a normal rainstorm are present—thunderclaps sound and lightning flashes—but the moisture continues to hover without ever reaching the ground. Virga may also be seen aloft, trailing from alto- or cirrocumulus clouds, for instance, as wisps of water droplets or ice falling from the cloud and evaporating in the air.

Thus, even as one learns to read what is written in the clouds, their message may be interrupted or garbled by other meteorological factors. Nevertheless, in a total picture where many of these factors are elusive and hard for the layman to measure, or so vast that he cannot experience them personally, the ever-changing clouds will remain for many people the visible and powerful embodiment of weather.

EVAPORATION AND CONDENSATION

Water provides a means for air to gain or lose heat. When water evaporates, it cools both itself and the surrounding air, because heat has been used to change liquid into vapor.

Conversely, when water vapor condenses—into clouds, for example—it adds heat to the air, because the heat absorbed when liquid changed to vapor is released when the vapor changes back to liquid. Unlike the cooling from evaporation, however, this heat will not be sensed by the observer as a rise in temperature. The cooling that causes condensation will always be greater than the heat released by condensation. If condensation could raise air temperature, the heat liberated would evaporate any water that was formed.

CHAPTER 6

ILL WINDS AND GOOD

Wind—air in motion ❖ Where the winds are born ❖ Foehns
—the family of warm winds that includes the fabled chinook ❖
The strange Santa Ana ❖ Tornadoes, waterspouts, dust devils

CAPRICIOUS AND ELUSIVE, wind has long been a source of mystery and fascination. To primitive man it must have been puzzling indeed—it hid from his eyes and could be seen only in its effects; it spoke to him now in a whisper, now in a howl; tall trees bowed when it passed, and small objects fled before it. Small wonder he tended to personify it. Today people speak of "witch's winds" and "dust devils," give a human name to the wind, such as "Maria," and assign a whole procession of feminine names to the tropical hurricanes.

But like other weather phenomena, wind has yielded many of its secrets to scientists' relentless quest for understanding. It has long since been discovered that the origin of the winds lies, not in the puffed-cheeked gods that illustrated early mariners' charts, but in the small pressure differences that abound on the earth's surface: air of a given pressure tends to flow to a region of lower pressure, as one may see when air escapes from an inflated balloon.

Atmospheric pressure, measured by a barometer is the weight of a column of air above a given location. Differences in atmospheric pressure are the result of temperature differences in the atmosphere. When heated, air expands and thus is less dense (lighter) than colder air. Being lighter, warm air rises above colder air. As warm air rises, more air must flow in at the lower level to replace it, creating the horizontal air movement called wind. If instead of being warmed, the air is cooled, the entire process is reversed; the cooled air sinks below the warm air and spreads horizontally as it nears the ground.

This simple explanation is complicated by the rotation of the earth which forces the winds into curving paths. The effects of this force (the Coriolis force, to be discussed on page 75) range from the benevolent trade winds to devastating tornadoes.

Three broad classifications of wind affect the American West: global, cyclonic and anticyclonic, and local. All begin with atmospheric temperature differences, and the dividing line between them is not sharp. They often interact, with two or even all three types occurring simultaneously. Whatever its type, the wind feels the same; without a weather map one cannot distinguish them.

Global, or prevailing, winds extend around the earth and are part of the overall circulation of the atmosphere. The prevailing winds over most of the United States blow from west to east, a fact from which meteorologists can infer future movements of storms. (Winds are named for the direction *from* which they blow.) *Cyclonic and anticyclonic winds* are those that rotate around the centers of high and low pressure systems, and may come from any point of the compass. *Local winds* depend upon local temperature differences found above such places as cities, newly-plowed fields, south slopes of hills, or the shadows of passing clouds, and can shift direction quickly.

There are few locations where the global winds are predominant at the surface, but they can usually be felt on the oceans, and on the high mountains of the West. In parts of Texas, Oklahoma, Kansas, Iowa, and neighboring states, however, southeast winds at the surface are related to a variable, but permanent and therefore

Concentrating energy from a midwestern thunderstorm, this malevolent twister unleashed its fury against Topeka, Kansas. Hidden by the ragged black cloud is the wind's deadly swirl.

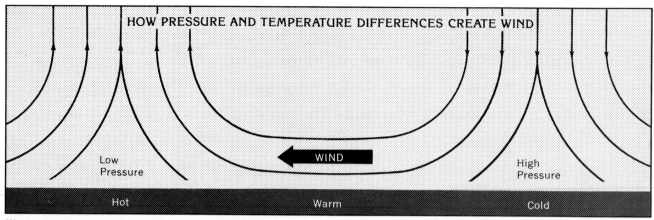

HOW PRESSURE AND TEMPERATURE DIFFERENCES CREATE WIND

Low Pressure

WIND

High Pressure

Hot   Warm   Cold

Warm air rising over a hot region on the earth's surface, such as a parking lot or desert, draws air in at the bottom, while cool air descending over a cold region, such as the shadow of a cloud or an ice field, pours air out at the bottom; either situation creates wind. The mass of warm or cold air can range in size from a few feet to thousands of miles. Over large areas, cyclones ("lows") may develop around areas of relative warmth and lower pressure; anticyclones ("highs"), around areas of coolness and higher pressure. The resulting winds blow from high- to low-pressure regions.

global, system of high pressure off the southeast coast.

In the Northern Hemisphere winds flow clockwise around highs and counterclockwise around lows, thus these winds are predictable. For example, if a low is to the north of a weather observer the winds experienced by him come from the west, whereas if the low is to the south, the winds will come from the east. As the position of a weather system changes with respect to the observer, he experiences a shift in the wind. Hence there is a basic rule that is useful in determining the direction to the center of a weather system: with the wind at one's back, lows are always to the observer's left, highs to his right.

Global winds and cyclonic and anticyclonic winds are described further on pages 76–79. This chapter focuses on local winds and winds that have acquired local renown.

The West has many windy localities, but the statistics are averages that do not portray the personality of the wind—its extremes or steadiness. Tatoosh Island, Washington, has average monthly wind speeds ranging up to 20 miles per hour, among the highest of nonmountainous regions. Abilene and Amarillo, Texas, range areas where "the wind blows free" across miles of open land, have average monthly wind speeds reaching 15 miles per hour. Surprisingly, "The Windy City," Chicago, annually averages only 9 miles per hour, a figure equaled by San Francisco, Denver, Boise, Albuquerque, and Salt Lake City, and exceeded by Kansas City, Billings, Omaha, Tulsa, and Rapid City. All through the Great Plains and

Midwest prairies, wind is a constant presence. This one consistency in an otherwise capricious climate has long been a valuable aid to farmers and ranchers who rely upon windmill-driven pumps to supply them with water.

Important local winds—called *diurnal winds* because of daily habits—result from the air density differences brought about by solar heating during the day and radiative cooling at night. Two common diurnal winds are land and sea breezes, and mountain and valley winds (see diagrams on pages 123 and 140). Briefly, solar heating of the land warms the air above it, causing air to flow upward along the land's slope; at night the air flow is reversed, as radiation cools the land, chills the air above it, and the air flows downslope like a stream. The powerful winds that accompany the advancing inferno of a forest fire are extreme examples of the same principle.

The chinook—named for the balmy breeze that blew from "over Chinook camp," bringing unseasonable springlike weather to Astoria, Oregon, during the days of the early Hudson's Bay Company—is a familiar weather phenomenon in various parts of the West. Though historically a chinook meant a warm, moist, southwest wind along the Oregon and Washington coasts, the term is now usually used to describe a characteristically warm, dry wind that blows on the leeward side of mountains. Chinook is the American name for a foehn (pronounced *fern*), which can be found worldwide.

Paradoxically, rain and snow are the source of the

warmth and dryness of a chinook. Air that is forced up over a mountain range expands and cools. The cooling releases water from the air, as clouds, rain, or snow, but in return for its freedom, the moisture leaves heat behind in the air (see box on page 55). As the air rushes down the leeward slopes, it is warmed not only by compression, but also by the heat given off in the process of precipitation. Lacking the moisture it dropped on the windward slope of the mountain, the chinook is a very thirsty wind.

Neither seasons nor the sun directly affect the development of a chinook, which may come sweeping down the slopes night or day during any time of year, though more frequently in winter, a season when the chinook is most welcome. Sometimes referred to as the "snow-eater," this weather phenomenon has given rise to numerous Bun-

yan-like tales. In Alberta province of Canada, according to the folklore, a sled-driving settler once tried outrunning a chinook, but the best he was able to do was to keep his sled's front runners in the snow while the back ones scraped over dry ground.

A falling barometer, which generally encourages a chinook, heralds its coming. Suddenly, out of the blue, horizontal white streamers appear along the mountaintops, forming a crest cloud, the "chinook arch." West of this cloud cap, rain or snow fall.

The warm descending air of the chinook quickly evaporates any remains of its own cloudy moisture; it is parched and moving at high speeds when it reaches the foothills or high plains. Temperatures may jump twenty to forty degrees in ten to fifteen minutes, the record rise being forty-nine degrees in two minutes at Spearfish,

Bowled over by a "Boulder wind," January 1972. Such destruction as this is usually reserved for tornadoes and hurricanes, but at their most furious, chinook winds too may exceed one hundred miles per hour.

BOULDER DAILY CAMERA

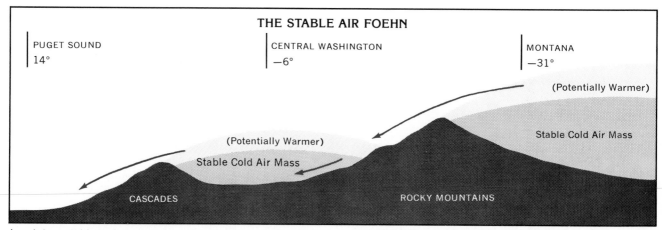

THE STABLE AIR FOEHN

PUGET SOUND
14°

CENTRAL WASHINGTON
−6°

MONTANA
−31°

(Potentially Warmer)

Stable Cold Air Mass

(Potentially Warmer)

Stable Cold Air Mass

CASCADES

ROCKY MOUNTAINS

In winter, stable polar air pools up over the plains and is pushed against the eastern slope of the Rockies. Like water over a dam, the upper level of air, the potentially warmer part, slips over the crest and down into the Great Basin, forming a body of air that is warmer than the air mass it left but colder than the air it displaces. Farther west the process is repeated as air flows over the Cascades. Again it displaces relatively warm air and spills toward the coast as a cold wave.

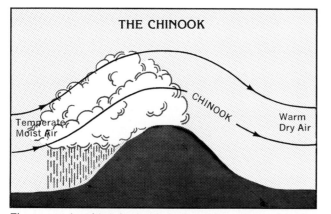

THE CHINOOK

Temperate Moist Air

CHINOOK

Warm Dry Air

The warm, dry chinook wind is born on the western slopes of mountains. Temperate, moist air moves up the slopes, cools, and condenses its water vapor to clouds, which leave rain and snow on windward slopes. The heat added to the air by condensation and by the warming of the air as its descends leeward slopes makes the chinook warm and dry. If no precipitation is left behind in the mountains, there will be no chinook.

South Dakota. The warmth and extreme dryness of the chinook evaporate ice off ponds and reservoirs, and virtually "eat up" banks of snow at rates as high as an inch an hour.

During its warmest period a chinook wind may hit speeds over fifty miles an hour. Occasionally the winds can become almost hurricanelike in speed and destruction. The U.S. Weather Bureau at Denver reports that buildings have been blown down during chinook windstorms registering seventy-five miles an hour. On January 7, 1969, a chinook, or "Boulder wind," burst upon that city at speeds recorded as greater than a hundred miles an hour. Shingles flew off roofs, fences were uprooted, car windshields were etched by wind-driven sand, and grass and prairie fires were ignited by downed power lines.

When a chinook pays the prairie a visit, it may stay from an hour to several days. The chinook may hug the mountain slopes or may blow on past the crest, touching down to earth a hundred miles or more beyond. In its path temperatures climb while on all sides the weather may be hovering around zero. In 1898 the city of Helena, Montana, was shivering in subfreezing temperatures while a mountain weather station a few miles from the city was basking in 32° F. weather.

Unusual events reportedly accompany a chinook. Boulder residents were able to hear a train whistle at Tabernash, Colorado, eighty miles and a mountain range away. Metal objects, insulated from the ground, are said to pick up positive charges in a chinook wind, a phenomenon called "wind static" because of its interference with radio communications. Wire fences occasionally accumulate enough charge to kill livestock, and there is an unconfirmed report that the voltage of a chinook wind kept a neon lamp burning for several hours.

Intemperate as chinook winds may be, the clear, balmy

weather they bring is generally advantageous. They have helped keep tracks cleared and railroads running in winter. In extreme winters, they have kept many of the vast stock ranges from having to be abandoned. Sometimes a chinook will arrive in the nick of time, saving a herd from both freezing and starvation. In November 1896 a series of chinooks moved across Idaho, raising temperatures far above normal and softening the soil sufficiently for some farmers to start plowing. To the westerner, the chinook is usually a welcome guest.

The same cannot be said for the stable-air foehn, which can bring chill air west from the cold interior of the continent. In winter the Rockies and the Cascades normally protect the Pacific Northwest from the full westward onslaught of stable polar air that frequently hits with fury the states east of the Rockies. But under certain meteorological conditions the upper levels of the stable air mass can slip over the mountain barrier. This air is said to be "potentially warmer," meaning that it would be warmer than air from the lower levels in its air mass if the two could be compared at the same altitude.

As the cold upper-level air flowing over the Rockies descends the west slope, it is compressed and warmed, reaching the lowlands at a temperature higher than the air it left behind at a corresponding altitude east of the Rockies (the *stable-air foehn* effect). It is still not as warm, though, as the milder air it replaced in the lowlands, so it is experienced as a cold wave. The air mass continues to move westward until it meets the next barrier, the Cascades. There the entire sequence is re-enacted, as the air, slipping over the peaks and downslope, is warmed more and eventually displaces still warmer Pacific air.

In summer, the stable-air foehn functions in reverse. Relatively stable air, flowing eastward from a cell of high pressure located over the Pacific, moves first against the coast ranges and then against the Cascades, with the air at higher levels always crossing the barriers first. Upon descending the lee side, the air is warmed, bringing higher temperatures to the interior plateaus. The stable-air foehn's source of heat is its "potentially warmer air," whereas the chinook's source is heat given off in the process of condensation on the windward side of the mountain.

"Drainage winds" emanate from extensive pockets of cold air that settle over mountain-sheltered inland plateaus and intermontane basins. Frequently the remnants

of an arctic cold wave, this mass of air may be much colder than that immediately adjacent to, but outside of, the mountainous region. Being colder, it is also denser, and once started in motion toward lower elevations, it flows at an increasing pace, bringing strong winds and significantly colder temperatures to the surrounding lowlands. Like a chinook, the air is warmed by compression, but it starts as such a cold mass that it is always at a lower temperature than the air it replaces. This cold blast of air, generally called a *bora*, occurs frequently along the Rockies, and often sweeps through the Columbia River Gorge to the Pacific. When the air is channeled through a canyon, the bora comes, often without warning, in a fierce, concentrated onslaught.

The most notorious of the drainage winds in the United States is the *Santa Ana*. This dry, sometimes hot, sometimes cold, wind is named for one of the low mountain canyons through which the wind exits to the Pacific Ocean. But what may sound like a very local disturbance is really the product of a far-reaching weather phenomenon. These winds have their source over the Great Basin, but their blast is most strongly felt in the Los Angeles metropolitan area. Their influence may extend as far north as Ventura, California, and as far east as the Colorado River between California and Arizona.

Richard Henry Dana described a Santa Ana wind in *Two Years Before the Mast* in 1836, and Commodore Stockton mentioned it in his diary in 1847; these are considered the earliest descriptions of the Santa Ana, although neither writer named it. As with most natural events that are also dramatic, strange and unusual tales accompany the Santa Ana. California Indians, the story goes, would throw themselves into the sea when the Santa Ana blew. This wind, blowing from the shore to the sea, may cause the Pacific to turn still and glassy near the shore. The surf dies, a yellow color lights the sky, and people talk about "earthquake weather," so still and tense is the mood before the wind.

The Santa Ana, or "witch's wind," can be a killer. Late in Southern California's dry season, in the fall or early winter, the chaparral-covered hills are tinder-dry, and the combination of fire and the anticipated Santa Ana is a double-barreled threat. In 1970 it was blamed for the loss of fourteen lives, in various ways, and injuries to one hundred Los Angeles County firemen in a siege of fires that the wind fanned and spread. In eight

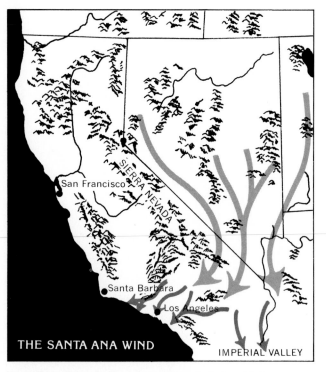

THE SANTA ANA WIND

The driving force behind Santa Ana winds is a high-pressure region that often forms over the mile-high Great Basin, trapped between the Sierra Nevada and the Rockies. But an escape path does exist to the south, along which the relatively cool air of the high drains to lower altitudes, sometimes aided by the attraction of a low off the coast of Southern California. Once the air breaks free of the desert through passes in the San Gabriel and San Bernardino mountains, it speeds across the Los Angeles and Santa Ana basins and the San Fernando Valley, then down numerous coastal canyons. Alternately, it may take a route to the east over the Salton Sea or along the Colorado River. The Santa Ana is a drainage wind, but it warms by compression like a stable air foehn, thus tempering the air of the high, which may arrive cold, mild, or warm, but always dry.

days, 795 houses and buildings were totally destroyed, and property damage reached $100 million in Los Angeles and six nearby counties. Perhaps the longest Santa Ana experienced in the Los Angeles Basin blew for fourteen days.

The Santa Ana also seems able to whip man's psyche to the flash point. It has been blamed for murder, suicide, and violence of all kinds. People in its path become irritable, depressed, nervous. High levels of static electricity sometimes make even handshakes between friends a shocking experience. Scientists have discovered that other psychological and physiological effects of the Santa Ana are also related to this static electricity.

Joan Didion, writing in the *Saturday Evening Post*, observed "the violence and the unpredictability of the Santa Ana affect the entire quality of life in Los Angeles,

accentuate its impermanence, its unreliability." Though indeed a local wind, the Santa Ana has, in legend if not in fact, achieved national notoriety.

COMPRESS THE SOUND AND FURY of a sizable thunderstorm into a diameter of one hundred to one thousand feet, add dirt and smashed debris, and stir. That is the tornado, the prairie twister; its winds of 200-400 miles per hour are the most violent and concentrated of all.

Photographs, the earliest taken in 1884, reveal that tornadoes assume three basic shapes: the classic funnel, the straight-sided cylinder, and the hourglass figure. They usually rotate counterclockwise and range in color from gray to black, the degree of darkness depending upon the amount of cloud formed inside the column. Produced by a variety of conditions, tornadoes strike with a fearful suddenness.

This terrifying funnel cloud usually originates when two bodies of air—one warm and humid, the other cool and dry—collide. Conditions necessary to create tornadoes occur primarily in Australia and in the midwestern and southwestern parts of the United States.

Tornadoes are ordinarily born in the turbulence of severe thunderstorms, adjacent to the boundary between cold and warm air. Just beyond this boundary, or front, a mass of rain-cooled air from ten to twenty thousand feet up sinks toward the ground. Ahead of the front, warm air is forced to rise over the intruding cold air. Expanding and cooling as it rises, the water vapor is condensed into clouds and rain, and the tornado forms in the zone of conflict between the sinking cold air and rising warm air. Fed by the energy released in condensation, the tornado grows, spinning faster as it concentrates the winds into a smaller area, much as an ice skater quickens his spin by drawing in his arms.

The funnel moves at the same speed as its parent cloud, typically thirty to forty miles an hour. Fortunately, the life cycle of a tornado in "Tornado Alley"—including Texas, Oklahoma, Kansas, Nebraska, Missouri, Iowa, and Illinois—is normally less than an hour. On an average it touches the earth for only eight minutes and, unbelievable as it is to anyone who has never seen its destruction, spends only about fifteen seconds at one spot. The tracks of nearly half of all tornadoes are less than three miles long, but a few exceed twenty miles. By

Lying in the path of the Santa Ana, this house in Chatsworth, California, was consumed by wind-driven fire.

lifting up from the earth, leaving the ground untouched as the funnel passes above, and then touching down again, some have traveled two hundred to three hundred miles before dissipating.

Plains farmers survived the terrible funnel wind by building protective cellars underground. If caught in the open, a farmer fled at right angles to the storm path; as a last resort he lay flat on the earth.

Tornado weather is hot and humid. At first, a gentle wind blows, commonly from the south, and a line of thunderstorms forms in the west, low at first but swiftly rising until huge thunderheads dominate the heavens. In the depths of these storms are the swirling winds from which a tornado may be born.

"A roar like a thousand freight trains" was the description provided by retired army Captain Roy S. Hall as he recalled the approach of a tornado that engulfed him and his home in Texas. There was hail and lightning, combined with a tremendous wind. Suddenly, a calm pervaded, "as if hands had been placed over my ears, cutting off all sound. [A light appeared of] a peculiar bluish tinge . . . so unnatural in appearance that I held the thought for a moment that the house was on fire. . . . [The funnel] extended upward for over one thousand feet, and was swaying gently and bending slowly toward the southeast. Down at the bottom, judging from the circle in front of me, the funnel was about 150 yards across. Higher up it was even larger, and seemed to be partly filled with a bright cloud, which shimmered like a fluorescent light. This brilliant cloud was in the middle of the funnel, not touching the sides, as I recall having seen the walls extending on up outside the cloud."

A relative of the tornado, the *waterspout*, occurs only over water. In futile attempts to dispel this demon, sailors were known to pepper it with cannon fire, taking careful aim at the rising column of water and its cascade of spray. A waterspout can be fierce but its energy is usually spent in the midst of an uninhabited ocean.

A *dust devil* is the tornado's mild, fair-weather cousin. Averaging about a hundred feet across and rarely reaching more than a few hundred feet in altitude, the tiny twister starts as a local updraft on the hot desert floor, in a furrowed field, or between city buildings on a hot summer afternoon. The rising hot air of the dust devil draws air in from the sides at its base, and as in a tornado, air currents spin rapidly in a tight spiral. (Unlike a tornado, however, it is as likely to spin in one direction as the other.) Not having the storm-fed power of a tornado, the dust devil does little more than stir a few leaves and raise a pocket of dust during the brief minutes of its existence.

WHETHER IT BLOWS GOOD OR EVIL, wind is as much a part of weather as the sun or clouds. It is air in motion and as such is the workhorse of weather. It carries heat, moisture, and the rotating weather systems, cyclones and anticyclones, to all parts of the globe. Without wind, temperatures over much of the earth would soar to intolerable levels, rain would fall only over bodies of water, and weather would take no dramatic turns. Wind is weather's breath of life.

CHAPTER 7

ICE AND SNOW

Snow, sleet, frost, and rime—how they differ ❖ Hailstones and
how they develop ❖ The white destruction of avalanches ❖
Glaciers—what causes them and where they can be found in the West

THE WINTER SOLSTICE—DECEMBER 21—represents the dividing line between fall and winter, between the golden days of falling leaves and the long white nights of storm and snow. In many parts of the West, however, the trappings of winter precede its official beginning. In the high mountain ranges, a few snow flurries may occur during any month of the year, and it is not unusual for these areas to have a full-fledged blizzard in early September. By the end of September, Trail Ridge Road, a scenic highway between Estes Park and Grand Lake, Colorado, is usually closed by snowdrifts.

Early mountain snows have had tragic consequences. It was only the first of November, 1846, when the emigrants in the Donner party found themselves and their oxen caught in an unexpected Sierra Nevada snowstorm. Storm followed storm in that early winter, marooning seventy-nine men, women, and children just east of the summit; before their spring rescue came, thirty-four people had died.

All forms of frozen moisture are generally associated with the cold months of winter, although sleet and hail, ice and glaciers can be found year-round somewhere in the West. Permanent glaciers exist in the Cascades and Glacier National Park, and Iceberg Lake in Rocky Mountain National Park, Colorado, contains ice throughout the year.

Winter storms of unusual severity, sweeping down from Canada into Montana and the Great Plains, are accepted as a part of life by the westerner, who endures, but does not welcome, them. Weather Bureau records reveal dozens of dramatic and often tragic storms. A long-lasting blizzard in 1856–57, aptly named the Massacre Winter, completely wiped out the last prairie elk from Iowa. In 1887 one of the most severe storms on record—later referred to as the Great White Ruin—had a devastating effect on the mountain and plains states.

In this century the West was paralyzed by the Blizzard of Forty-nine. Moving quickly out of the north with little warning, the storm brought viciously high winds and a lashing, fine snow. More than a dozen states became snowbound, from Montana south to Arizona and as far east as Kansas and the Dakotas. At times, snow even covered the Mojave Desert.

Highway and railroad plows faced a herculean task, and virtually all automobile and train traffic came to a halt. Fifty passenger and freight trains were stalled between Omaha, Nebraska, and American Falls, Idaho. Stores, gas stations, and private residences along highways were jammed with stranded motorists. At the crossroads town of Rockport, Colorado, 343 people found refuge for three days at a small tavern. Business boomed and spirits were high until the food and drink ran out.

To some caught out on the roads, the storm brought tragedy. Near Hillsdale, Wyoming, a rancher, his wife, and their daughter were less than a mile from home when their Ford coupe stalled. Much later, the three were found dead in the car, blanketed by the fine snow that had blown in through the doorjambs and around windows. Officials attempting to reconstruct the story of the family's vain struggle for survival reported that the man

Fresh snow overlies an ancient glacier at the entrance to Mount Rainier ice caves. Icicles at left
have fused into a column capable of surviving the massive crack at its top.

65

KEITH GUNNAR

SOME MAJOR TYPES OF SNOW CRYSTALS

Examples	Name	Size Range (inches) of Single Crystals	Description
	Hexagonal Plates	0.01–0.2 (diameter)	Thin, semi-solid or solid crystals which, when small and present with small stellar crystals, are called "diamond dust."
	Stellar Crystals	0.03–0.5 (diameter)	Simple or branching rays which have become the symbol for snow. They often form bundles that are known as snowflakes.
	Hexagonal Columns	0.01–0.1 (diameter)	Ice prisms, usually transparent, that may contain air pockets within the crystal. When aloft in clouds, they produce halos around the sun and moon.
	Needles	0.2–0.4 (length)	Long, thin, often irregular hexagonal crystals with sharp points on each end, often found in bundles with their jagged points grown in several directions.
	Spatial Dendrites	variable	Plumed combinations of plates and stellar crystals.
	Capped Columns	0.01–0.2 (diameter)	Hexagonal columns, the end or ends of which carry hexagonal plates. Sometimes a third plate grows around the crystal's midsection. "Snowflake" Bentley called them "collar button" crystals.
	Irregular Crystals	variable	An asymmetrical grouping of small, plate-like particles clustered about a formless center, this is perhaps the most abundantly produced crystal type; like the stellar crystal, these too clump to form snowflakes.

Beginning life as a micro-sized germ of ice, no larger than the speck of dust on which it forms, the snow crystal grows by collecting water from the cloud vapor around it. Liquid water is not involved; the change is directly from vapor to solid. Tumbling and floating through the storm cloud, the budding crystal acquires its size, shape, and design. If it develops corner crystals, it will become plate-shaped; if long branches, star-shaped. The crystal eventually breaks free of the cloud and begins falling to earth, usually reaching the ground battered and imperfect.

Even so light and transient a substance as the snow crystal has not eluded the probing of scientific study or the photographer's lens. The first man to photograph snow crystals successfully was Wilson A. "Snowflake" Bentley. In the late 1880s he captured snow, while it was falling, on a smooth, black board. In an ice-cold shed the sample was inspected with a magnifying glass. If perfect, it was gently transferred to a microscope slide and then pressed against the cold glass by a stroke of a small feather. If the crystal remained intact, it was photographed in natural light with a bellows camera and a low-power lens.

Many of these mechanical procedures have not changed since the early days of photomicrographs; cool natural light that will not melt a crystal is still used in taking daytime snow crystal portraits; at night illumination is by electric lamp equipped with a heat-absorbing filter. Today, most photomicrographs are taken with oblique light, which enhances the crystal's rugged surface topography and reveals more clearly air pockets and white crystal borders.

At the National Center for Atmospheric Research in Boulder, Colorado, some researchers let snow crystals replicate themselves in a thin layer of plastic diluted with a solvent. The solvent (NCAR uses hexane) evaporates rapidly, leaving a thin plastic cast of the crystal. Another technique is to catch snow in a cold liquid that does not dissolve ice, eliminating the need for the ice-cold room.

had apparently dragged a fence post to the car, broken it into pieces, pulled a hubcap off the car, and lit a fire inside the vehicle, using the hubcap as a stove.

On the white-blanketed rangeland, livestock went unfed for weeks, and their only water was what they managed to get from the snow that surrounded them. The losses would have been great if Operation Haylift had not been initiated. Hay bales were thrown out of giant C-82 transports (the "flying boxcars" of World War II), their wings and tails painted bright red so that they could more easily be spotted if they were forced down. Mercy missions were flown from Denver; Ely, Nevada; Rapid City, South Dakota; Kearney, Nebraska; and Ogden, Utah. It is estimated that the haylift operation saved more than a million sheep and a hundred thousand cattle. Wild animals were not so fortunate, and the toll among them was horrendous. Starving deer were wandering helplessly along streets of Salt Lake City, and the pheasant population of South Dakota was decimated.

Snow, despite its potential hazards, is nonetheless a vital product of nature, bringing needed moisture to the plains and building vast snowpacks in the mountains that will help maintain forests on the slopes and, come spring, provide runoff for rivers and reservoirs. Snow is also a natural insulator, and its presence moderates soil temperature in the winter.

Meanwhile, ingenious man, in his effort to profit from everything, turns snow into gold on the ski slopes of the Sierra, the Cascades, and the Rockies. It is not unusual, when driving near Steamboat Springs, Colorado, or Jackson Hole, Wyoming, or Sun Valley, Idaho, to see a flurry of bumper stickers saying, "Think Snow."

Of all forms of frozen precipitation, snow is probably the most beautiful and the most useful. Sleet and freezing rain are rarely aesthetic and often dangerous, adding destructive weight to trees and power lines, and covering roads with a hazardous glaze. Both these icy culprits begin as rain and fall through a subfreezing zone near the ground. If the drops freeze before reaching the surface, they become sleet; if they freeze on contact, they are called freezing rain.

Some of winter's other forms of frozen water are not really precipitation. Frost is a light, feathery deposit of ice that results from the freezing of moisture that condenses on grass, windowpanes, rooftops, or other objects whose surface temperature is below both dew point (see

The famous Coffeyville, Kansas, hailstone—the largest ever recorded. Projecting spikes formed as it rotated in its descent to earth.

page 52) and freezing. Rime, a close cousin of frost, forms in moist cold air, developing horizontally and often projecting straight out into the wind. It is found on the windward side of unprotected fence posts, solitary trees, or other objects exposed to the wintry elements.

HAIL IS ANOTHER FORM of frozen precipitation, roughly spherical in shape. Paradoxically, of its several varieties, the most damaging kind occurs during warm rather than cold months, a by-product of thunderstorms. This large, or true, hail develops only within a cumulonimbus cloud in which there are extremely strong updrafts. These currents carry raindrops to high altitudes, where they freeze into the ice grains that form the nuclei of hailstones. Falling into the lower reaches of the cloud, the ice grains pick up a wet coating of rain. Then they are again carried aloft, where the additional water freezes and the stones grow. They may repeat this cycle many times, adding another onionlike layer with each round trip. Only when they are finally too large to be supported by the updrafts do they escape from the cloud and fall to earth.

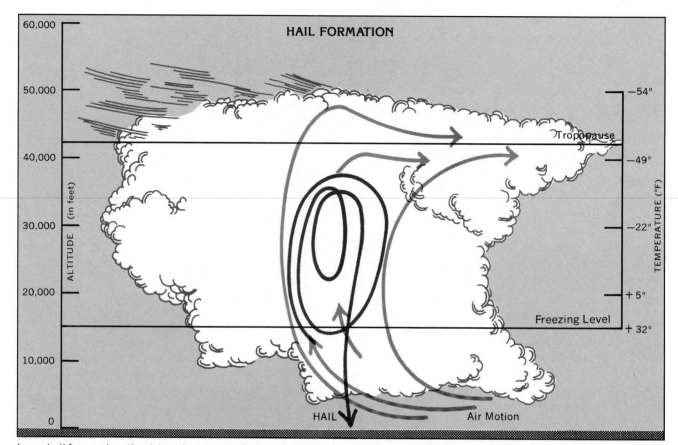

HAIL FORMATION

60,000

50,000 — −54°

40,000 Tropopause −49°

ALTITUDE (in feet)

TEMPERATURE (°F)

30,000 −22°

20,000 +5°

Freezing Level +32°

10,000

0

HAIL   Air Motion

Large hail forms when the rising air currents of a thunderstorm carry what is initially a small grain of ice on repeated trips from the rainy area low in the storm up into the subfreezing region. When the air currents can no longer support the weight of the hailstones, they fall—with sometimes devastating impact. If the freezing altitude is high, as is usually the case in late summer, or the air currents are weak, the hailstones will be small or even melt to rain before reaching the ground.

The more violent the thunderstorm, the larger the hail, although only about one thunderstorm in ten actually produces hail that reaches the ground. Hailstones range from the size of a small pea to that of a large grapefruit. The largest on record in the United States measured five and one-half inches in diameter and weighed 1.67 pounds; it fell during a storm over Coffeyville, Kansas, in September 1970.

No section of the United States is totally free from hail, but the damaging variety is most frequent in an area extending from Montana south to central Texas, and from the Missouri and Mississippi valleys to the foot of the Rockies. In the southern part of this "Hail Alley," hailstorms may occur as early as March, increasing in number during April and May. By May and June, they have moved northward into eastern Colorado and Wyo-

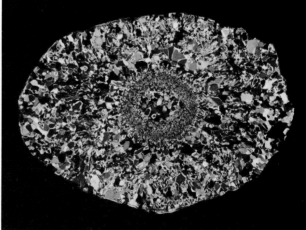

Cut open and viewed in polarized light, a hailstone reveals growth rings of coarse and fine crystals.

ming, while June, July, and August are the prevailing months for hail in Montana. Thus hail's physical capacity to destroy crops is compounded by its occurrence during the peak of the growing season. In the coterminous United States, total crop losses from hail are estimated at $300 million.

There are also two less destructive kinds of hail; soft hail (also called snow pellets) and small hail (also called ice pellets). Both are small clusters of ice crystals, which fall from storms containing snow and rain. Soft hail shatters on bouncing from a hard surface, whereas small hail does not. Small hail has a thin layer of ice over its core that has formed either by having water freeze on the surface or by falling first through a warm layer, which melts the surface, and then through a subfreezing layer, which hardens it again. Soft and small hail are generally the only types found on the West Coast.

JUST AS FLOODS are the result of too much rain, avalanches are the result of too much snow on steep terrain. Fortunately, they are confined to mountain country, usually far enough from cities and towns that their tremendous powers of destruction are spent, harmless and unseen, on the mountainside—with some dramatic exceptions.

Many tales are told of early gold-mining prospectors who found death instead of fortune when they were buried by avalanches or snowslides in the Cascades, the Sierra Nevada, or the Rockies. Perhaps the greatest avalanche catastrophe in the United States occurred in 1910, when a snowbound train with ninety-six passengers on board was swept into a canyon near Stevens Pass, Washington.

One of the most tragic years in Colorado avalanche history was 1884. On March 10 of that year, an avalanche swept over the railroad camp of Woodstock in the southwestern part of the state, resulting in fourteen fatalities among the seventeen inhabitants. Eyewitnesses recounted how two slides began moving simultaneously, joining forces just before hitting the town. "Suddenly the air became surcharged with snow so fine and so dense, it was like a snow fog, and there was a crashing and roaring like the tearing away of the mountainside." On that same day, other slides in Pitkin County took nine lives.

Silver Plume, in the granite mountains just west of

A passing truck narrowly escapes this avalanche accidentally triggered by skiers (on horizon).

historic Georgetown, Colorado, was partly buried on February 12, 1899, as two slides moved into the valley, killing ten residents. Ten days later another avalanche swept down Cherokee Gulch into the same town, crushing the Seven-Thirty Mine building and taking three more lives.

In the late 1960s, disaster struck Twin Lakes, a small resort community eighteen miles south of Leadville, Colorado. Early reports indicated that the slide originated on 14,431-foot Mount Elbert—the highest peak in Colorado—but U.S. Forest Service experts later traced its beginning to Mount Perry. The slide occurred around five-thirty in the morning, ripping apart buildings of the Gordon Mine several hundred feet above the town, then smashing two frame houses on the northwestern side of the valley, claiming seven victims. Two people and a family dog survived. It was the first avalanche in the area in over seventy years, and one of the most violent ever recorded there. The Forest Service computed that the slide reached a velocity of 130 miles per hour and not only leveled the trees in its path but stripped the branches bare of their needles.

The number of avalanches in the West runs well into

After an accident rescuers must probe systematically,
as the avalanche victim usually cannot save himself.

U.S. FOREST SERVICE

the thousands each winter. During a single month (January 1972) six hundred slides occurred in the vicinity of Stevens Pass, Washington.

Dr. Edward LaChapelle of the University of Washington, an authority on avalanches, points out that, while the force of gravity instigates a slide, the aging of the snow makes the mass more susceptible to movement. Time tends to smooth and round the individual crystals, reducing their cohesiveness.

IF AVALANCHES ARE THE WEST'S OUTLAWS, then glaciers are its heroes. Worldwide, the frozen assets of glaciers represent three-quarters of all fresh water reserves—the equivalent of approximately sixty years of global precipitation. John D. Ives, director of the Institute of Arctic and Alpine Research at the University of Colorado, points out that "during a hot, dry summer, when streams run low and lake levels fall, hydroelectric plants and farmers count on the extra glacier melt to balance the water supply."

By definition a glacier is "a field or body of ice, formed in a region where snowfall exceeds melting, and moving slowly down a mountain slope or valley." Only a small portion of the thousand or so ice fields in the contiguous United States—those in the highest Cascade and Olympic mountains—are living glaciers. The other long-standing ice areas collect, not more, but less snow than melts and are thus gradually shrinking. Seldom are these glaciers found in the path of direct sunlight; they lie behind the high mountain cirque walls, which prolong their survival.

Ice fields were not known to exist in the Sierra Nevada until October 1871, when naturalist John Muir discovered the Black Mountain Glacier in what is now Yosemite National Park. About seventy Sierran glaciers have since been recorded; Palisade Glacier, half a square mile in area, is the largest in the Sierra and the southernmost glacier in the United States.

The strangest glaciers are those known colloquially as "bug collectors." The largest and most accessible is Grasshopper Glacier in the Beartooth Range, northeast of Yellowstone National Park, which summertime hikers reach by a two-mile uphill trail over alpine tundra. Millions of grasshoppers buried over the past two or three centuries in this thick layer of glacier ice have been preserved in their sealed and frigid tomb. Evidence indicates that these insects, either blown off course or caught in summer snowstorms, succumbed to the cold mountain air and plummeted to earth.

Hallet's Glacier, north of Longs Peak in Rocky Mountain National Park, another bug collector, melted down substantially during the drought year of 1934, exposing thousands of insects, which were fed upon by the native bear population for several years. On the St. Vrain ice fields of Colorado, insects were so numerous that Major John Wesley Powell wrote that they "literally could have been gathered in wagonloads."

Perhaps three-fourths of all the West's glaciers are found in the state of Washington, where snowfall is heavy and summers are generally cool and humid. Anderson Glacier and a few other Olympic ice fields have developed entirely below timberline—a phenomenon that is unique in the Northern Hemisphere.

This rugged backcountry of Washington's Olympic Peninsula is the home of at least sixty-one glaciers, with recent aerial studies indicating that there may be many more. Blue Glacier on Mount Olympus, reaching a maximum thickness of 900 feet at its active midsection, is

Glacial ice is a sensitive climate indicator that scientists survey regularly for any sign of change. Crevasses, here on Blue Glacier in the Olympics, result from slow movement of the ice.

larger and moves faster than the average glacier in the United States. The ice crawls downslope a few hundred feet per year, melting at its snout, while building at its uppermost points, so that its overall size remains fairly constant.

Located below the North Pacific storm track, glaciers in Glacier National Park in Montana are well fed. A topographic map published at the turn of the century shows the park's Blackfoot Glacier as the largest in the American Rockies, a title it has since lost to Gannett Glacier in the Wind River Range of Wyoming, owing perhaps to climatic change.

Of the few glaciers south of the Wind River Range, most are confined to the Front Range of north-central Colorado, with a concentration in Rocky Mountain National Park.

The 1884 U.S. Geological Survey discovered glacial ice in the Snake Range amid the arid Great Basin of eastern Nevada and, possibly anticipating skepticism, stated in its report that "a region more unfavorable for the formation of glaciers could scarcely be found." Hav-

ing uncovered the survey's report, naturalist Weldon Heald rediscovered the glacier in 1955, located on 13,061-foot Wheeler Peak, in a cirque with walls so high that it was almost entirely obscured. This unique desert ice field is the only known American glacier lying outside the confines of the Cascades, the Sierra Nevada, or the Rockies.

BLIZZARD AND SLEET, hailstorm and avalanche assault man's comfort and convenience—sometimes his very life—so dramatically that they cast a negative pall over any discussion of frozen precipitation. And yet, the same combination of water and cold can, in a gentler mood, produce some of the most cherished products of western weather: the snow-capped peaks and glacier-carved valleys; the thin lace of morning ice on a mountain lake; a pristine ski slope after a snowstorm; the icicle fringe on a farmhouse roof; or a dusting of snow on red desert mesas. In all their guises ice and snow can bring a delicate beauty to the somber days of winter.

WHERE WEATHER IS BORN

From the larger perspective of space, ingredients of the global weather machine become clear. The earth's cloudy face and its vast, glittering oceans are part of a grand design that spreads rain and snow over the continents. The motions of the clouds reveal patterns that are too regular to have appeared by chance. Observed worldwide through a period of many days, they follow earth-circling wind belts of which the trades and westerlies are best known. On a smaller scale, clouds of all kinds swirl into spiraled knots of storm energy. In either view, the flow of air has been imbued with the characteristic curving action of the Coriolis force, a consequence of the earth's rotation. Unseen is that the atmosphere moderates the power of the sun, the distant but essential element that energizes the weather machine. On this and following pages is a potpourri of such concepts important to the behaviour of the atmosphere and weather.

THE ATMOSPHERE

The atmosphere, normally a tasteless, odorless, and colorless mixture of gases, is only 0.1 percent as dense at sea level as water, yet is so great in volume that it weighs some 5.6 million billion tons. It presses down with a force of one ton over each square foot of the earth's surface. Air pressure declines with altitude, dropping to half its sea-level value at 18,000 feet, and only 1 percent at eighteen miles.

The atmosphere is a security blanket for the earth below, intercepting most meteors, solar corpuscles, ultraviolet radiation, and cosmic rays.

Ninety-nine percent of dry air consists of the gases nitrogen, oxygen, argon, and carbon dioxide. By volume, air is nearly four-fifths nitrogen alone, and one-fifth oxygen. The principal remaining gases—hydrogen, neon, helium, krypton, xenon, ozone, and radon—are all present only in traces.

Scientists have discovered that the atmosphere consists of several layers, which they define by the manner in which the temperature varies through the layers. Separating each from the next is a "pause."

The bottom layer, or *troposphere* (from the Greek *tropos*, meaning "to turn, or mix"), consists of the six to ten miles of the atmosphere closest to the earth. Turbulent and energetic, it is the realm of clouds, storms, and convective air currents, and is the densest part of the atmosphere, containing nearly all suspended solids and water vapor, and 75 percent of all air. Convective air currents are stronger over warm regions, so the troposphere is pushed higher over the equator than over the poles, and higher in warm months than in cold.

Above the swirling winds and commotion of the troposphere lies the *stratosphere*, in which temperature changes relatively slowly. It is a layer that becomes warmer with height, heated in a process that uses ultraviolet radiation from the sun to combine oxygen molecules into ozone molecules. Ozone protects living things from the sun's harmful ultraviolet rays. Air temperature at the stratopause is nearly the same as at the earth's surface.

Whenever warm air lies above cold—as in the warm stratosphere above the colder troposphere—the condition is called an *inversion*. An inversion prevents the upward movement of air (see page 75), so the stratosphere is shielded from weather of the troposphere.

Temperature trends in the troposphere and stratosphere are echoed by the two layers above them. The *mesosphere* drops in temperature about the same rate

THE GREENHOUSE EFFECT

In many ways—storms, winds, thunder, and lightning—the atmosphere is boisterous and flashy, yet it performs one of its more remarkable tasks quietly. For all its apparent lack of substance, the atmosphere is responsible for keeping the earth warm and moderating its daily temperature range.

If there were no atmosphere, the temperature of the earth's surface would average an icy 15° F. instead of a mild 63° F. Temperatures could plunge to −300° F. at night, and soar to 200° F. by day, nearly the boiling point of water. Not every sort of atmos-

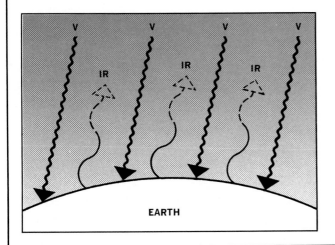

EARTH

phere would produce as temperate a world as ours. Two gases in the air, water vapor and carbon dioxide, have the special property of letting visible light pass through but absorbing infrared radiation, a light beyond red that is invisible to our eyes.

Most energy of the sun's rays is concentrated near the visible wavelengths of light (labeled ''V'' in the diagram) and penetrates the atmosphere. When it reaches the ground, the earth absorbs the energy and is heated by it. The ground, in turn, loses some of this heat as infrared radiation (labeled ''IR''), which is absorbed by water vapor and carbon dioxide in the air. By temporarily trapping heat that might have been directly radiated to space, and reradiating some of it back to the earth, the atmosphere stays warmer than it would otherwise be. Meteorologists call this process the *greenhouse effect* because a greenhouse works in the same way, using glass instead of water vapor and carbon dioxide to trap the heat.

Water vapor is usually more abundant than carbon dioxide, and its greenhouse effect is correspondingly more significant. The amount of water vapor in the air is highly variable, however; desert air, for example, contains little, and consequently the nights there cool quickly. The same is true at high altitudes. By contrast, the prairies are humid, and their summer nights remain warm.

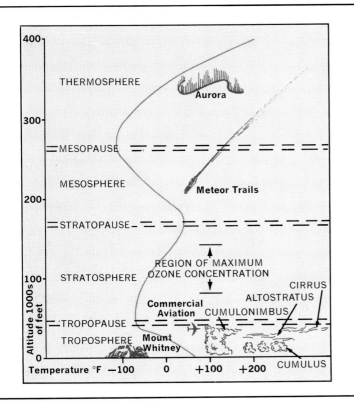

as does the troposphere, but because of its initially colder temperature and greater thickness, it attains a frigid −130° F. Like the troposphere, the mesosphere is turbulent, but the rarefied air and lack of moisture discourage anything resembling surface weather.

The beginning of the *thermosphere*—commonly called the *ionosphere*—is marked by a temperature minimum, called the *mesopause*, like that at the beginning of the stratosphere. The thermosphere is heated by cosmic rays and solar corpuscles, which,

One hundred miles up, the tenuous atmosphere is still dense enough to slow spacecraft. At two hundred fifty miles temperatures soar as high as 1700° F.—a figure having scant meaning, for in such thin air there is no sensible heat. Finally, about fifty thousand miles out, the earth's atmosphere merges with that of the sun in the inky vastness of space.

if not stopped, would be nearly as hazardous to life as ultraviolet radiation.

Cosmic rays and solar corpuscles ionize, or electrically charge, the gases in the rarefied upper atmosphere, making them into electrical conductors that reflect radio waves. Thus the thermosphere is a giant mirror off which radio waves can be bounced.

STABLE AND UNSTABLE AIR

Smog, cumulus clouds, and thunderstorms are related through an atmospheric quality called *stability*, which implies its opposite, *instability*, as well. Stability refers to the way in which air responds to forces, such as wind, that might displace it vertically. Stable air resists those forces while unstable air is highly susceptible to them. Stable air changes slowly and predictably; unstable air is unsettled, often stormy.

The stability of an air mass is determined largely by the way its temperature varies with height. The temperature measured at different heights in the atmosphere changes with altitude, generally decreasing an average of 3.5° F. per thousand feet. However, cloud-free air that is forced to rise cools by expansion at 5.5° F. per thousand feet. Thus its temperature can be different from that of the air into which it has risen, and the bubble will be heavier or lighter than the surrounding air.

In the case of the diagram labeled "Stable Air," a meteorologist might measure the temperature of an air mass at two intervals a thousand feet apart and find, for this example, that the temperature varies only 2° F. above and below the level at 70° F. If he raises a bubble of air from this level up one thousand feet, it expands, and cools by 5.5° F. It is then colder than the air around it, and when released, sinks. Similarly, if he pushes the air bubble down one thousand feet from the original level, it compresses, and warms by 5.5° F. It is then warmer than the air around it, and when released, rises. In either case, the air resists displacement, and is stable.

Unstable air behaves oppositely. In the case of the bubbles labeled "Unstable Air," the meteorologist might measure, for example, that the atmospheric temperature profile changes by 7° F. for each thousand feet of altitude. Now when he raises the bubble of air, he finds that it cools at the same 5.5° F. per thousand feet, which is less than the air around it, and a thousand feet above the level at 70° F., it is warmer than the surrounding air. Thus the bubble will keep rising. When he pushes the bubble down, it warms more slowly than the surrounding air, and a thousand feet below the level at 70° F., it is colder than the air around it. Thus it will keep falling. Once the bubble starts moving in either direction, it tends to continue moving that way, and the air mass is said to be unstable. In reality, the bubbles are any part of the air mass that is displaced vertically.

The cottony cumuli one sees on almost any fair day are there because the surface air is unstable from intense heating of the earth's surface by the sun. The air is sufficiently warm that it rises considerably, at least to the condensation level, before it mixes with the surrounding air and loses its unstable characteristics or cools to the surrounding air temperature.

Stable and unstable air have been described so far only for cloud-free air. Cloudy air behaves quite differently. As it rises beyond the condensation level, heat is continually released to the air as clouds multiply (see the box on page 55), reducing the rate of cooling. Whereas a bubble of cloud-free air cools 5.5° F. per thousand feet of altitude gained, a bubble of cloudy air cools at rates from about 5.5° F. down to about 2.5° F. per thousand feet gained, the latter figure for air containing large amounts of water vapor. The relatively slow cooling rate of a bubble of cloudy air means that a cloudy air mass can be unstable even if the temperature measured at different heights decreases little.

An air mass may start out cloud-free and stable, but when forced to rise, turn unstable as clouds form. For example, the ascent of air over a mountain range is one possible way to produce the unstable air that powers mountain thunderstorms. Clouds showing vertical development, such as thunderclouds, are a characteristic clue to the presence of unstable air. In the hot and very moist air over the prairie in summer, so much heat is released by condensation as cumulus clouds grow that strong updrafts draw up still more air and moisture, building immense anvil-headed thunderstorms, a common but awesome result of atmospheric instability.

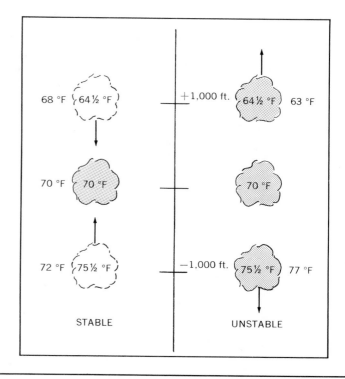

68 °F 64½ °F   +1,000 ft.   64½ °F 63 °F

70 °F 70 °F   70 °F

72 °F 75½ °F   −1,000 ft.   75½ °F 77 °F

STABLE   UNSTABLE

Inversions

An important special case of stable air is called an *inversion*. It occurs whenever warm air lies above cool. The denser, cooler air has absolutely no tendency to rise, and is trapped by the warm air. Where inversions are frequent, in some valleys, basins, and coastal regions, residents have become aware of the natural consequence that pollutants accumulate, occasionally reaching hazardous concentrations. A meteorological effect of some inversions is that they block the upward movement of air containing water vapor and thus prevent showers. This is at least a partial explanation of the origin of deserts.

There are two types of inversions: *upper air* and *surface*. In each, the air temperature varies in a characteristic manner, shown below. Temperatures in the inversion layer are warmer, rather than cooler as is normal, at higher altitude.

Surface inversions are common, and their most frequent cause is the nighttime radiation of heat from the earth. Because land radiates heat more effectively than air, it can cool rapidly after sunset; by conduction, the adjacent air cools, too, while higher air remains relatively warm. Surface inversions are often found in low areas to which cold surface air has drained—basins and valleys. Warming rays of the morning sun usually destroy the inversion.

Upper air inversions are common on the West Coast where they arise from a combination of warming, descending air from the North Pacific High and a cool layer of marine air at the surface. Within that layer, temperatures, starting near that of the Pacific Ocean, fall with increasing altitude. Roughly a thousand feet up, the marine layer encounters the warmer air of the high, and an inversion results.

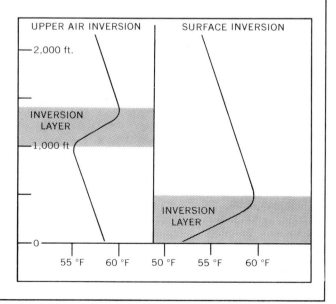

THE CORIOLIS FORCE

Air moving over the face of the earth cannot move in a straight line because of a force, not obvious in everyday life, to which the winds, seemingly free, must respond. Called the Coriolis force, it arises from the rotation of the earth.

To understand the Coriolis force, it is helpful to look at the earth from afar. Any point on the earth must make a full rotation every day. But the earth is larger at the equator, so the surface speed there is greater than at any other latitude—about one thousand miles per hour. Since the whole atmosphere rotates with the earth, air at the equator is also moving west to east faster than at higher latitudes.

If air moves directly northward from the equator, it maintains its same eastward speed due to the rotation of the earth (though in reality friction decreases it somewhat), but the farther north it travels, the slower the earth turns below it. The result is that the air acquires an eastward trend with respect to the surface. To an observer on the surface, who cannot sense the rotation of the earth, it appears that a force, the Coriolis force, is pushing the air eastward. If the air had begun its northward journey from a higher latitude, the result would have been the same. On the other hand, had the equatorial air headed southward, it would instead have swerved to the west.

The Coriolis force always turns winds to the right in the Northern Hemisphere and to the left in the Southern Hemisphere. It causes the rotation of air around highs and lows and, along with atmospheric pressure differences and air friction, determines other features of atmospheric motion.

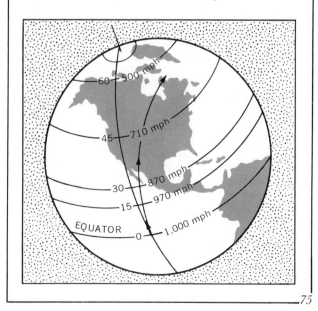

HIGHS AND LOWS

The general circulation of the atmosphere is often masked by an endless procession of atmospheric disturbances and associated weather fronts, just as eddies and whirls of a river can nearly obscure the downstream flow of the main current. Traveling west to east in the middle latitudes, they are here today and gone tomorrow; inconspicuous on the average seasonal charts of winds and pressure, their presence usually brings the weather of any given day.

The traveling atmospheric disturbances are called cyclones and anticyclones, or lows and highs, because the air pressure in them is either lower or higher than surrounding air (at the same altitude). On weather maps, the wind patterns show as whirls, their direction depending on whether the system is a high or low. Since air moves from regions of high pressure to those of low pressure, it will stream toward a low and away from a high. In response to the Coriolis force, air in the Northern Hemisphere will veer to the right of the center of a low and, seen from above, will circulate counterclockwise. The reverse is true of highs, with the wind circulating around them clockwise. The faster atmospheric pressure changes with distance from the center of a high or a low, the faster the winds will circulate around it.

The air moving at ground level into a low must go somewhere: it goes up. Therein lies the reason that lows are associated with cloudy weather. As the air rises, it cools, and eventually clouds may form. If they are thick enough, rain or snow may fall. Conversely, the air spreading out at ground level from a high has come from above and, in descending, has warmed, enabling it to evaporate whatever clouds it may have contained. Thus high pressure regions are associated with dry weather and clear skies.

Cyclonic storms, the lows that bring much of the nation's rain, are more complex than this simple description. They evolve from the conflict between contrasting air masses along *fronts*, or boundaries, separating them. Names of fronts are based upon the relative motions of the contrasting air masses.

In a *warm front* (figure 1a), advancing warm air overrides cooler air. The front gently slopes because the retreating cold air is retarded by friction along the ground. Clouds form at all levels along the front, and the rising warm air releases widespread precipitation before the front passes at the surface. On its arrival, a falling barometer becomes steady, winds shift direction, temperatures rise, rain diminishes, and humidity—high during the rain—remains high. Behind the front there is usually clear air.

In a *cold front* (figure 1b), advancing cold air displaces warmer air. The front is steep because its lower layers drag along the surface and may become rounded (as shown). Like a wedge, the cold air thrusts the warm air upward, producing clouds. If

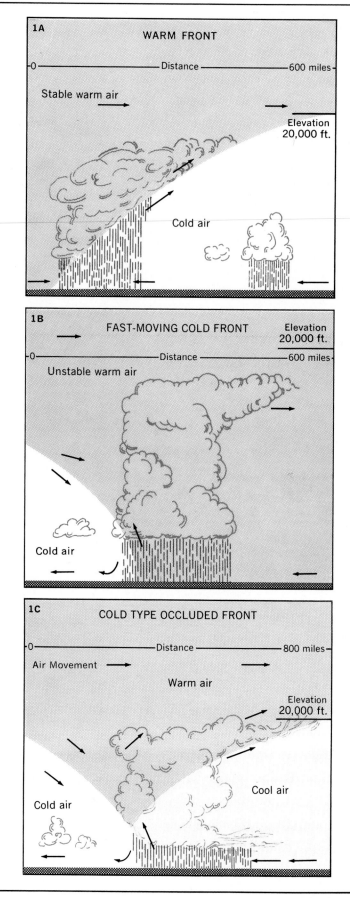

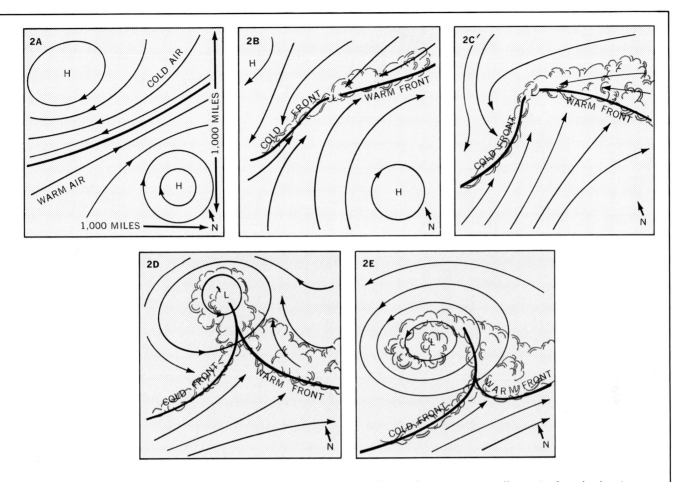

the warm air is unstable, they may be part of a thunderous squall line. Precipitation is showery. In a slow-moving cold front, warm air overlies the cold for a distance behind the front, and precipitation there is widespread. In a fast-moving front (shown), precipitation falls in a narrow band, primarily just ahead of the front. Once the front passes, barometers rise rapidly, the wind shifts and picks up speed, temperature and humidity suddenly drop, and showers and squalls along the front diminish, then stop. A cold front is usually followed by a short spell of clear weather, then by brief showers from cumulus clouds, and finally a general clearing of the skies.

An *occluded front* (figure 1c), a composite of warm and cold frontal systems, occurs when a cold front overtakes a warm front. Air behind the cold front may be colder, as in a cold front occlusion (shown), or warmer, as in a warm front occlusion, than air ahead of the warm front. The warm air mass between the two is forced entirely above them. The clouds of an occluded front are initially those associated with both the cold and warm fronts separately. The ascent of so much warm air usually brings precipitation, heaviest just ahead of the juncture of all three air masses while the occlusion is young, then diminishing when the occlusion is older and the continued ascent of the warm air has wrung most of the moisture from it. Weather following the passage of an occlusion is that of the cold front that caused it.

These fronts are usually part of cyclonic storms, often called wave cyclones because of their resemblance to a water wave in cross section, a model originally formulated by the Norwegian meteorologist Jacob Bjerknes around 1919. A cyclonic storm often forms in a region of relatively low pressure between two highs that differ in temperature and humidity (figure 2a; the arrows indicate wind direction). A typical combination over the Great Plains would be a cold, polar high from the north and a warm, moist high from the Gulf of Mexico.

The cyclonic storm is born as a kink in the boundary between the highs (figure 2b). On the right, warm air is riding over cold as a warm front, while on the left, cold air is advancing as a cold front. As the front moves past an observer, the wind direction changes. When a warm front passes, the wind shifts from southeasterly to southwesterly, while for a cold front the shift is from southwesterly to northwesterly.

A distinctive wedge of warm air to the south of the low pressure center, called the *warm sector* (figure 2c), narrows as the cold front eventually overtakes the warm front, forming an occlusion (figure 2d). At this stage, the winds begin to circle the low. Air may orbit the center several times, twisting bands of clear and cloudy air into a tight spiral (figure 2e), signaling the final fling of the storm. Its supply of warm moist air cut off, the storm slowly dissipates.

THE MARCH OF STORMS

Lows and highs move eastward in an alternating sequence around the poles (figure 1). They are ripples in the sinuous boundary separating polar from tropical air, where most lows and highs in the mid-latitudes are spawned. This boundary and its accompanying belt of storms retreat poleward in summer and advance toward the equator in winter.

Many lows that reach the West Coast originate far away over the North Pacific. Days later they arrive, often occluded and wound into a tight spiral. Broken up by the West's mountains, they may regroup and head for the East (figure 2). Those formed in Wyoming, Colorado, and Texas move across the Midwest while relatively young, but already very potent.

Highs traveling across the United States from the Northwest are really intervals between lows, and their air is relatively mild. The highs from Canada, occurring as polar air makes deep plunges southward, are more severe.

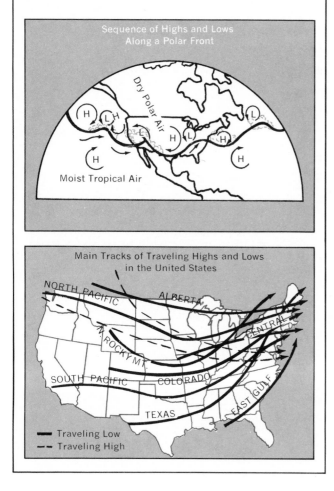

Sequence of Highs and Lows
Along a Polar Front

Dry Polar Air

Moist Tropical Air

Main Tracks of Traveling Highs and Lows
in the United States

NORTH PACIFIC
ALBERTA
CENTRAL
ROCKY MT.
SOUTH PACIFIC
COLORADO
EAST GULF
TEXAS

— Traveling Low
-- Traveling High

GLOBAL AIR CIRCULATION

The earth's atmosphere has a general circulation, powered by solar energy, that carries air, heat, and moisture from the equator to the poles. Because the sun's rays fall almost vertically at the equator and obliquely at higher latitudes, most atmospheric heating occurs in the equatorial region. Simplistically, the equator is an earth-girdling low while the poles are highs. One might expect a surface flow of cold air from the highs at the poles to the low at the equator. The warm air of the equatorial low would rise, travel aloft in mid-latitudes, and descend over the ice caps to complete the circuit. Circulation vaguely similar to this does occur, but there are complications.

If equatorial air were to reach the poles directly, the Coriolis force would cause it to race around them at roughly a thousand miles an hour. Instead, complicated forces acting on the atmosphere break the circulation into three zones in each hemisphere (shown below)—an equatorial zone, a mid-latitude zone, and a polar zone—each having relatively slow winds. In the equatorial zone, warm air rises over the equator, flows poleward at high altitude, sinks in the vicinity of latitude 30°, and returns along the surface to the equator. The Coriolis force swings the southward-moving surface air to the west, so the winds in

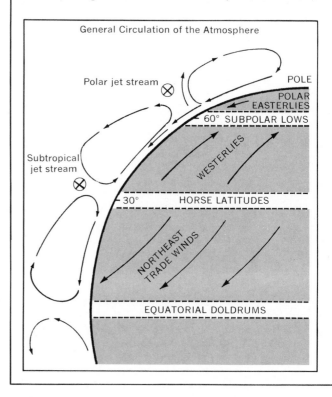

General Circulation of the Atmosphere

Polar jet stream
POLE
POLAR EASTERLIES
60° SUBPOLAR LOWS
WESTERLIES
Subtropical jet stream
30° HORSE LATITUDES
NORTHEAST TRADE WINDS
EQUATORIAL DOLDRUMS

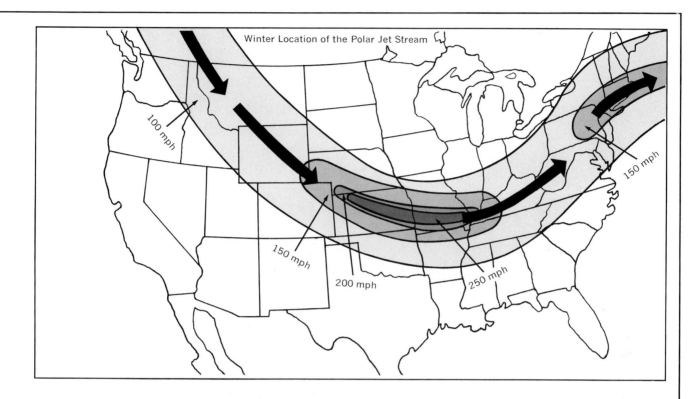

Winter Location of the Polar Jet Stream

100 mph

150 mph

150 mph

200 mph

250 mph

the equatorial zone, the trades, are easterlies. The air that sinks around latitude 30° is also part of the mid-latitude circulation zone that extends to about latitude 60°, where the polar zone begins. Since surface air in the mid-latitude zone has an average poleward motion, the Coriolis force turns the air eastward, so winds there are westerlies. Weather systems of the mid-latitudes almost obscure the westerlies, whereas the trade winds are reasonably steady. Finally, cold air sinking at the poles returns toward the equator along the surface, giving rise to polar easterlies.

Early mariners on the seas of the Southern Hemisphere, where there is little land to slow the wind, referred to the windy regions as the Roaring Forties; as they penetrated to higher latitudes, they encountered the Furious Fifties and the Shrieking Sixties. Westerlies in the Northern Hemisphere, landlocked throughout large portions of their global journey, are meandering and less vigorous.

Where the equatorial air subsides, around latitude 30°, are found ''stationary'' anticyclones that affect weather patterns. The two important ones for western weather are the North Pacific, or Hawaiian, High and the North Atlantic, or Bermuda, High. The North Pacific High is responsible for the relative dryness of California and much of the Southwest, while the North Atlantic High does the opposite for the prairies as

it circulates moist Gulf of Mexico air into the Midwest, creating thundershowers in summer and cyclonic storms the remainder of the year. In a similar way, rising air in the vicinity of latitude 60° gives rise to the Aleutian Low, which spawns storms that dampen the Northwest. Though basically permanent features of atmospheric circulation, these stationary cyclones and anticyclones vary in both strength and position with the seasons.

Special features of the general circulation are the jet streams. These are bands of very high velocity winds, sometimes exceeding two hundred fifty miles per hour, that are found six to eight miles up in the troposphere along the boundaries of the circulation zones. The diagram above shows an example of the location of the polar jet stream over the United States in winter, with representative wind speeds.

The lateral extent of the ''core'' is about two hundred miles, its depth less than one mile, though the jet streams often extend completely around the earth. The jet streams are highly variable in speed and position, but they can be charted and predicted by weathermen for the benefit of aircraft pilots, who use them to save time and fuel. Meteorologists, having found that cyclones follow the curving path of the polar jet stream, use this fact to aid in the prediction of storm tracks.

CHAPTER 8

THE CIRCLE OF SEASONS

Characteristics and timing of the seasons in different parts of the West ❖ The natural responses of living things to the passage of the year ❖ Reasons for the seasons

THE GREAT DIVERSITY OF CLIMATE in the West is perhaps nowhere more evident than in the ways the seasons are experienced in various regions. In the Southern California desert, summer seems eight months long, while in the high country of the Rockies it is winter that seems to last three seasons. On the prairies and eastern Great Plains, there are years when spring is almost nonexistent, while in coastal California it often seems to begin shortly after Christmas and last through May. Inland the differences in seasons are sharp and unmistakable; as one nears the Pacific, they become ever more subtle. Yet, every place does have its seasons. And in each place living things—through thousands upon thousands of revolutions of the earth—have come to understand their local cycle of seasons and year after year perform their ancient rituals of response.

As spring gathers in the earth, knowledge of the coming season reaches all living things. In the plant world, the humble skunk cabbage is first to send up shoots from its swampy dwelling place. Sheathed by a slender hood, and retaining heat released by the oxidation of carbohydrates, the skunk cabbage is able to melt frozen ground and push toward the surface with gentle strength.

Hibernating animals stir in their snug hideaways, and snow-melt torrents roar down the mountain streams. Migrating mule deer will soon begin their seasonal trek from the foothills to summer feeding stations on the mountains, with preying coyotes and mountain lions not far behind.

As life awakens in the North, migratory birds return instinctively to their breeding grounds. Song sparrows, grackles, redwings, and some robins often return to a still-snowy landscape; in fact, some especially hardy robins never leave the northland.

Spring is an assorted weather season. Killing frosts and bursts of sunshine intermix in the Rockies; until mid-June, snowfall is possible at high elevations on the Colorado Front Range, and even lowlands remain vulnerable to ice and windstorms. Remnants of a cold mound of high pressure, though less intense and more ephemeral than in winter, still hover over the Canadian Arctic, while over the southwestern United States a cell of low pressure is building. Incursions of arctic air sporadically pour down the meridians, flowing close to the earth. British meteorologist Sir Napier Shaw once estimated that $3\frac{1}{2}$ trillion tons of cold arctic air flows south each year in late winter and early spring; and with every new influx comes a change in the weather.

Hence, freak weather conditions and record storms are not uncommon in spring. The Easter blizzard of 1873, for example, swept a huge swath across Kansas, Nebraska, and South Dakota, blowing wet snow into drifts and killing many new settlers; in 1906 a rare east wind drove fire from the San Francisco earthquake dangerously across the city; one spring day in Los Angeles registered 100° F., and another in Eagle Nest, New Mexico, a numbing —36° F.

Although Robert Frost is closely associated with New England, his words about the vicissitudes of spring apply as well to the mountains and valleys of the West:

When the annual thaw swells mountain streams to roaring cataracts, all living things know that spring is at hand.

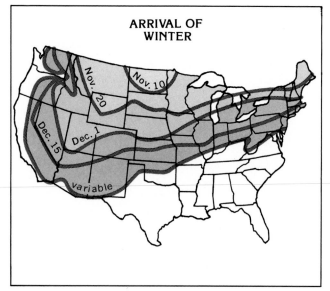

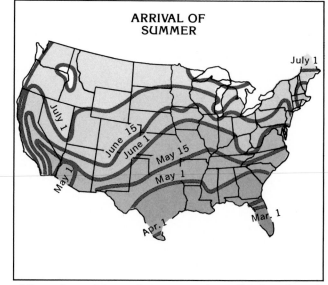

Average dates for the onset of winter (left), based on the retreat southward of 32° F. temperatures, and summer (right), based on the advance northward of 68° F. temperatures. Over most of the nation, winter and summer arrive well before the solstices (about December 21 and June 21, respectively) but in certain climates one or the other seems never to come at all.

The avalanche lily is among the first to reclaim the earth from the bleakness of winter.

You know how it is with an April day:
When the sun is out and the wind is still,
You're one month on in the middle of May.
But if you so much as dare to speak,
A cloud comes over the sunlit arch,
A wind comes off a frozen peak,
And you're two months back in the middle
    of March.

Throughout much of the inland West, winter yields reluctantly to spring. When crocuses are already peeking through last year's leaves on the eastern seaboard, it would take a keen observer to hear the trickle of melting snow only beginning in the Rockies or feel a slight softening of the bitter wind across the northern plains.

In understanding summer weather, one word is of primary importance: *convection*—the vertical exchange, along with partial mixing, of large air masses. The ascending air currents can literally hold up a summer cumulus cloud until the main supply of energy from the sun is cut off toward evening. "The full moon eats clouds" was an old French saying, and indeed it is true that, instead of falling to earth, cumulus cloud droplets can vanish (evaporate) into thin air at the end of the day— a phenomenon usually noted with a bright, full moon.

The typical summer storm usually originates locally, convectionally produced by heating of moist, unstable masses of air. Rainfall comes in showers, often thunderstorms, but usually does not last all day. Because summer moisture in the West comes from either the Gulf of Mexico or the Gulf of Alaska (which lies athwart the wind track of the prevailing westerlies even in summer), the likelihood of rain decreases with distance from these sources. Least accessible to either are Nevada and Southern California, regions of long summer drought. In California the "dry season"—that is, summer—lasts about half the year, browning the grasslands and encouraging punsters to call it the "Golden Bare" state.

Summer is the season of that king of convective storms, the thunderstorm. For the country as a whole, July is by far the most thundery month; in the most northerly tier of midcontinental states, two out of every three thunderstorms occur between June and September. The only western region where thunderstorms occur at all in the winter is along the West Coast, and then infrequently.

Summer heat and humidity are called "corn weather" in Iowa. Bearing down on the flatlands of the Corn Belt around the beginning of July, the temperature may be still in the high 90s—with humidity the same—even in the small hours of the morning. Sleeping on such a night may be unthinkable. Growing so fast that one can hear it, the corn may be six inches taller by morning.

Heat makes the tomatoes grow in the Great Central Valley of California, too. Although nights are cool, daily temperatures over 100° F. are common, baking all the rainless earth except for the fields and orchards that are hooked up to a life-line of irrigation ditches and canals.

There are several field-tested methods for ascertaining the approximate air temperature without benefit of a thermometer. They sound like folk wisdoms, but meteorologists say they work. One involves timing the speed of ants; another, pacing a worm; and a third—perhaps the simplest test—counting the number of chirps per minute

MARY RANDLETT

In the Palouse country of western Washington, midsummer is the time of the great wheat harvest. Rarely are Palouse wheat ranchers threatened by either hail or heavy pre-harvest rains, two natural enemies.

With the coming of summer, the cyclonic storms that have controlled western weather all winter give way to a succession of brief but intense thunderstorms.

of a particular katydid: divide by 4, and add 50! Similar formulae work for crickets, too.

Many people think that autumn is the most beautiful time of the year. Nights are crisp and clear; days have a lingering warmth and can even be hot; inland lakes, though cooling, are still swimmable; and the air is soft and aromatic.

In the western states autumn blazes with the color of yellow aspens and tamarack, and red vine maple and poison oak. The pigments bringing these tones have been part of the leaves since spring, but their color was overwhelmed by the leaf's green chlorophyll. With the cessation of chlorophyll synthesis brought on by fall's short days and cool weather, the vibrant pigments are revealed, and the red and purple even increase in concentration. Weather is critical to the display. Drought decreases the intensity of the color, while too much rain may cause persistence of the food-making process and a correspondingly sodden autumnal display. When conditions are perfect, Yosemite Valley glows with new color, from its tall meadow grasses to the Kellogg black oaks, the maples and dogwoods and poplars. In Utah the birch trees turn yellow; in the foothills of the Coast Range and the Sierra, clumps of red berries ripen on the toyon, and willows illumine every streambed.

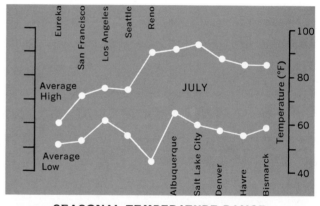

SEASONAL TEMPERATURE RANGE

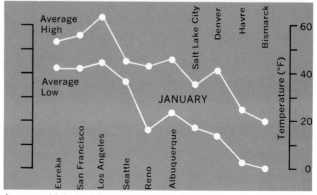

Average high and low temperatures for summer and winter vary little on the coast, more widely inland.

THE SEASONS

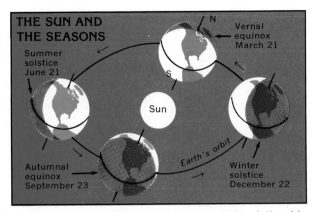

THE SUN AND THE SEASONS

Summer solstice June 21

Vernal equinox March 21

Sun

Earth's orbit

Autumnal equinox September 23

Winter solstice December 22

N

S

The seasonal cycle depends on the geometric relationship between the earth's tilt and the sun's rays.

The origin of the seasons is found in astronomy, in the fact that the earth's axis of rotation is not parallel to its axis of revolution—they differ by 23½ degrees. Because the axis of rotation maintains a nearly constant orientation in space as the earth orbits its star, the North Pole leans toward the sun for one half of the year, and away from it for the other half. However, since the North and South Poles tilt in opposite directions, the seasons are reversed in the Southern Hemisphere; in the Southern temperate zone, June is cold, January hot.

Whatever the location, the seasons are defined as beginning at an instant fixed by astronomical events. In the Northern Hemisphere, summer and winter begin when the North Pole tips the full 23½ degrees toward or away from the sun (the solstices), respectively; spring and fall, when the poles tip neither toward nor away from the sun (the equinoxes).

The familiar yearly cycle of warm and cold temperatures results from seasonal variation in the intensity of the sun's rays reaching a given part of the earth's surface—the insolation (*incoming solar radiation*). In spring and summer, the sun's rays strike the ground at an angle nearer to vertical and for a longer time each day than in fall and winter. Thus spring and summer are the warm seasons.

Curiously, although spring and summer each bring the same quantity of sunshine, summer is warmer than spring, because spring's heat has accumulated in the land and the oceans, similarly, fall is warmer than winter.

As insolation declines in the fall, temperatures of the land and water decrease, but stored heat keeps them warmer than insolation alone would indicate.

Even though days grow longer from the first day of winter on, land and water continue to cool as they lose excess heat. Their temperatures reach a minimum sometime after the beginning of winter. As summer approaches, land and water temperatures lag, now from winter's effects, and do not reach their maximum until sometime after the beginning of summer. Water stores more heat than land, thus causing greater temperature lags. For example, on the coast of Washington the highest temperatures come about seven weeks after the beginning of summer, whereas in northeast New Mexico, far inland, the lag is only about three weeks.

Another effect of the seasonal cycle is that the earth-circling zones of atmospheric circulation follow the sun, strengthening some weather systems and weakening others. Thus the North Pacific High moves northward in summer, and its influence spreads to include most of the Pacific Ocean north of the equator. In winter, the high weakens, drifts southward, and the Pacific falls under the dominance of the Aleutian Low, which was absent during summer. Cyclonic storms that would have been blocked in summer by the North Pacific High move freely into the Pacific Coast states in winter, adding a cycle of storms to the cycles of seasons.

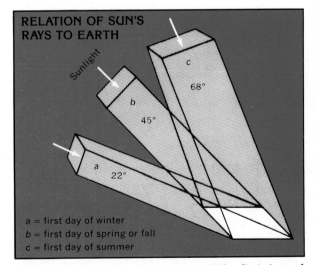

RELATION OF SUN'S RAYS TO EARTH

Sunlight

c 68°

b 45°

a 22°

a = first day of winter
b = first day of spring or fall
c = first day of summer

Between the first days of summer and the first days of winter, the sun's position at noon drops from 68° (90° is directly overhead) to only 22° at Portland's latitude. With winter's low sun angles, a given area on the earth's surface receives a smaller bundle of solar rays—and thus less heat—than it would receive in summer.

The four major flyways for migratory birds—down the Atlantic Coast, the Pacific Coast, the Mississippi Valley, and southward from Montana and Wyoming—are busy with seasonal commuters on their way to winter quarters. At the Bear River Migratory Bird Refuge in Utah, flocks gather before heading to their wintering grounds. Some proceed directly south, some turn west to the Pacific route or east to the Mississippi, and a few take the long way via the Atlantic Coast. Another large wildlife sanctuary outside Sacramento provides a waystop on the Pacific flyway where millions of waterfowl gather. And on Monterey Bay, in October, wintering monarch butterflies congregate in the pine trees of their sanctuary at Pacific Grove.

Autumn's first warning of winter occurs with an influx of cold polar air from the north. Along the Canadian border it may come by the end of September, and repeated onslaughts strike deeper into the country as the season progresses. But suddenly, just when cold seems to have swept in and taken charge, Indian summer may arrive. Strictly speaking, this name applies to a late fall stretch of warm, hazy, euphoria-producing days and cool nights that visits the central and eastern United States as the unpredictable gift of winds from the Gulf of Mexico.

But it has grown to mean any unseasonably warm spell that comes along after fall has settled in. The term "Indian summer" is part of eighteenth-century America and was first used on the frontier of western Pennsylvania. Some say it came from the Indian strategy of attacking when settlers had relaxed their guard in the pleasant, mild weather; others say that the air was smoky from Indian fires, or that the good weather allowed the Indians to harvest their corn, squash, and pumpkins.

By autumn's end, almost all the northern third of the United States has had some snow, with the snow line descending like a miniature ice age.

Though winter does not begin or end on the same day for the myriad forms of life, there is a rule of thumb that when the mean daily temperature falls below about 43° F., plant processes in the mid-latitudes cease. But nature has proven to be foresighted: in the autumn trees develop the buds that hold the potential for new growth they will tap in the spring.

In the insect world, crickets, katydids, woolly bears, grasshoppers, and ladybugs crawl into hibernation. Bats hang in suspended animation in their caves; frogs have burrowed into the mud of streams; the marmot is underground, and the muskrat has retreated to its den. On the coast, the grosbeak, finch, and junco appear, having abandoned chill nesting places in the high country. The chinook, or king, salmon has made its spawning run to the high waters of the Columbia River and died.

After the first day of winter, the shortest day of the year, the weather grows more blustery. Spilling down southward from Canada, the polar air becomes colder as winter deepens. Snow cover reflects incoming heat from the sun, rather than absorbing it as the ground does. Thus wind blowing over a snow- and ice-covered landscape has a biting cold in the new months of the year that was not there in December.

Cold waves, when the thermometer suddenly plummets, obey age-old rules of the atmosphere and sometimes can be easily forecast. The principal ingredient is a strong high pressure system located over the Northwest Territories and the Yukon, poised and ready at any moment to slip its chill across the border. The catalyst to action is a low pressure system in the Great Lakes region that draws the cold air southward in its wake. The faster the low travels and the greater the pressure difference between it and the high, the more rapidly the cold advances.

BOTH PAGES: GRANT HEILMAN

Golden aspens brighten the fall landscape of Colorado as winter readies its assault.

In the vast reaches of the continent's interior, winter is a time of waiting. Here rays from the pale sun form a halo on cirrostratus clouds that brood over a snowy Colorado ranchyard.

In the northern border states—Minnesota, North Dakota, and Montana—cold waves are legend. Montana plains may be locked in the grip of a cold wave for as long as two weeks. In the Mississippi Valley the same cold wave may last only two days. In its southward venture, the life span of a cold wave is diminished, and there is a tendency for its replacement to be a warm spell of comparable intensity. The warm spells and cold spells are, in fact, characteristic of winter in the Middle West.

Sometimes the meaning of a season is best illustrated in its myths. Groundhog Day—February 2 in most states—celebrates one such myth. If the groundhog (woodchuck), emerging from his burrow that day, sees his shadow, he will return to the burrow, and winter will continue for another six weeks. But if the skies are cloudy and he sees no shadow, he will go about his business and spring will be early. In fact, long-range predictions cannot be forecast by a single day's sunshine or cloudiness, and the groundhog is less a weather omen than a study of life renewed.

During his winter hibernation the groundhog—or in the western United States, his cousin the marmot—takes a mere ten or twelve breaths an hour, his body temperature a cool 38° or 40° F. Then on an early spring day, within just a few hours, he awakens. In what must be a miracle of spring, his temperature rises nearly sixty degrees, his respiration quickens to thirty or forty times a minute, and he emerges at the chimney of his hole to greet a world that is perhaps still alternately freezing and thawing, not quite ready for renaissance.

To paraphrase Ecclesiastes, for every place there is a season, or rather a cycle of seasons. The rich variety that western America offers in other ways—landforms, plant and animal life, historical development, day-to-day weather—is true also of its seasons. The northern plains swing from arctic cold to Saharan heat in half a revolution of the earth, while a coastal city like Eureka, California, must look beyond its thermometers to know that the season has changed at all. Montanans experience four very distinct seasons, while residents of the coast often think in terms of only two—rainy and dry. But seasons they are, all the same.

The seasons existed before life, roll on unaffected by it, and may continue to do so long after it disappears. Life has had to adapt to the seasons, building their rhythms into its very structure. Even man, while he can sometimes modify the weather, cannot stop the relentless procession of the seasons.

COLOR SPECTACLES AND SKY PHENOMENA

No part of the world has a monopoly on the strange and beautiful manifestations of earth's weather, but few people would deny that the sweeping skies of western America offer a theater par excellence for observing and enjoying them. Over vast expanses of the West's plains, deserts, mountain tops, and seashores the heavenly stage stretches, unbroken by wall or tree, from horizon to far horizon.

The very size and diversity of the West allow it to include a wide range of weather marvels—often with several visible from a single vantage point. In the Pacific Northwest one may see such exotic phenomena as the aurora borealis and strange looming mirages that send boats sailing upside down along the horizon. In the desert Southwest residents are treated instead to brilliant sunrises and sunsets, rainbows, and phantom lakes spread shimmering over the sun-seared land. Everywhere in the West there are colors and wonders to be seen in one display or another. One has only to look. And to look with understanding makes the show all the more enjoyable.

The sun, as it retreats toward the horizon, often appears distorted because of the same irregular atmospheric refraction that causes mirages.

Puffy white cumulus clouds are usually a sign of continued fair weather, but when they tower and roil as this one does, they may become showery cumulonimbus.

*Seemingly menacing, these mountain wave clouds formed in air rising over
the isolated peak of Mount Adams, Washington, as did the fog below.*

Bubbles of air from weather systems, in effect miniature fronts aloft,
can cause a cloud line to come in from out of the blue. This one displays
a hard edge but also a slight degree of turbulence.

KENT & DONNA DANNEN

JOSEF MUENCH

Mile-deep Grand Canyon has weather of its own design, here lying under broken stratus clouds while surrounding
plateaus enjoy a cloudless sky. Note the color of foreground shadows, illuminated only by blue skylight.

OVERLEAF: *Beneath a sky black with clouds, a late afternoon cloudburst nearly blocks the sun*
with the kind of deluge that fills desert arroyos and brings flash floods.

JOSEF MUENCH

NATIONAL OCEANIC AND ATMOSPHERIC ADMINISTRATION (NOAA)

*A tornado (right) and waterspout
(below) have much in common, but the
weather conditions which spawn the
two twisters are different, and rarely
does the power of a waterspout equal that
of the weakest tornado. Note the wind
tracks as air spirals in to the waterspout.*

JOSEPH GOLDEN, NATIONAL SEVERE STORMS LABORATORY

LARENA BROWN, PHOTOGRAPHY UNLIMITED

Was this fire started by lightning? Every year some 10,000 blazes
in the United States are. Fanned by its own upslope breeze,
the fire has spread, its smoke reddening the setting sun.

Within a stream-carved cave the frozen assets of Mount Rainier's Paradise Glacier are slowly meted out, then rapidly carried away. Sometimes a cold drainage wind can be felt escaping from the mouth of the icy chamber.

Icebergs along the Inside Passage, Alaska. When air flows across a stretch of frigid open water, sea fog may form and be blown inland, sometimes to wreath the coastal islands.

Cloud iridescence—irregular color bands seen in thin altocumulus clouds illuminated by the partly obscured sun at left. Young clouds have the uniform droplet size necessary for the best color.

Atmospheric oxygen atoms struck by charged particles from the sun give this eerie display of the aurora borealis its greenish glow.

While storm-born winds kick up dust, a double rainbow arches over the Utah desert. Note the darker sky between the primary and secondary bows, a "blind" spot for scattered light from the raindrops.

With spring come the snowmelt, showers, and abundant sunshine that renew the annual cycle of life, as here in the high mountain meadows of Olympic National Park, Washington.

Summer is the season of maturity. Fruit forms, and seeds begin to set while late bloomers, like these in Kaibab National Forest, Arizona, keep the landscape colorful.

In fall the first tentative forays of polar air signal the change from summer to winter weather patterns and set trees ablaze with color, like these aspens near Telluride, Colorado.

Winter brings the sparkling yet tranquil beauty of snow; here in Yosemite it is but an echo of the Ice Age glaciers that carved the valley.

The West has probably never known a more appreciative observer of its weather and other natural phenomena than John Muir. For him both earth and sky fairly scintillated with color and pattern, light and motion to delight the senses. Passages like this one abound in his writings:

July 20 — Fine calm morning; air tense and clear; not the slightest breeze astir; everything shining, the rocks with wet crystals, the plants with dew, each receiving its portion of irised dewdrops and sunshine like living creatures getting their breakfast, their dew manna coming down from the starry sky like swarms of smaller stars. How wondrous fine are the particles in showers of dew, thousands required for a single drop, growing in the dark as silently as the grass! What pains are taken to keep this wilderness in health—showers of dew, floods of light, floods of invisible vapor, clouds, winds, all sorts of weather, interaction of plant on plant, animal on animal, etc., beyond thought. How fine Nature's methods! How deeply with beauty is beauty overlaid!

—MY FIRST SUMMER IN THE SIERRA

As if to climax the day, clouds, sun, and atmosphere combine at sunset to produce some of the most gorgeous displays of weather pageantry.

CHAPTER 9

WONDERS AND PAGEANTRY

Facts and misconceptions about lightning ❖ The dramatic light phenomena of sunsets and sunrises, rainbows, halos, and sundogs ❖ The aurora borealis ❖ Those "magic" images of mirage

STONE AGE MAN, peering at the clear western sky thousands of years before Galileo trained his telescope on the heavens, probably saw it merely as a background for the sun by day and the stars by night. When towering thunderheads appeared on the horizon, when lightning flashed beyond the mouth of his cave and thunder reverberated in the valley below, he may have imagined that a furious god was challenging the pacific, endless sky. And when a rainbow shone against the blackness of the storm, the caveman's primitive mind may have concluded that this was a symbol of truce between the gods of the storms and the sky.

Today these dramatic and colorful phenomena are no longer seen as miracles wrought by mysterious forces lurking in the infinite heavens, but they are no less beautiful and awe-inspiring.

Most of what is seen in the sky results from optical effects of light on the contents of the atmosphere—water droplets, ice crystals, or dust. Only a few optical phenomena such as mirages and blue sky can intrigue the eye without the presence of substances other than the natural gases of the atmosphere.

A clear vault of blue is a sight seldom enjoyed in the cities or the lowlands, where dust and humidity frequently spoil the sapphire hue; it is usually reserved for the crystalline air of mountain tops or deserts. The sky is perceived to have color because light from the sun's rays is scattered by the gas molecules of the air. Blue is scattered preferentially over other colors, so it predominates. Having thus lost a portion of its blue light, the sun itself appears yellow rather than its true white. Unlike atmospheric gases, dust and the relatively large water droplets in clouds scatter all colors equally and thus make the sky appear white. As large quantities of dust and water droplets accumulate in the air, the deep blue is smothered by a white pall.

The sky is frequently the backdrop for a variety of spectacular shows that are staged in the atmosphere. Along the eastern slope of the Rockies, for example, on almost any summer afternoon a thunderstorm matinee is presented. From behind the Front Range, puffy cumulus begin to build, rising as they start their eastward trek. Gradually the clouds darken, thunder rumbles an overture, and lightning flashes start the action.

Lightning, one of nature's most dramatic phenomena, is the climax to a complex chain of events. (See diagrams page 109.) This "flying flame," as Tennyson called it, actually consists of 3 to 10 strokes, each lasting less than 1/1000 of a second, but all occurring within the space of half a second. Lightning can cleave deep holes in the earth, split apart huge trees, and toss slabs of bark fifty paces or more.

The ancient Greeks and Romans were convinced that thunder and lightning must be weapons of Zeus, the father of the gods. They remained objects of myths and mystery until 1752, when Benjamin Franklin, kite string in hand, proved that lightning was directed by neither demons nor deities but was a form of electricity, to be harnessed rather than feared. The flash is actually a giant electrical discharge—related to the spark that

Sunlight, penetrating a gap in the clouds, illuminates dust and water droplets in the air.
Though it's called "sun-drawing-water," nothing but the observer's gaze ascends the beams.

Each lightning bolt in this time-exposed picture is composed of several individual strokes, but branches usually appear only on the initial stroke. Note that the paths are curved and kinked, not zigzag.

sometimes jumps from one's finger to a doorknob after one has walked across a nylon carpet.

The thunder following a lightning flash moves a slow 1,100 feet per second and is the sound of explosively expanding air. As the lightning bolt sears its sinuous path through the sky, its intense heat increases the temperature of the air, raises its pressure, and forces the air from its path, causing audible sound waves. While the reaction is virtually simultaneous throughout the bolt, the sound is drawn out because different parts of the bolt are at varying distances from the listener. Rumblings following a thunderclap are sometimes mere echoes of the original sound. Under most conditions thunder is not heard from lightning strokes more than about eighteen miles away.

Effects are many when lightning hits a target connected to the ground. Electrons—the electrical charges of a bolt—spread out radially like the concentric ripples a stone makes when tossed into a pond. In April, 1959, lightning struck in the middle of an Illinois cornfield and blasted out a crater one foot deep and twelve feet across. Sometimes lightning leaves a more subtle trail. Near Dodge, Nebraska, in 1935 a branching hole was found within the earth, marking the path the lightning had followed. It burrowed vertically for eight feet, dived another seven feet not quite vertically, then spread laterally in several sections, disappearing into moist soil.

Sometimes, instead of a hole, lightning leaves fused mineral matter, so-called "petrified lightning," or *ful-gurites*. These are hollow, glass-lined tubes, very brittle

LIGHTNING

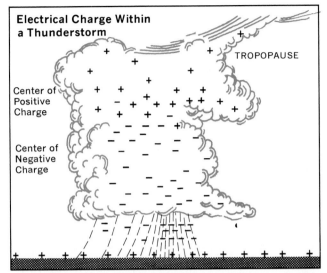

A thunderstorm is a giant electrical generator that collects a positive charge at its top and a negative charge at its bottom. In a way not fully understood, it may charge cloud droplets and ice crystals by friction, somewhat as static electricity is created by shuffling one's feet on a carpet. Voltages in the cloud, or from it to the earth, may exceed 100 million volts.

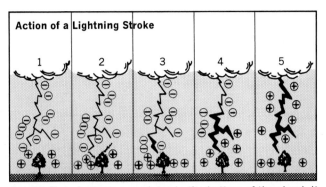

As negative charge accumulates in the bottom of the cloud, it attracts positive charge in the ground below. To reach it, the cloud puts down "stepped leaders," lightning's precursors, in faintly luminous bursts roughly 150 feet long about every 50 millionths of a second. In response, positively charged fingers stretch upward a few hundred feet from high spots on the ground, such as trees or television antennae. When the two meet, negative charge pours into the earth from the bottom of the stepped leader, initiating a bright lightning stroke. It climbs upward, from earth to sky, seeking the charge contained in the cloud. Once it has a conductive path, lightning may use it several times in the next fraction of a second, finally ceasing when the cloud is drained of charge.

and therefore hard to recover intact. Often they are found at beaches, where wave action has gently revealed them, and atop mountains as pieces of rock consolidated and fused, or as a vitrified streak on the rock. One such fulgurite has been found on Mount Thielson, a Cascade volcano in Oregon.

Florida, Mississippi, Georgia, Arizona, and New Mexico are the states with the greatest number of lightning-producing storms, while the Pacific coastal regions—Northern California, Oregon, Washington—have relatively few.

One misconception, perpetuated through mining town folklore, is the belief that lightning is attracted by mountains containing a high percentage of iron. In fact, topographical features play a more important role than mineral composition in determining where lightning touches down. Mountain slopes and forests, their tall trees providing attractive antennae, are frequent targets. Among man-made objects, power lines, forest watchtowers, radio towers, and tall industrial smokestacks usually take the brunt of any lightning in the area. One of the most powerful lightning flashes ever recorded hit the Anaconda Copper Mining Company plant at Butte, Montana. Striking the 585-foot smelter stack, it was measured

at 160,000 amperes and 15,000,000 volts, more than a hundred thousand times greater than the voltage in an ordinary household circuit.

Hikers and climbers must count lightning among the major dangers of the mountains. The higher the terrain, the closer it is to the thundercloud and the greater the probability that lightning will strike. Idaho's Clearwater Forest is the West's tinderbox, with most fires starting at or above the 7,000-foot elevation.

In recent years man has become more diligent and more efficient in controlling forest fires, both lightning-created blazes and man-made conflagrations. Some people question these efforts, such as lightning researcher Martin Uman: "It would seem obvious that lightning-induced forest fires should be suppressed, but this is not necessarily the case. In California until recently, for example, frequent fires kept the forest floor clean; the fires were small and did not damage the trees. Ironically, efforts to prevent and contain forest fires in California enabled the brush to grow more thickly on the forest floor and, as a result, more fires are now big ones. In fact we may be indebted to ancient forest fires for California's giant sequoias. The seedlings of these trees can germinate in ashes but not under the thick layer of needles covering an unburned forest floor." Some ecologists say the answer is to continue forest fire control but to use controlled burning or other underbrush removal techniques to fill any natural void.

The giant sequoia, virtually immune to fungus, disease, and insects, and having no resin to feed forest fires, is nevertheless an easy prey to lightning. Both the General Sherman and the General Grant trees in Sequoia National Park were topped by lightning generations ago. Walter Fry, first superintendent of the park, saw a 300-foot sequoia shattered by lightning in the late summer of 1895. In his words, "This tree looked as though it had been passed through a gigantic rock crusher and the product symmetrically piled."

In 1933 a lightning fire wiped out the vast Tillamook Forest, the last large stand of virgin timber in Oregon. However, the gravity of the loss is disputed. Some naturalists maintain that these woodlands had already been abandoned by most of the wildlife, that those remaining were unhealthy, and that the forest had been heading toward an ecological demise. Since viable natural communities were established after the burn, natives say that lightning was the creator of a new and better life.

Several types of lightning have been described. The most often viewed and most widely photographed is *streak lightning*, which in a winding, twisting path connects ground and cloud. *Sheet lightning* discharges over broader areas, generally within or between clouds. "Silent" and diffused flashes, beyond the eighteen-mile sonic range of thunderclaps, are commonly called *heat lightning*.

By far the most controversial type is *ball lightning*, fiery spheres whose specific description seems to vary considerably from one reported sighting to another. Eyewitnesses have claimed variously that it can float across a floor, down a tree, or across the sky. Its colors range from red to orange to yellow, blue, or white. Its lifespan is said to be from several seconds to several minutes, with some fireballs disappearing quietly while others explode suddenly with a bang.

One typical account of ball lightning came from a resident of Iowa: "While outdoors during a particularly violent thunderstorm . . . I heard a heavy rushing noise like an extra strong wind. This caused me to look about me and I saw a ball of fire, yellowish white about the size of a wash tub bouncing down the dirt road. The ball traveled a little faster than one could run. I didn't see

from where it came. I watched the ball travel about a city block, when it struck a small shed, maybe 10 feet by 12 feet in which a horse was stabled. The shed seemed to explode and the horse was killed."

It has been estimated that only 5 to 10 percent of the population has reported seeing ball lightning. Almost everyone else—including scientists, who are stumped to explain the phenomenon—is quite skeptical that it exists.

ANOTHER, MORE WELCOME LIGHT may also grace the skies in the transition between shower and sun—the rainbow.

It is hardly surprising that something at once so beautiful and so mysterious has long been an object of myth to primitive men. To the Pueblo Indians of the Southwest, for example, rainbows had both practical and symbolic significance, especially as representative of the dead, the Cloud People. The Zuñi believed that their ancestors originally had lived in the "worlds below," and that their passage into this world was upon rainbows given to them by the Sun Father. They were led by the "Divine Ones," two sons of the Sun Father. One son, named Rainbow, was believed to have it in his power to command the rainmakers to go where he wished. Since rain was the essence of Zuñi survival, clearly Rainbow was a deity not to be offended.

In our own culture the familiar idea of the pot of gold at rainbow's end is no longer so much myth as fable, for the elusiveness of that treasure is based in scientific fact: the rainbow, created as it is by the particular geometric relationship between the sun's rays, the rain, and the beholder, moves with the beholder, ever to elude him.

A rainbow shines not of its own light but rather from sunlight reflected and refracted by raindrops. Some light penetrates the drops, and, reflecting one or more times inside, finally escapes in a direction different from the one at which it entered. The light rays that enter and leave the raindrop are refracted at the surface, and, in a manner identical to that of a simple prism, are split into bands of color known as the spectrum.

The laws of physics prescribe those directions in which the raindrop most intensely sends back the tinted beams. If the light reflects only once inside the raindrop, it creates a primary rainbow, at an approximate angle of 42° from the entering light. If it reflects twice, it creates

A double solar halo. The larger, with 46° radius, forms from light refracting through the ends, rather than sides, of ice crystals; it is not formed by multiple reflections as a secondary rainbow is.

an additional, secondary arc at an approximate angle of 51°. Rainbows formed by light reflected more than twice are rarely seen.

Not all rainbows manifest the full spectrum. Sometimes at sunrise or sunset, when only red light is present to enter the raindrop prism, a dramatic all-red arch will stretch across the sky.

Akin to the rainbow is the *halo*, a colored ring formed by refraction through hexagonal ice crystals rather than raindrops (see diagram on page 113). A halo may be seen around either the sun or the moon. When it occurs around the sun, it is readily visible but may be painful to see because of the sun's glare.

Three hundred sixty-five days of the year the sun rises and sets, and each time many places in the West experience an assault of color so grand that it defies man to take its familiar glory for granted. Yet, like the rainbow, its colors are an ephemeral display. With only a slight change in the dustiness or cloudiness of the local atmosphere, any evening's beautiful sunset might have been a leaden affair.

The red colors of sunsets and sunrises exist for the same reason that the sky is blue—the colors in the blue end of the spectrum have been extensively scattered by the ten or twenty miles of atmosphere through which they must pass when the sun is near the horizon. Only the redder light remains to illuminate the clouds and the sky near the sun. When backlit by the low sun, opaque clouds screen out its rays and appear dark while clouds carrying less moisture glow as the light passes through. Overhead, gentle undulations on the undersides of broken clouds are brushed with a reflection of glancing rays from the low sun.

Haze and dust concentrated near the surface of the earth contribute to the pageantry. After every major volcanic eruption (such as Babuyan in 1831, Krakatoa in 1883, Pelee in 1902, and Katmai in 1912), beautiful sunrises and sunsets occurred for months or years all over the globe. During the 1970 brush and forest fires along the California coast, sunsets were particularly ruddy. The grand sunsets seen in the Great Valley of California are the result of dust raised by agricultural activity. Within limits, the dirtier the air, the more beautiful the sunrises and sunsets. Atmospheric dust also colors the moon—the dust produced in bringing in the crops is responsible for the yellow "harvest moon."

When light interacts with particles, such as water droplets, whose size approaches that of a light wave (a hundredth the diameter of a human hair), a variety of atmospheric color effects become visible. One of the most

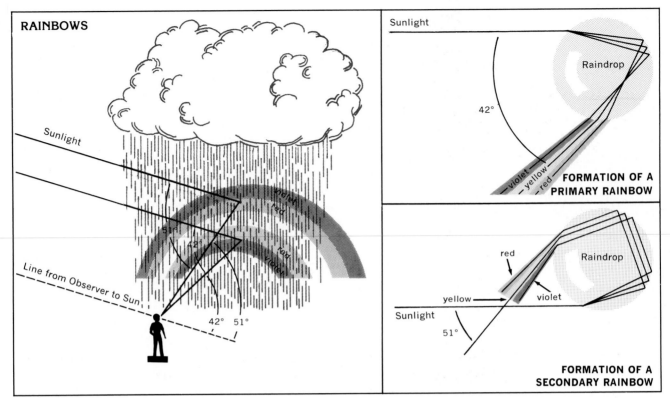

RAINBOWS

Sunlight

Line from Observer to Sun

42° 51°

Sunlight

Raindrop

42°

violet
yellow
red

**FORMATION OF A
PRIMARY RAINBOW**

red

Raindrop

yellow

violet

Sunlight

51°

**FORMATION OF A
SECONDARY RAINBOW**

Light entering a raindrop is refracted, reflected once or twice, then refracted again on exiting. Dispersion accompanies each refraction, giving the rainbow its colors. The diagrams of light rays in raindrops for primary and secondary rainbows show that colors in the two are reversed. The rays exit at angles, measured from the entering rays, of approximately 42° and 51° for primary and secondary rainbows, respectively. The same angles are the radii of the rainbows as shown in the third diagram. If the sun is high, the center of the rainbow will be below the horizon, and if it is higher than 51°, neither rainbow will be visible unless the observer can look downward as from a cliff or an airplane.

common of these is the *corona*, concentric faintly colored rings around the sun or the moon (or other bright light), having an angular diameter typically less than a few degrees. Usually the rings result from diffraction of light off water droplets, but occasionally off very fine ice crystals or dust particles. A special form of corona is the iridescence of clouds, in which they often appear green or purple, the hue and intensity being dependent on the distribution of the sizes of water droplets in the cloud. On rare occasions, scattering of light by smoke or volcanic dust has turned the sun or moon a peculiar green or deep indigo, hence the expression "once in a blue moon."

The lovely spectacle of a low and hidden sun sending a fan of golden shafts across the eastern or western sky is called the "crepuscular ray" phenomenon. The beams, though they appear to radiate from a central point, are actually parallel. Their convergence is due to perspective, the same illusion that makes a road seem to narrow as it stretches away into the distance. The rays that seem to spread out overhead often can be seen to converge again on the opposite horizon. There is a daytime counterpart, the "sun-drawing-water" phenomenon, in which beams seem to streak down to the ground. Impressive though both are, they can be readily understood by comparison to the beams of sunlight one often sees streaming across a room, reflecting on the myriad dust particles floating in the air. The beams are often divided into multiple shafts by window mullions or other obstacles to the light's passage. In the case of the larger displays in the sky, it is clouds, either visible or just over the horizon, that break up the light into rays, but it is again dust or moisture in the atmosphere that makes them visible.

THE HORIZON IS THE STAGE for another remarkable phenomenon, the mirage, which has been hoodwinking humanity for centuries and, for all our scientific sophistication, continues to do so. Illusory ice floes in the

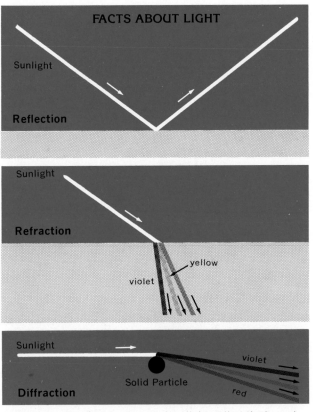

FACTS ABOUT LIGHT

Sunlight

Reflection

Sunlight

Refraction

yellow

violet

Sunlight

Diffraction

Solid Particle

violet

red

Reflection and refraction occur when light strikes the boundary between two materials through which it travels at different speeds, such as air and water. *Reflection* (top) is the bouncing of the rays from the surface; *refraction* (center) is the bending of rays upon penetrating the surface. Both usually occur together. For refraction, the transition can be abrupt, as between glass and air, or gradual, as between layers of air of differing densities. Blue light is refracted more than red light—a phenomenon known as dispersion. *Diffraction* (bottom) is the bending of light around objects, such as dust particles. The redder the light and the smaller the objects, the greater the amount of diffraction.

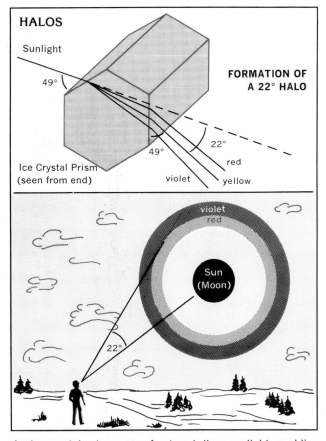

HALOS

Sunlight

49°

FORMATION OF A 22° HALO

22°

red

49°

Ice Crystal Prism (seen from end)

violet

yellow

violet
red

Sun (Moon)

22°

An ice-crystal prism can refract and disperse light, enabling colored halos to be formed. Rays passing through the sides of the usual hexagonal ice crystal (upper diagram) are refracted by approximately 22 degrees from their entering angle. Because there is no reflection to send the light backward, as with a rainbow, the halo is seen *around* the sun or moon (lower diagram) rather than opposite it. A large group of phenomena called "halos" are formed by reflection and refraction. Not all appear around the light source. One of these is the rarely seen *parhelic circle*, which rings the horizon.

polar seas have prompted ships to turn from safe channels and run aground in a frantic effort to avoid collision. In 1913 the American Museum of Natural History spent $300,000 to subsidize exploration of an arctic mountain range thought to be blocking the much desired Northwest Passage, but as climbers approached the supposed mountain barrier, it mysteriously disappeared.

One notable mirage in American history occurred in 1878, as General George Custer and his small army of men left Fort Abraham Lincoln in the Dakota country to play their part in the Battle of the Little Big Horn. Those left behind in the fort beheld a spectacle that might well have been read as an omen: the departing column passed out of sight behind the hills, then reap-

peared a few moments later in a mirage, marching away across the sky!

There are four general kinds of mirage: the *superior mirage*, in which the image appears above the source; the *inferior mirage*, in which the image is seen below the source; *towering*, in which the source appears elongated vertically; *stooping*, in which the source appears contracted vertically. The Puget Sound area has frequent incidents of both towering and superior mirage, the latter accounting for the inverted images of ships, islands, and cities reported there from time to time. The familiar illusion of water, so common in arid regions of the West and observable on almost any highway in the country on a clear, hot day, results from inferior mirage. The water,

PHOTO BY JOHN W. McGEE, M.D., FROM FPG

Three phenomena can be seen here: The vertical band is an arc of a 22° halo, the horizontal is a parhelic circle, and at their intersection is a sundog, or mock sun. The latter two result when the majority of ice crystals have their sides vertical. Light reflected off the crystals creates the parhelic circle; it includes the sun, always lies parallel to the horizon, and may circle it. Sundogs are refracted light, like a 22° halo. Because of the vertical crystal alignment, they shine as spots, brighter and more colorful than a halo, to the right and left of the sun.

actually an image of the sky, is simulated even to the quivering reflection of objects on distant shores.

One of the first persons to offer a proper explanation of mirages was Gaspard Monge. Late in the eighteenth century he reasoned that mirages were the product of differences in air temperatures, which resulted in layers with differing density lying near the earth. Over land, surface air is usually hotter than the air above, whereas over water it is often cooler. In passing through these layers of varying density, light is refracted, that is, bent in a curve, changing the apparent direction from which it comes.

A sky decorated with shimmering curtains of green and red, dancing rays, and wavering arcs—and accompanied by the very low frequency cackles, hisses, and pops in radio reception—that is the unearthly display of the *aurora borealis,* or northern lights (*aurora australis* in

the Southern Hemisphere). It is not really a weather phenomenon at all, but rather, visible evidence of an attack on the atmosphere by charged particles spewed by the sun's fiery surface in times of solar storms. Highly agitated by the intruders, atoms of atmospheric oxygen and nitrogen emit light—yellow-green and the deepest reds from oxygen, purple and other reddish hues from nitrogen.

Charged particles traveling across a magnetic field follow a spiral path toward the strongest part of the field. Thus the charged particles reaching the earth from the sun spiral into the polar regions, where the earth's magnetic field is strongest. As a result, dramatic auroral displays are limited to the more northerly states. When the aurora is strong enough to be visible at all in Phoenix and Albuquerque, the skies of Spokane and Bismarck appear to be on fire. Indians of the Midwest used to say that on nights like those, northern medicine men were making stew of their enemies.

A number of scientists believe that a bright aurora may be a weather indicator, since these displays often end with the sky veiled in high, thin (cirrostrus) clouds.

MIRAGES

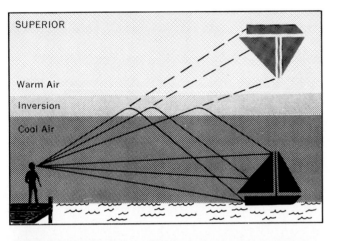

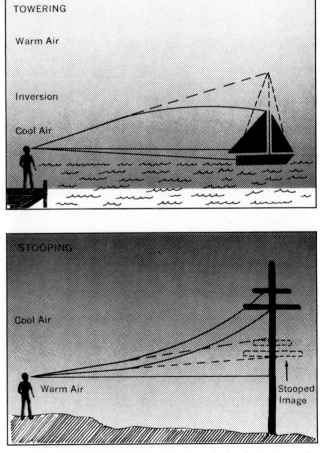

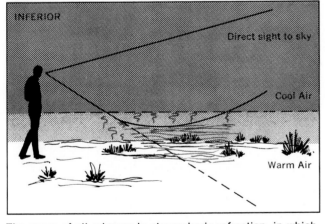

The cause of all mirages is atmospheric refraction, in which light rays bend in traversing air layers whose temperatures change rapidly with height. Light rays curve away from warmer layers. Mirages are usually very distant from the observer. *Superior mirage:* An observer in cool air below warm sees one or two images above the source; if one image only, it may be inverted (shown) or not; if two images, the upper is erect while the lower inverted; the source need not be directly visible.

Inferior mirage: If the observer is in cool air above warm, he sees the source directly and a lower, inverted image. *Towering and Stooping:* Different curvatures of light rays from the upper and lower parts of the source cause towering and stooping. Either can happen with either warm or cool air uppermost. Towering is shown for warm air above cool, and stooping for the reverse. In these cases, the upper rays curve most. Inferior or superior mirages may show towering or stooping.

Cold air above a warm layer heated by Puget Sound produced this inferior mirage (inverted). The upright image shows towering.

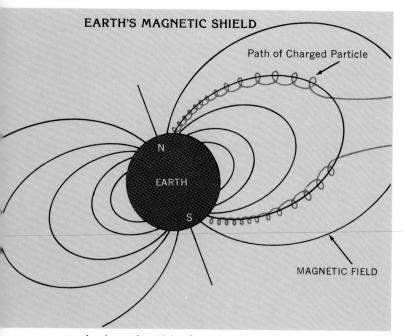

EARTH'S MAGNETIC SHIELD

Path of Charged Particle

EARTH

MAGNETIC FIELD

As charged particles from the sun (corpuscles) stream toward the earth, they spiral in toward the strongest parts of the earth's magnetic field. Thus they pour toward the poles, where they produce auroral displays, and away from the equator, where the aurora is rarely seen.

Though this idea has been disputed, there is other evidence to suggest that the low pressure systems that bring winter storms from the Gulf of Alaska to the West Coast intensify following bright auroral displays.

MODERN MAN'S GROWING UNDERSTANDING of exotic weather phenomena, aided by ever more sophisticated tools for observing, measuring, and interpreting them, has taken him a long way from the cave. Gone are the terror and the myths. Gone are the primitive sacrifices to appease angry gods or win their favor. Most of the mysteries have now been solved (except perhaps for ball lightning), and many scientists are turning their inquiries outward to other planets and other suns. Rocket-launched instruments are probing the atmospheres of Venus and Mars and beyond, destined no doubt to find weather wonders not yet imagined.

And yet, as one stands at sunset watching the vapor trail of one of those very rockets turn pink against a darkening sky, explanations pale, and one can still feel some of the ancient awe that man has always felt for the colorful pageant of the sky.

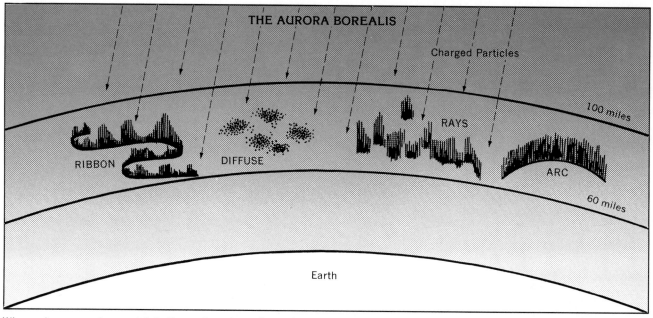

When solar corpuscles crash into the earth's atmosphere, they excite atoms of oxygen and nitrogen to glow like a neon sign. The electrical and magnetic forces that exist between the infiltrating corpuscles, and between them and the earth's at- mosphere and magnetic field, forge swarms of corpuscles into the ribbon, ray, and arc patterns of the aurora borealis. Very active displays may form looping folds hundreds of miles across. The lines in the aurora follow the earth's magnetic field.

Part 3
A CHOICE OF CLIMATES

*The range of temperature, precipitation, days of sunshine,
days of fog is so great in the West that climate, like
life-style, can be a matter of choice. But today's population
follows closely the patterns of pioneer settlement,
showing that there has been little change in American
ideas of where life can best be lived.*

CHAPTER 10

THE CONGENIAL COAST

The lush rain forests of the Northwest ❖ Northern California's maritime climate ❖ The gentle fogs of San Francisco and the central coast ❖ Southern California's mild Mediterranean climate

MOVING GENERALLY EASTWARD around the deep Aleutian low pressure area, moist temperate air from the North Pacific flows over the coast, where it splits into two streams, one coursing northeast across British Columbia into the Yukon and the other flowing south over Oregon and California. From these beginnings come the mild coastal weather of the Northwest and the ideal year-round climate of California.

The northerly flow becomes an identifiable air mass known as the maritime polar Pacific system, which with its numerous accompanying cyclones is capable of drawing raw, moist polar air into cold regions and warm, wet air from the mid-latitudes into mild regions. In contrast to this vigorous northern branch, the southern flow forms relatively stable, dry air that not only controls much of the Southwest's weather but often stretches out eastward as far as the eastern slope of the Rockies.

Typically, coastal weather from San Francisco north to the Canadian border consists of rainy winters and cool, dry summers—a *maritime* climate. The winter rains result from storms originating over the North Pacific and are accentuated by the coastal mountain ranges. On the Olympic Peninsula in Washington, the heavy rains have produced one of the world's few temperate zone rain forests, and one of the densest growths of trees in the Western Hemisphere. As one of the folk songs of the Northwest says, "For four years I chopped and I loggered, but I never got down to the soil." While the Olympic Mountains average 100-plus inches of rainfall annually, a short distance to the northeast the city of

Port Angeles averages 23 inches and Port Townsend only 18. Despite their relative dryness, these communities do not enjoy an abundance of sunshine, since fog and clouds drifting inland along the Strait of Juan de Fuca keep skies overcast for most of the winter and for a third of the summer.

But seasons are not always typical. Occasionally a winter month in the North passes without a single storm. Or a rare outbreak of arctic air will pour into the Pacific Northwest, creating unusual winter storms. The cold wave of January 1916 and the blizzard of January 1950 were two of the worst winter assaults on record in the state of Washington. In the more recent storm, thousands of trees in Seattle suffered broken limbs from the weight of twenty-six inches of snow; the dome of St. James Cathedral collapsed, with damage estimated at $35,000; and a section of the stadium at Denny Field on the University of Washington campus sustained multiple fractures. In November 1955 an unusually early cold spell damaged fruit trees and ornamental shrubs still in the growing stage. Apples were still being picked and potatoes, onions, carrots, cabbage, and sugar beets were being harvested when the cold struck, resulting in multimillion-dollar crop losses.

The North Pacific storm belt ends near Cape Mendocino, California. South from San Francisco to the Mexican border the climate is *Mediterranean*—three months of winter rain followed by a hot, dry summer.

The big storms that hit Southern California are of the Sonoran type, sweeping north from the Gulf of Mexico

Seen from the window of a Puget Sound ferry, the Olympic Mountains are almost hidden by rain and low clouds; in this maritime climate storm will follow storm until winter is past.

during July, August, and September, but these are infrequent. One such storm, on an extraordinary excursion northward in September 1904, dropped five inches of rain on San Francisco in four days. Most of Southern California's rainfall is left by the dregs of the numerous winter storms that sweep the coast from the Northwest.

Today California weather is generally regarded as ideal, particularly along the coast. Strangely, in earlier times the climate of the Golden State was often criticized. "From July to November San Francisco and nearly all California is an excellent place to keep away from," advised a journalist in an 1880 issue of *Scribner's* Magazine. "Dust and intense heat in the interior, dust and cold winds and heavy fogs on the coast, make it a most undesirable place of residence." Observing that the climate of Santa Barbara was dry and hot, a tourist in 1875 said that its citizens and admirers must be from

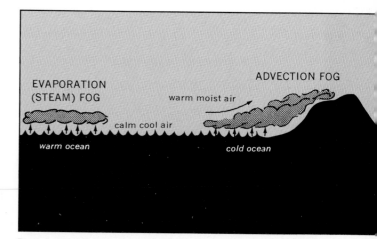

Fog—a cloud that lies at or near the ground—forms in two ways: when a moist body of air cools, raising the relative humidity to 100% and condensing water vapor to droplets, or when moisture is added to the air until saturation is achieved and

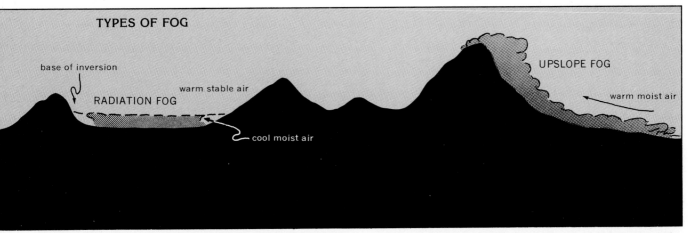

TYPES OF FOG

base of inversion

RADIATION FOG

warm stable air

cool moist air

UPSLOPE FOG

warm moist air

condensation occurs. A kind of drizzle often results from fog, and the air usually feels raw and wet. There are four major types. *Evaporation fog* forms when water vapor rising from a warm, moist surface meets a colder air layer; *advection fog,* when warm air is transported over a cold surface and cooled to saturation; *radiation fog,* when nighttime cooling of the ground lowers the temperature of humid air; *upslope fog,* when wind forces warm, moist air upward against a mountainside.

"some worse place—probably often from the interior; no one from Puget Sound ever praises it."

Apparently, later travelers did not agree with those disgruntled early writers, for San Francisco has become one of the most visited cities in the world, and its natives relish their weather, even the fogs, which help to air-condition their city.

PROBABLY THE MOST STRIKING element of coastal weather is sea fog, which can occur on a daily basis in the spring and summer seasons, and less frequently in winter. It forms over the ocean's surface, sometimes hugging close to the waves, sometimes towering high above them. It is called *advection* fog, a type that in due course moves inland from the shoreline. It floats on the wind, through the natural gaps that connect the coast and the interior, such as straits, valleys, and mountain passes, or in lieu of these, it vaults its barriers. It comes in the night, when the earth's surface is cool; by morning, when the sun is rising, the inland valleys and perhaps even coastal highlands are sodden and cool beneath an overcast. The low clouds are a confusion to easterners more familiar with humid climates of summer storms, where such clouds normally bring rain; on the West Coast they bring sunshine, as the fog screen usually evaporates by noon.

By definition, advection means that horizontal movement is required to make a sea fog. When warm, maritime air makes contact with, and flows over, a surface that is colder than itself, such as cold ocean water, the air cools, and its relative humidity rises. Condensation begins when the air can no longer contain the moisture as a gas. Water droplets, often with beads of salt from sea spray as cores, form fog, a cloud on the surface of the earth. Turbulence within the air is common with an advection fog, occurring because wind drag against the wavy surface of the water induces a slight mixing motion of the air. The cooling that began within the lowest layers of air spreads upward to higher levels, increasing the depth of the fog. As the air continues to flow over the cold water, the air becomes colder, until it, rather than the water, chills fog into the air. The fog thus formed is above the water and is called high fog, or stratus fog, the major and most dramatic of sea fogs along the West Coast. High fog is capable of rushing landward like a river in the air, spreading into inland valleys and cascading over coastal hills.

The fog belt of the West Coast is found between central Oregon and Point Conception, California. This range is no coincidence, but is the by-product of a zone of cold water that hugs the shoreline. The cold water appears first in May off Cape Mendocino and reaches its maximum north-south extent by August, when the

Winds sweep across miles of ocean, transfer their energies to the water, and build waves that pound the coast. The scattered droplets of seawater, on evaporation, can form salt haze.

A salt-spray haze and low clouds romanticize the sea stacks on one of Oregon's many crescent-shaped beaches. The salty air and stiff wind have sheared the shoreline of all but a few tough trees.

ocean's surface along an eighty-mile belt averages about two degrees (F.) lower west of San Francisco than it did in July. Off the coast of San Francisco, surface water temperatures have reached about 56° F., or slightly colder than the waters off Cape Flattery, the northernmost point on Washington's coastline. Spring and summer ocean temperatures within the cold-water belt are in fact colder than in winter.

The cold water is an upwelling from deep within the ocean that is present throughout much of the year, but most pronounced in summer. Winds sweeping around the North Pacific High blow along the Pacific Coast in summer and drag the coastal water with them. The ocean currents, like the winds, are deflected by the Coriolis force (see page 75), which turns them away from the coast. Somewhere below, cold water flows toward the shore and up to the surface, to replace what the wind and the ocean currents took away. Thus, every

spring a cold ocean strip forms near shore and provides the cooling that builds sea fogs.

Distribution of fog is the work of the wind. Along the fog belt of the central California coast, the wind is strong and steady, blowing from the northwest or west with constancy. It does not even allow development of the onshore and offshore breezes whose diurnal rhythm is characteristic of most coastlines, including the Los Angeles region. The reason for this is twofold: high atmospheric pressure from the Pacific High and low atmospheric pressure from a trough extending northward from the deserts to the Central Valley. The result is a great landward movement of air on a one-way street, termed by some meteorologists a monsoon.

The striking dissimilarities of climate that exist between the usually cool coast and the usually warm interior occur because of the relief etched on the landscape. There is a very short coastal plain, immediately backed by mountains that rise, in the Santa Cruz range, to just over 3,800 feet. In the shadow of the Coast Ranges lie San Francisco Bay and the coastal valleys, including the Santa Clara and Salinas valleys. Beyond them is a second mountain chain, and finally the Central Valley as close as forty miles from the coast. Over that distance, air temperatures rapidly increase with distance from the coast. One major gap in the Coast Range, the Golden Gate, and one inland waterway, the Carquinez Strait at the north end of the bay, connect the ocean to the interior. At the end of that route, because of infiltrating ocean air, summer temperatures are the lowest of any part of the Central Valley.

It is primarily through the Golden Gate and over the peninsular hills that the wind brings in the sea fog. The process is predictable, beginning late in the afternoon,

after the hot part of the day. When fog first passes through the Gate, it mixes with warm air and evaporates. Over the hills, it cascades down eastern slopes, evaporating on the leeward side, where the descending air is warmed by compression. Usually it is not until after sundown that the fog is able to form a continuous and spreading cloud mass. The winds determine which valley sections are fogged first. Most often the fog spreads from the eastern side of the bay back to the leeward sides of the coastal hills, and to the northern and southern ends of the bay. Winds through the Golden Gate split, pushing the fog north into the Napa Valley and south to San Jose. Even inland valleys such as the Livermore Valley can sometimes have fog.

As the sun rises in the morning, the fog at first holds fast, reacting slowly to incoming solar radiation. Then

Onshore

Offshore

Land heats and cools more quickly than water, so wherever the daily temperature range is wide, winds form: onshore from cool water to warm land during the heat of the day, offshore from warm land to cool sea at night.

San Francisco often disappears beneath a summer fog bank, borne inland through the wind gap of the Golden Gate.

Big Sur, California: Flowing over the choppy sea, wind can lift a fog bank from the water's surface. The "high fog" that results may ride the sea breeze wherever it blows.

gradually the edges and base of the fog bank begin to dissipate. The white top of the fog, because it tends to reflect solar heat rather than absorbing it, does not evaporate quickly. Holes in the fog may break first on the leeward sides of the hills, where air descending to the valley floor is warmed because of compression, or where the edge of the fog rests against hillsides newly warmed by the sun. The fog layer breaks leisurely at first, but then dissipates at accelerating rates. The windward slopes, such as the Berkeley Hills and ridges east of Monterey Bay, clear last, as they are in the mainstream of upward moving, and therefore cooling, air. While the fog bank proper retreats toward its source, the ocean, remnants may linger for hours, or even until the fog's return in late afternoon; in full retreat the fog will leave the coastline but remain offshore for the next daily cycle.

This rhythm—morning overcast, daytime retreat, evening advance—is only the most conspicuous of the fog bank's cycles. In an approximately weekly pattern, cool, foggy marine air rushes inland to the warm Central Valley, pulled by the low pressures of its interior. There it reduces temperatures, equalizes pressures, and, in response to the declining interior pressures, penetrates less each day. Once the fog no longer reaches the interior, the pressure and temperature imbalances slowly return, and fog is again drawn inland from the coast. The full cycle occurs roughly once every seven days. There is also a seasonal cycle, waxing in spring, waning in fall—the same cycle displayed by the offshore upwelling, the fog's progenitor.

On cooler days, fogs tend to be wet and drippy. What is called "Oregon mist" collects on the leaves and branches of trees, and forms wet spots where the moisture is shed. Measurements of fog drip in the Berkeley Hills, directly opposite the Golden Gate, show the gathering of approximately ten inches of moisture, or an amount nearly half as great as Berkeley's annual rainfall. Such fog usually begins far out at sea, having had time for the droplets to merge and grow in the fog mass. Dry fog does not have drip characteristics, being formed just offshore or over the coastal hills.

It is no accident that the fog belt and what remains of the coastal redwood groves coincide. Because redwoods can absorb water through their needles, the steady summer fogs help to ease them through what would otherwise be a long dry season.

During the winter certain areas of California have a different kind of fog, described as *radiation* fog. The winter rains thoroughly soak the earth, and humidity remains high, even during the periods when the rain ceases. In the longer nights of this season, the land cools by radiating its heat, chilling the moist air until the dew point is reached and condensing water vapor to fog. The inland areas, without benefit of the warming influence of the ocean, are more susceptible to radiation fog, which forms most frequently over swamps, rivers, and ponds. Because tules (and other marsh plants) grow in these areas, the fog is known in the Central Valley and San Francisco Bay region, where it is found, as *tule* fog.

If a cold, windless spell persists, the tule fog accumulates with each passing day. Fog depths of several hundred feet often occur in the Sacramento River Delta or the Livermore Valley. In winter the inland areas are colder (and air pressures therefore higher) than the coast, with the result that the high pressure pushes the tule fog into the San Francisco Bay Area through Carquinez Strait, the Hayward Pass, and other low points in the East Bay hills. Thus, in winter San Francisco's fog comes overland, and in summer it comes from the ocean.

Local climate is affected to a large extent by the geography of the area, some of it submarine. Along the southern coast of California, there is an oceanic platform with canyons and ridges whose peaks form such islands as Catalina, Santa Barbara, Santa Cruz, Santa Rosa, and several small islands extending west to San Miguel Island and south to San Clemente Island. The irregular ocean floor concentrates some water along channels and allows other water to remain quiet, almost motionless in its basins. The still waters warm in the summer sun and are therefore less likely to form fog than waters north of Point Conception. Moving south along the California coast from San Francisco, the incidence of fog decreases

dramatically, with Santa Maria showing an average of 88 days of fog a year; Los Angeles airport, 53 days; and San Diego, 30 days. When fog does occur in the Los Angeles area—usually during the colder months—it is not the result of warm air flowing over cold water but is, rather, radiation fog formed in the Los Angeles Basin.

Los Angeles has the unenviable reputation of being the smog capital of the United States. Aside from the concentration of population and heavily used freeways, the city's geographical location and topographical features combine with weather conditions to create ideal circumstances for smog. The meteorology is this: air cooled from traveling over the surface of the Pacific Ocean covers the Los Angeles Basin. This air is covered by a layer of warmer air, which has not been in contact with the cool water, for it comes from aloft, warming and drying as it descends from the upper reaches of the North Pacific High toward the desert regions of the Southwest and Southern California. In the Los Angeles Basin, the result is an inversion of normal atmospheric temperatures (see chapter 16). This prevents the upward dispersion of smoke, automobile exhausts, and industrial pollutants, while the mountain barrier that partially surrounds the Los Angeles Basin precludes any eastward escape of the smoggy air.

NORMAL WEATHER ALONG the 1,200-mile coast, from the southern Canadian border to Mexico, is mild, with uniform temperatures near the shore and more continentallike temperatures inland. The moderating effect of the ocean upon coastal weather is reflected by relatively slight temperature extremes. At Tatoosh Island, the northwesternmost point in the coterminous United States, recorded temperatures have never been lower than 14° nor higher than 88° F. Once the thermometer dipped to 28° F. at San Diego; it has been as high as 104° F., but during a typical year that southern coastal city has expected lows and highs of 32° and 90° F. Compare these with inland cities at similar latitudes, where high-low ranges of 120 degrees are not uncommon.

In the Pacific Northwest, day-to-day changes in average temperature seldom exceed ten degrees. Gentle, misty rains last for days and sometimes weeks. Gray clouds blanket the Washington coast much of the time, and "continued cool and cloudy" is a common forecast.

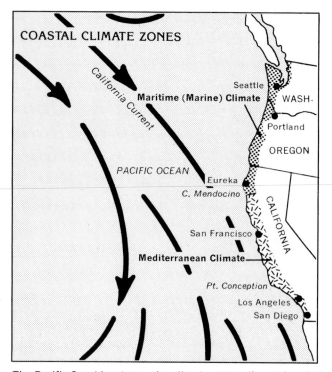

The Pacific Coast has two major climate zones: the cool, moist *maritime* and the wet-winter, dry-summer Mediterranean.

A mature cyclone approaches the coast, bringing rain to the Northwest but leaving California dry.

Perhaps the coolest California town in summer is Eureka in Northern California. Backed up to Humboldt Bay and facing the Pacific with virtually no defense against the wind, Eureka's thermometers seldom climb as high as 75° F. during the summer and frequently have only a two- or three-degree variation during a twenty-four-hour period.

Eureka is one of the foggiest of the coastal cities. So pervasive is the overcast that the navy established a base near the town to test a fog dispersal system for airports (FIDO, for "Fog, Intensive Dispersal Of"). What the Weather Bureau classifies as "dense fog" decreases from 51 days annually at Eureka to 19 at San Francisco.

In most of the exposed places along the coast north of Point Conception, the landscape is barren of vegetation except for a few gnarled pine and cypress trees that defy the constant wind. Such a shorescape may be seen around Monterey, while on nearby coastal lowlands, cool weather crops flourish: artichokes, peas, beans, and brussels sprouts. Laurels, live oaks, and stately redwoods grow in the sheltered valleys of Northern California,

from the Big Sur coast north to the Oregon border.

Areas inland from the ocean often undergo severe summer droughts, but despite its dryness the land just beyond the coastal ranges supports sugar pines, incense cedars, and red and white firs; farther from the moist sea breezes only grasses and scrubby chaparral can survive. During the winter months these inland northern valleys are green, exploding with multicolored wild flowers in early spring before drying to the summer yellows and browns of Mediterranean climates and landscapes of Southern California. Hence, they belong to the land of transition, not wholly maritime nor Mediterranean.

An imaginary line from Point Reyes on the coast to Santa Rosa, about twenty miles inland, would mark the approximate point where maritime and Mediterranean climates meet. North of this line lumbering is the main support of a large portion of the population, while to the south it becomes a minor industry. The northern climate resembles that of the British Isles; the southern is more closely related to that of southern Europe and the northwestern coast of Africa. The northern forest is Douglas fir; the southern one, a dwarf forest of dense, thorny scrub, or chaparral.

Mediterranean climate reaches fruition in the lowlands along the coast from Santa Barbara southeastward to San Diego. This region is ideal for citrus growing, particularly close to the coast where freezes are infrequent. Among the citrus fruits lemon trees are the most susceptible to cold and are usually grown closest to the ocean shore, with oranges just beyond—many on low hills in preference to night-cooled valleys—and the hardy kumquats and grapefruit still farther inland. Brief drops to 22° F. may prove fatal to a lemon tree, and temperatures that remain as low as 28° F. for an hour or more can ruin an entire crop.

In temporary cold spells citrus growers use smudge pots to warm the air or wind machines to disperse the cold air. These crop-saving devices are particularly useful in areas around Santa Barbara, San Fernando, and Pomona, which have registered readings as low as 23° F. Asuza, Claremont, and Redlands lie at the edge of the citrus belt; areas beyond are too unreliable for citrus growing, even with smudge pots.

Fortunately, damagingly low temperatures can usually be predicted sufficiently in advance to give warning time to growers. In four of the major freezes experienced in Southern California since citrus-growing weather records have been kept, a low pressure area was located over the Southwest, and a high pressure ridge extended over the Pacific from the Arctic Ocean to the tropics; there were also high winds aloft and an absence of any temperature inversion. When these conditions exist, a freeze is sure to follow. R. W. Durrenberger, a geography professor who has studied this aspect of weather and its effect upon the California citrus industry, warns that freezes can be expected to occur in Southern California every ten or fifteen years.

THE PACIFIC COASTAL STRIP IS, then, a land of many weather contrasts within two broad climatic zones: maritime in the north and Mediterranean in the south. The two meet, and to some degree overlap, around San Francisco Bay.

That great breach in the coastal battlement is a convenient landmark of climate zones, but they are caused, not by topography, but by differences in the great

DAVID MUENCH

Mediterranean vista: Santa Barbara, California, where winter rain often comes from towering cumuli.

global weather patterns under whose domination they fall. Nevertheless, the differences are readily apparent in the landscape as one travels from one zone to the other. The great conifer forests of the north give way to oak woodlands and chaparral, with only a few pockets of giant coast redwood to be found south of San Francisco. As the habitat changes, so do its residents. In the animal world, too, the sharpest boundary between different coastal species falls at the Golden Gate.

Even in the affairs of man, climate plays its role. It was probably no accident of history that settlers from Russia's northerly latitudes never ventured farther south than Fort Ross, some seventy miles north of San Francisco; or that the Spanish, with a cultural heritage that was literally Mediterranean, extended their chain of missions only to San Rafael and Sonoma.

In twentieth-century America differences in the human populations along the coast are more subtle but still detectable. Surely many factors have contributed to these differences, but few observers would deny that climate has played some part.

CHAPTER 11

THE FERTILE VALLEYS

America's bountiful gardens: the Willamette, Sacramento, Napa,
San Joaquin, and Imperial valleys ❖ Differences in seasonal
patterns and temperatures ❖ That all-important element—water

BETWEEN THE SALT-SPRAYED Pacific coast ranges and the high masses of the Sierra Nevada and the Cascades lie some of the most productive agricultural valleys in the world. In Oregon's Willamette Valley, down the long trough of the Sacramento and San Joaquin valleys, and in the Coachella and Imperial valleys of California's southland, are fertile Pacific lowlands with differing climates and long growing seasons conducive to a wide variety of fruits, vegetables, and nuts. The land is usually gently sloping, steep enough for drainage but level enough for easy cultivation. Water is available naturally in some valleys through rainfall, and in all through irrigation. These valleys are, or have been, outlets of mountain watersheds, and their earth, the dust of the mountains, has been washed down and deposited over long geological time.

Located within fifty or one hundred miles of the coast, these valleys share its predominant storm patterns: in the north, cyclones spun off from the Aleutian Low; in the south, the weakened remnants of these storms and an occasional Sonoran storm from the Gulf of Mexico. Rainfall in the valleys is lighter than on the immediate coast, variations in daily and seasonal temperatures are greater, and sunshine is more plentiful. The high landscapes surrounding the valleys often blunt the severity of storms and exert influences of their own.

In general, the extent to which the weather of a valley differs from that of open countryside at the same latitude depends on the size and elevation of the valley, the height of its surrounding mountains, and its position with respect to the sources of moisture. Valleys that lie in the rain shadow of mountains can be quite dry. On the other hand, if the normal path of storms is into the mouth of the valley, rainfall can be very heavy, for the clouds are forced higher at the head of the valley, causing precipitation. Thus the Great Valley of California, east of the Coast Ranges, is dry while the western valleys of the Olympic Peninsula are deluged.

Smaller valleys nestled deep in the mountains, as Yosemite is, are not subject to severe rain shadows because the clouds remain high while passing over them en route to succeeding ridges. Even if a valley is dry, precipitation that passes over it is captured by the peaks, sometimes banked in the vast reserves of the winter snowpack, but eventually sent coursing down mountain-born rivers to the valley below.

Temperature in valleys can have a wide daily range. Daytime highs are comparable to those of open countryside and are influenced by the same factors. Thus, dry valleys receive plenty of sunshine to heat the ground, which in turn heats the air above. Moister valleys have less sunshine, because water vapor is available for cloud formation, and so heating of the air by the ground is not as pronounced. The coolness may be enhanced by a cover of forest or other thick vegetation on the valley floor. Vegetation does not become as hot as bare ground, and it also provides direct cooling by evaporation from its leaves.

At night valleys collect the cold air that drains down the mountainsides (see explanation of mountain breezes,

The abundance displayed in this Coachella Valley grapefruit orchard exemplifies the productivity of the many agricultural valleys found in the Far West.

JOSEF MUENCH

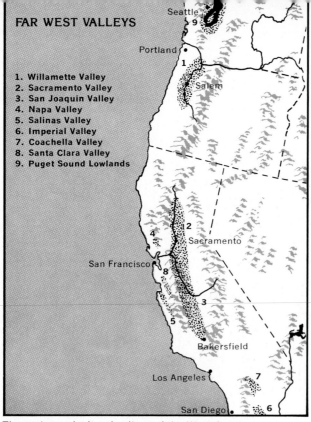

FAR WEST VALLEYS

1. Willamette Valley
2. Sacramento Valley
3. San Joaquin Valley
4. Napa Valley
5. Salinas Valley
6. Imperial Valley
7. Coachella Valley
8. Santa Clara Valley
9. Puget Sound Lowlands

The major agricultural valleys of the West Coast.

page 140), thus reducing temperatures considerably and stretching the daily temperature range. This cold air creates fog if the valley air it meets contains sufficient water vapor, and frost if its temperature dips below the freezing point. Fog and frost are intrinsically related to the topography of valleys, and architects, engineers, and agriculturalists routinely consider them in selecting locations for buildings, highways, and crops.

Another consequence of cold air drainage is that inversions frequently occur over valleys. This condition coupled with man's propensity for settling in valleys, farming then, developing industrial plants, and jamming valley highways with automobiles, causes severe air pollution, which the valley's natural air circulation system cannot eliminate. When that system fails, clouds, fog, or pollution itself block out the sunlight, keeping the land cool and sustaining the inversion.

Far West valleys have always been associated with agriculture. A few agricultural settlements had been established by European explorers along coastal California and in the Oregon country before the great emigration of Americans that started in the late 1840s. In California dry farming techniques and the raising of livestock were introduced by Spanish missionaries in the late eighteenth century. Bringing with them seeds and tree crops that could flourish in the dry summer weather, they culti-

vated large tracts of mission land and diverted water from the streams of the Coast Range for irrigation. The Spanish farming methods were an efficient use of the land and climatic resources, suiting a population that produced for its needs alone and exported little.

North of the 42nd parallel (the historic boundary between California and Oregon), the pattern of pioneer settlement was decidedly different. In the Northwest, the trapper and Indian trader came first, followed by the missionary and the frontiersman, and finally the pioneer settler, who started farming on public land. Many of the crops with which the emigrants were familiar from earlier days in the East and the Mississippi Valley grew easily in Oregon. Abundant winter rainfall was sufficient to maintain a supply of groundwater during the summer season, prompting the rapid growth of fruit trees. On a six-month journey from Iowa to Oregon, Henderson Luelling and his family undertook to transport a traveling nursery of some seven hundred vines, shrubs, and grafted trees, standard varieties of apples, pears, peaches, plums, grapes, and cherries common to Iowa. Near the townsite of Milwaukie, six miles south of Portland, Luelling planted in 1848 the first orchard of grafted fruit trees in the Pacific Northwest. His foresight proved of such tremendous importance to the growth of this new land that some Oregonians claim that load of trees brought more wealth to Oregon than any ship that ever entered the Columbia River.

As one moves southward along the Pacific Coast, the total annual precipitation decreases and the need for irrigation increases. With more intensive use of the land by increasing numbers of immigrants, a supplementary source of water became more and more important, although only in the dry interior valleys and in Southern California was natural water so scarce that the land would not yield something on its own.

OREGON'S WILLAMETTE RIVER VALLEY is bounded on the west by the Coast Range, on the east by the Cascades, on the north by the Columbia River, and on the south by the Calapooya Mountains. The valley, generally considered to be that portion below an elevation of five hundred feet, was originally settled by Finns and other northern Europeans, who proceeded to strip the slopes of the virgin Douglas fir and clear the lowlands

More than half the population of Oregon—industrial and agricultural alike—enjoys the benefits of the Willamette Valley's moist marine climate. Mount Hood dominates the horizon.

for farming. Alders promptly replaced the fir, spreading from streamside to become the second growth. On the cleared lowlands fruit trees, oats, and other forage crops and cereals were planted.

In the valley today agriculture is widely diversified, yielding particularly significant crops of hops, pears, walnuts, and prunes. Apples are also grown in the valley, but not in quantities to equal the Hood River Valley and other small, irrigated valleys east of the Cascades. The Willamette climate does not have the autumn chill that colors apples nor the wide variation between winter and summer temperatures that is a factor in reducing spoilage.

Dairying is well suited to the Willamette and to the Puget Sound region as well. The cool, humid climate not only provides a long pasturing season but produces luxuriant, green forage that is both succulent and cheap. Economics and the ever-increasing value of farmland have been making inroads into the dairying industry, with more acreage now being devoted to higher-income-producing specialties such as berries, nuts, fruit, and forage seed crops.

Wind movement over the Willamette Valley is dominated by weather systems over the Pacific. In winter, when the North Pacific high pressure center is farther south, southwest winds move relatively warm ocean air inland and bring precipitation to the lowlands and adjacent areas. In summer the pressure center lies due west of the Northern California coast, and the circulating winds flow in a more northerly direction—a condition that tends to decrease relative humidity and reduce the amount of cloudiness and precipitation. In spring and autumn intermediate conditions occur causing alternating wet and dry spells. Although normally dominated by maritime influences during all the seasons, the valley occasionally—particularly in midsummer and midwinter—is affected by east winds bringing in continental air.

One characteristic of weather in the valley is the pattern of rainfall, with over 15 percent occurring in each of the winter months of November, December, and January, and only 1 percent each in July and August.

NORTH OF THE SAN FRANCISCO BAY REGION, from Petaluma east to the Sacramento Valley, the weather is transitional—displaying characteristics of both the marine climate of the north and the dry-summer, subtropical climate of the south. The southern edge of this climate zone is noted for its orchards of plums and prunes, grazing lands occupied by herds of beef cattle or flocks of sheep, and, especially in the Napa Valley, thousands of acres of vineyards.

When Father Serra and his small band of Franciscans landed in California, they rejoiced at finding wild grapevines festooning the trees along creeks and riverbanks— an indication that their cultivated vines, so essential for the making of sacramental wines, would probably flourish. Today wine-making is one of the most important industries in the southern and central California valleys, where the vineyards are lavishly endowed with plenty of sun, cool air, and a long growing season. In Napa, the sandy soil and climate are ideal for the growing of the finest quality grapes.

The ripening of wine grapes is a delicate process, requiring optimum temperature and moisture conditions. Grapes will thrive only in places where the average annual temperature is between 50° and 68° F., and where the growing season is long enough to produce the high content of sugar essential for conversion into alcohol. The climate should also be cool so that acids, important contributors to the dryness of table wine, will be retained rather than transpire out of the fruit. Too warm a climate causes the grape to lose the subtle flavor needed for fine wine, and sometimes its color as well. Thus grapes from southern Spain, Sicily, Cyprus, and Southern California, while suitable for sweet dessert wines, cannot qualify for the making of great table wines.

Perhaps the chief adversity growers face in the Napa Valley is the occurrence of early and late killing frosts. To avoid frost damage, they have taken a lesson from nature: temperatures are less extreme in windy weather because the wind continually mixes the air and prevents stratification into cold and warm layers. Thus, the growers fan their fields with giant wind machines in frosty weather. Another technique, surprising to the layman, involves sprinkling the vines with water; as it freezes on the vines, the water gives off heat and prevents them from freezing.

To many San Franciscans, "the Valley" means Napa's vine-covered fields; in Hollywood it is probably the San Fernando Valley; to John Steinbeck it was the Salinas, the locale of several of his novels. But to all Californians, "the Valley" is also California's immense Central Valley, or Great Valley, a long, banana-shaped depression through the heart of the state. The Central Valley produces rice and cotton, peaches and oranges, tomatoes, asparagus, sweet potatoes, and scores of other crops, which make California one of the finest agricultural states in the United States.

Flatter than most of the Middle West, this food basket cradles approximately 25,000 square miles of productive land, stretching from the Klamath Mountains in the north to the Tehachapis in the south. The southern portion, the San Joaquin Valley, was known to the Spanish as the Tule Valley, or Valley of the Lakes (which today would be inappropriate, to say the least). The northern part, the Sacramento Valley, was then a sea of grass, broken only by patches of white oak. The Spanish were unimpressed by the Central Valley, preferring to settle in the mild and pleasant valleys by the sea.

The Great Valley's climate is classified as "interior Mediterranean." Southwesterly portions of the San Joaquin Valley, around Bakersfield, are subtropic desert, as hot as the Colorado Desert, with winters even milder than the Mojave. July temperatures in Bakersfield average 84° F., and the highs are hardly within the comfort range for human beings. To the north, Fresno's climate may be just as warm in the summertime, but winter rains are twice as frequent. Dependent on the remnants of North Pacific storms, annual rainfall in the valley ranges from twenty inches at Red Bluff and seventeen inches at Sacramento to only three inches around Bakersfield. The west side of the Sacramento Valley is in the rain shadow of the Coast Range and has less precipita-

Verdant in the rainy months of winter and spring, burnished gold through summer and fall, Pine Valley in Monterey County shares the Mediterranean climate common to the central California coast.

tion than the east side. For instance, Orland, on the west edge of the valley receives an average of 17.5 inches annually, whereas Chico, at the east edge, enjoys an average of 23.5 inches.

Winds are frequent in the Central Valley. In summer intense heat expands the air over the valley, generating a low pressure cell. The pressure difference between the Pacific high and this valley low draws cool air in from the ocean to bring welcome relief from 110° F. temperatures. Residents of Mendocino, on the coast, predict Sacramento Valley temperatures by the pull of their onshore fog banks. Soupy fog at Fort Bragg means sizzling heat in the valley.

The greatest gap in the Coast Range occurs where the Sacramento and the San Joaquin rivers converge and flow into the San Francisco Bay. Blowing over the dry peat of this Delta region, summer winds create dust storms in the southwestern parts of the San Joaquin Valley. Cool ocean air, flowing inland, tempers the

diurnal range of summer temperatures in the Delta by about ten degrees.

Cold winds bring the Central Valley its only significant weather hazard. The growing season, usually nine or ten months long, is sometimes abbreviated by subfreezing weather that blows in from the northeast in late spring or early autumn. This polar onslaught is referred to by the chilled residents as a "norther."

Another disagreeable weather feature is "tule fog," a low-lying fog that follows periods of heavy rainfall and high humidity. It occurs during December and January, when sunlight is less than other times of the year and unable to burn off the overcast. Weather below a tule fog is damp and cold, and skies are overcast day and night for periods of three to ten days. If the fog lifts in late afternoon, nighttime temperatures may plunge below the freezing point.

Fortunately, the Central Valley is not dependent on local rain alone for its agricultural survival. The water-

133

shed for the valley is the Sierra Nevada, whose snowpack provides a great natural reservoir. The Sierra does, however, fluctuate widely in the quantity of water it can supply: in 1906–1907 the watershed represented 63.3 million acre-feet; in 1923–1924, only 9.2 million acre-eet. Flooding is infrequent—only five flood years were reported between 1909 and 1955—but when it occurs the damage can run into many millions of dollars. Such floods normally result when winter storms from the central Pacific bring warm rain that prematurely melts the snowpack, causing a heavy early spring runoff.

One of the most overwhelming floods ever to inundate the Central Valley occurred in 1862. Mountain rivers swollen with heavy rainfall rampaged downstream, devastated towns and mining operations, and carried tons of silt and debris to the lowlands. A vast, shallow lake, estimated to have been as large in area as Lake Michigan, filled the Sacramento Valley, submerging everything in the countryside, including the new state capitol. The booming cattle industry was almost wiped out when hundreds of thousands of animals were destroyed.

Ironically, the following two years registered the most severe drought on record. Between 1862 and 1864, the foothill pastures of the San Joaquin Valley burned brown. Stockmen, desperate for forage, moved their animals up into the mountains to keep them alive, establishing in California the pattern of migratory grazing. Other ranchers shipped cattle outside the state for pasturage, while thousands of head, literally too thin to stand the trip, were auctioned off at distress prices in a bear market.

In 1933 the Central Valley Project (CVP), a multi-purpose program to improve and coordinate the use of water resources, was established, and its first priority was the San Joaquin Valley, which it considered to be California's area of greatest water deficiency.

ALTHOUGH IRRIGATION had been practiced by the prehistoric Hohokam people, who built canals in the Southwest, and by the Yuma and Mojave Indians, who cultivated the flood plain along the Colorado River, it was the Franciscan fathers who, during the Spanish colonial period, introduced this watering method to California's coastal valleys by digging ditches to irrigate the mission fields. The Mormons also practiced irrigation, and in the 1850s they watered some four thousand acres of outpost land in what is now San Bernardino. The idea began to catch on, and in 1856 Yolo County formed a water company to serve various wheat farmers.

As early as 1849, when most men in California were still dreaming of bonanzas from the mines, Dr. Oliver

Lush lettuce fields in the hot Imperial Valley are irrigated with water from the Colorado River.

JOSEF MUENCH

to the soil, the heat, or the long growing season, which lasts some two hundred days. Success came only as farmers began to plant such truck crops as lettuce, tomatoes, cantaloupes, watermelons, and carrots, and exploit this long season by employing the technique known as double-cropping, in effect doubling the yield of every acre. Their produce soon dominated the winter market. Today the fertile basin of the Imperial Valley—with just three inches of average annual rainfall but 470,000 irrigated acres capable of growing two or three crops a year—has become Southern California's natural hot-house and nursery.

Summers in the Imperial Valley are long, hot, and dry, with temperatures ranging from 100° to 120° F., while winters are short and mild. After Labor Day, when most of the country is in the midst of harvest, valley farmers are starting to plant, aiming for crop maturity in midwinter or early spring, when there is little competition from other growers.

Wozencraft proposed a grander and eventually far more lucrative dream: irrigation of the Imperial Valley. At that time both the Imperial and the smaller Coachella valleys were considered part of the "Great American Desert" and thus all but uninhabitable. In demonstrating that they could be irrigated by gravity flow of water from the Colorado River, Wozencraft changed the course of Southern California agriculture—and eventually of the Colorado River as well.

Settlement in the Imperial Valley began at the turn of the twentieth century and burgeoned for three decades as irrigation was expanded and agriculture flourished. Then, in the winter of 1905–1906, the life-giving waters of the Colorado turned on their master, broke through their channel, and poured into the Imperial Valley, forming the Salton Sea. So great was the damage that Congress ultimately authorized construction of Boulder (Hoover) Dam, completed in 1936.

Most of the early settlers came from the Midwest, enticed by the promotional efforts of the Imperial Land Company, which—with typical California-booster grandiosity—coined the name Imperial Valley for this hot and arid land. Nevertheless, the venture proved successful, and since the mid-1920s agriculture has been firmly established. Transplanted farmers soon found that the products they had planned to raise—wheat, grapes, deciduous fruits, potatoes, hogs, turkeys—were unsuited

EXCELLENT CLIMATE AND PLENTIFUL WATER have combined to make the agricultural valleys of the Pacific states among the most productive in the world. But another factor is not to be ignored: development and increased use of specialized and uniform hybrid crops, tailored to the soil and the specific climate conditions of the last thirty years.

Noted meteorologist Walter Orr Roberts believes that no period in the last thousand years has been as favorable to agriculture as these last thirty. Man has achieved the maximum in crop productivity at the very time when, because of spiraling population, his needs were the greatest. Unfortunately, Roberts also believes there is but one chance in a thousand that the next thirty years will be equally propitious. Should vagaries of climate result in shifts of temperature, rainfall, or humidity to such an extent that the weather is no longer suitable for growing hybrid crops, or should conditions arise that encourage disease or pestilence, the grower may find that hybrids lack the resistance of the original varieties, and extensive crop losses may occur. The changing availability of water must also be considered.

With such forecasts as a warning, man dares not take the resources of the great and productive agricultural valleys for granted.

Stretching half the length of the state, the ambitious California Aqueduct was built to transport the surplus from Northern California's winter rains to Southern California's parched acres.

CHAPTER 12

THE MOUNTAIN BARRIERS

Weather in the western ranges—the Sierra, the Cascades, and
the Rockies ❖ Weather effects that mountains create: rain
and rain shadow, mountain/valley breezes, and mountain wave clouds

"THERE ARE NO NEUTRAL MOMENTS" in a mountain town, according to author Theodora Kroeber, who spent her childhood in mile-high Denver. For that matter there are no neutral times anywhere in the mountains, so steeped are they in the drama of free-flowing weather. Every foothill, valley, canyon, and peak has a weather pattern as unique as a signature—bold, amplified, imprinted by the mountains themselves.

Skiers face violent storms and sub-zero temperatures to experience the new powder; climbers challenge cloud-piercing peaks in midwinter (an annual New Year's Day event in the Tetons) pitting human skill against alpine winds and blizzards; hunters spend bone-chilling nights in high mountain camps so they can begin their quest at first light. In late spring, even before the snow has disappeared, families pack into the mountains, spend the night, and pack out again, merely for the taste of what Mark Twain called "fine, bracing and delicious [air], the same the angels breathe."

To scientists, mountain weather represents a mosaic of microclimates fitted so intricately into the geographical patterns of slope, elevation, and exposure that it is virtually impossible to present them all on a climatic map. Sunny southern slopes, clear of snow and greening by mid-May, contrast with adjacent cool canyons, where sunlight penetrates only a few hours a day and snow-packs may survive until August. Weather, too, may change dramatically over short distances, creating marked differences in vegetation. The Cascade crest, for instance, generally separates west-side Douglas fir from east-side ponderosa pine. Hikers who have spent all day in the fog-filled valleys of the western slope, upon reaching the crest, can watch the fog blanket melt at the edge of "good weather" on the east side.

Throughout the world the principal mountain chains and high mountain basins of the middle and low latitudes are considered to have "highland climates." In North America these include the Cascades, the Sierra Nevada, and the Rocky Mountains. Variations in highland climate are determined primarily by altitude, local contours, and the effectiveness of the mountains as barriers.

Coloradoans are inclined to say, with some justification, that there is air at high altitudes that has never been breathed before. Mountain air is thinner, because of altitude, and ordinarily much freer of dust and smoke than lowlands. Thus it is more transparent to the passage of incoming and outgoing radiation. Even the cities along the foothills of the Rockies have a climate considered so salubrious that in the 1870s pamphlets advertising the strong sunshine and dry air were distributed throughout the nation by Denver's Committee of Asthmatics. Unfortunately, in recent years smog frequently forms along the foothills and over Denver, creating an atmosphere not so beneficent as it once was.

Under clear skies in highland climates, one can almost literally burn in the sunlight and freeze in the shade. The mountain air permits passage of the shorter, burning wavelengths of light (violet and ultraviolet), which are more attenuated by the air at lower elevations. At sundown, temperatures drop quickly, since the dry air has

Mountains are places of action. Cumulus clouds develop above Mount Stuart, fed by moist air rising over the Cascades, but erode away in the drier air to the east.

The Owens Valley lies in the rain shadow of the Sierra Nevada. Winds flowing over the mountains dip into the valley, then rise again forming a lee wave cloud (left); below it a rotor churns up dust.

little capacity for retaining heat; and bare rock loses heat rapidly by radiation, further fostering broad daily ranges of temperatures. Night frosts are possible anytime during the year in mountains as lofty as the High Sierra or the Fourteeners of the Rockies, even when daytime temperatures rise well above freezing.

Temperature drops an average of 3.5 degrees F. for every thousand feet of altitude gained. Along the slopes and in the high peaks of the Rockies, the frost-free growing season averages forty days shorter than in the valleys, and at the high weather stations it is eighty days shorter. In the mountains of northern New Mexico, average temperatures are as low as those in the interior of Washington or New York states, which are hundreds of miles farther north. In fact, northern New Mexico is cooler than any large geographical area in the Northeast and thirty degrees cooler than some lowland areas at similar latitudes in Southern California.

Moisture is easily condensed out of cooling air, such as that rising and expanding over mountains. This is one of the reasons why precipitation increases on the slopes, while the mountains, having captured most of the air's

moisture on their windward side, exert a rain shadow effect on lowlands to their lee. On the western slopes of the Cascades, the precipitation, about 100 inches annually, is six times greater than on the northeastern slopes. The western Sierra Nevada, because of its broad western flanks, receives ten times as much precipitation as areas immediately to the east. In Arizona several mountain weather stations receive three times the precipitation of lowland stations in their respective rain shadows. The rain shadow effect is most pronounced during generally dry years; in abnormally wet years, mountains seem to receive relatively little more rain than the adjacent lowlands.

Where ranges are in echelon, as in the Pacific Northwest, the first mountain range receives the largest amount of precipitation, and succeeding downwind ranges receive progressively less. The amount of precipitation received by the downwind ranges depends largely on elevation. Moisure averaging fifteen to fifty inches falls annually on the Blue Mountains in eastern Oregon and the northern Rockies in Idaho, because they are as high or higher than the Cascades to the west. To the lee of

In the thick of an upslope fog, hills and conifers appear and vanish again behind the mist. Muted by overcast skies, even the sun is dimmed.

these mountains and their spurs are several local dry islands, the largest of which is the Snake River Plain. Again, elevation differences determine the amount of precipitation: the lower portion of the plain receives about ten inches or less, the middle portion ten to thirteen inches, the upper portion more than thirteen inches.

Snowfall, likewise, is heavier at higher altitudes and remains on the ground for longer periods. Snowpacks may remain throughout the summer as far south as southern Colorado and the central Sierra. The farther away mountains are from the source of moisture for their storms, namely the Pacific Ocean, the drier is the air that reaches them, since earlier encounters with mountain barriers have removed much of the moisture. For this drier air to produce precipitation, it must be cooled more than moist air. Thus, the snowline in the Rockies of Montana is higher than in the Cascades, which, in turn, is above the Olympics' at comparable latitudes.

Fog—clouds at ground level—makes more frequent appearances on mountains than on nearby plains or valleys. On Pikes Peak (elevation 14,140 feet), there were 119 days of fog in one year, while nearby Colorado

Springs (elevation 6,072 feet) had only 14. As moist air near the saturation point is gradually lifted up a sloping plain or hilly region, it may cool and form upslope fog. This same phenomenon is common on the high plains east of the Rockies, where it is called "Cheyenne fog."

The primary causes of precipitation (frontal storms and convective air currents) are the same everywhere, but in mountainous regions they are intensified by the rising of air over the mountains—known technically as the *orographic effect*. Frontal storms impinge upon both mountains and lowlands, but the annual yield of rainfall is greater over higher country. Sudden summer thunderstorms, common to the Rockies and the Sierra Nevada, strike while most of the western lowlands are experiencing their dry season. Forming leeward of peaks in late afternoon, to the dismay of unprepared picnickers and hikers, they move across Denver or Reno, cooling a hot afternoon and washing the streets for an hour or so.

Occasionally these cloudbursts pour out a substantial amount of rain. In Denver, for example, there were times before the Cherry Creek Reservoir was constructed when the normally placid stream that passes through the heart

Wind sculpture occurs in the high country of the Cascades whenever a tree stands alone and unprotected.

dies down and whitecaps on the lake subside, the first large raindrops begin to hit the water. Lightning cracks high in the range, thunder claps, and the Tetons disappear behind a veil of rain.

In sunny summer weather, when air movement is generally light, the major breeze is a mountain-valley wind, blowing up the valley during the day and down the valley at night, often in contrast to higher air moving above the peaks or adjacent plains. A valley breeze (meteorologists name winds by the direction *from* which they come), flowing toward the peaks, starts to blow

Because temperatures in the mountains vary considerably from day to night, a local wind develops: upslope by day, when air rises over the warm slopes; downslope at night, when cooler mountain air sinks into the valley.

MOUNTAIN BREEZES

Upslope

Downslope

of the downtown section would become a rampaging river en route to its juncture with the South Platte.

Although the Cascades have thundershowers, they receive most of their rain from persistent cyclonic storms that come directly off the Pacific.

In mountain country, winds are greatly affected by the rugged terrain, usually moving around ranges and over ridges. Near Pikes Peak, forceful windstorms sweep down the mountain, frequently continuing for a day or two before blowing themselves out. Winds may be confined by canyons, such as Cascade Canyon near Jenny Lake in the Tetons, only to break free with startling suddenness and lash through the forest beyond. As a brief but dramatic summer storm approaches, a silver line of mist forms over the lake, and a gale whips through the pines like an orchestral crescendo. On September 23, 1933, a particularly violent blast through Cascade Canyon felled almost every tree in a quarter-mile swath, devastating much of the Jenny Lake campground. The wind is often the forerunner of a thunderstorm. When it

Cold weather moving in after a storm in the Sierra Nevada has left a dry snow that is easily blown by high winds around the summit of Mount Morrison.

shortly after sunrise, reaches its maximum near midday, and diminishes by sunset, to be replaced by a mountain breeze that flows from peaks to valleys. Southern slopes, being more intensely heated by the sun, produce the strongest winds, and northern slopes the weakest. When the valley wind is moist, cumulus clouds build up over the peaks, formed from the cooling, ascending air currents. These rising cloud masses often result in afternoon cloudiness and showers. On spring and fall evenings, mountain breezes may bring fog or frost to the valley floor while higher, more exposed slopes remain clear and mild.

Another effect of the mountain barrier is to delay a weather front, slowing it sufficiently to allow a subsequent front to override the first, a phenomenon called *occlusion*. If moist ocean air meets cold continental air in an occluded front, the result is heavy rainfall.

A prime example of how the barrier changes weather can be found at the great water gap of the Columbia Gorge, the only substantial break in the Cascade Range. East of the gorge, as far east as the edge of Idaho, the average January temperature is above 30° F., or almost

ten degrees higher than in surrounding areas. This climatic fluke is the result of warm, moist Pacific air squeezing through the Columbia gap. Cold air may flow westward from the interior through the same channel when conditions are favorable, exiting to the ocean side of the Cascades. Longview, immediately west of the gorge, has recorded the western Cascade's lowest temperature, —20° F. Towns not in direct line with the gap, and therefore not subject to the cold air, have more moderate temperatures. At times the air draining westward in the gorge can produce winds of destructive velocity. Similar gorge winds occur on the Fraser, Snake, and Thompson rivers, the Strait of Juan de Fuca, and the fiords of British Columbia.

Clouds may be the best graphic display that mountains disturb air flow on a scale sufficient to affect surface weather. Air forced up over a mountain or range continues on the lee side in an undulating pattern, a series of waves like ripples from a rock lying in a stream. Clouds form near the wave crests because the air, expanding and cooling in its ascent, chills sufficiently to condense some of its water vapor. In the reverse of this process, clouds

141

Clouds formed above a mountain barrier can develop vast proportions, like this cumulonimbus over the high country near Yosemite—so vast that sometimes they can persist independently of the slopes.

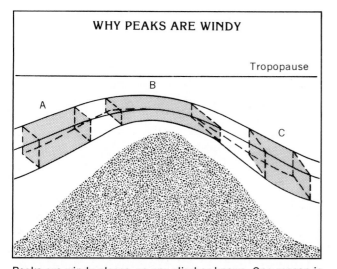

WHY PEAKS ARE WINDY

Tropopause

A   B   C

Peaks are windy places, as any climber knows. One reason is that mountains rise into prevailing winds, which increase in speed with elevation, so winds that encounter a mountain actually move faster over the crest. Too, peaks have little vegetation to break the wind. But most important, in order that air approaching the mountain not be dammed on the windward side, a volume of air equalling that approaching the mountain must pass over it. When air parcel A moves over the top of the mountain to become B, it squeezes between the crest and the tropopause, which blocks any upward movement of air since it marks an inversion. B must get thinner because air on both sides restricts it, so to maintain its volume, it lengthens. Since B passes the summit in the same time as A would pass the base, and B is longer, its air must travel faster. When B moves on to C, it is no longer constricted; the air mass then thickens and shortens to its former shape, and its air speed is reduced to that of A.

movement reaching fifty miles per hour at times, represent a particular hazard to the pilots of small aircraft. A pilot attempting to cross a mountain range from the lee side may find, when he encounters the descending portion of its mountain wave, that his aircraft will not climb fast enough to clear the mountain crest. Numerous wrecks of light aircraft attempting a westward crossing of the Rockies are found just east of the Continental Divide. Danger for pilots also lurks under very strong lee waves, where there is turbulence—a pilot's enemy—as air forms a countercurrent in a rotating pattern called a *rotor*. If the relative humidity near the ground is high, a tremendous cloud will be formed, releasing energy through condensation and increasing the turbulence.

The shape of the mountain barrier is reflected in its lee wave clouds. An isolated peak makes clean waves across the airstream, which lie in ever widening patterns. Beyond a series of peaks are lee wave clouds formed by the reinforcement of overlapping waves from the individual peaks. Similarly, a long ridge will have wave clouds parallel to it, and a second range paralleling the first may cancel or reinforce the waves trailing the first.

If general cloudiness prevails to the lee of a mountain range, wave clouds may not be distinguishable, but a "hole in the clouds" may occur. Sometimes a startling sight, this phenomenon results where air, descending between lee waves, is sufficiently warm to evaporate the cloudiness, especially if it is thin.

evaporate near the wave troughs. The position of the wave pattern is fixed in relation to the mountains. Since the clouds are generated at specific locations within the wave pattern, they appear stationary.

Wave clouds formed directly over mountains are called *mountain wave clouds*, as contrasted to those formed downwind, which are known as *lee wave clouds*. Most wave clouds are lenticular (lens-shaped), with arched tops, flat bases, and smooth contours. The level of the cloud bottom is determined by the altitude at which condensation occurs, and the rounded top conforms to the undulating shape of the airstream. Lee waves sometimes extend as far as two hundred miles downwind from the mountains, and there may be as many as twenty-five individual waves in the series.

These lee and mountain waves, with vertical air

IN MANY WAYS WEATHER is altered by the high barriers of mountains, and yet their very height is the seed of their destruction. They intercept the weather only to be destroyed by it. Millions of years of erosion by wind and rain, fracturing of the rocky flanks by repeated freezing of water in cracks, and scouring by glacial ice laden with abrasive rock fragments have sculpted the ranges. In the Sierra Nevada are some of the best examples of Ice Age sculpture in America: over twelve hundred lakes and tarns, paternoster (chained) lakes, U-shaped canyons, waterfalls, scores of rapids and cascading streams, and grandest of all, John Muir's beloved Yosemite Valley.

Thus in the mountains a thoughtful observer can see clearly the partnership of land and atmosphere, each constantly transforming the other, both collaborating to produce the ever-changing panorama called weather.

CHAPTER 13

EMPIRES OF THE SUN

Deserts and arid basins of the West ❖ The precious rains—how and when they come ❖ Flash floods, haboobs, dunes, and other desert phenomena ❖ How living things adapt to desert survival

A S THE INFANT UNITED STATES began to outgrow its cradle along the eastern seaboard, it found fertile, well-watered prairies and woodlands stretching away for hundreds of miles beyond the Appalachians. Farmers moved west, clearing and plowing, reaping a rich harvest with the skills they had honed back east. In time this westward pressure pushed the vanguard all the way to the Mississippi River, and beyond. There a curious thing happened. The explorers and trailblazers found that the half of the continent that lay beyond that great stream was anything but a mirror image of the half they had left behind. It could hardly have been more different. Not only did it have mountain barriers to dwarf the Appalachians, but it had deserts—thousands of square miles of them—unlike anything known east of the Mississippi.

The "Great American Desert" they called it. And given their agrarian background, one can hardly blame these westering easterners for placing the edge of that desert at the point where prairie turns into plains. Indeed most of the western half of the country, except for the Rockies, the Sierra Nevada, and part of the Pacific Coast, was considered desert.

By today's definition the desert region is more limited in extent. It is any land of little moisture, high daytime temperatures, low nighttime temperatures, strong winds, and streams that are dry washes much of the year. Nevertheless, it stretches—vast, sprawling, irregular, and interrupted—from Oregon south to beyond the Mexican border, and from California to west Texas. But part of

the early misconception remains—the idea of a single American desert. In actuality, there are several quite distinct deserts in the West, each with its own patterns and sources of weather, its own topography, and native plants and animals.

Another common misconception is that deserts are always hot. The very word calls up visions of lost prospectors crawling along endless miles of scorching sand under a relentless sun. The truth is that temperatures in the various desert areas of the West vary widely. In July, the average daily temperature range is from approximately 50° F. to 95° F. for the relatively high (4,000-foot) Great Basin and Chihuahuan deserts to approximately 75° F. to 105° F. for the lower Mojave and Sonoran deserts. Greenland Ranch in Death Valley commonly reports summer temperatures that make it the hottest spot in the nation. There, on July 10, 1913, an air temperature record was set: 134° F., two degrees below the world record (set on September 13, 1922, Azizia, Libya).

While temperatures in the Great Basin often dip below zero in winter, the Sonoran rarely has temperatures below freezing.

Aridity, more than heat, is the condition that characterizes deserts. Most portions of the Great Basin receive less than ten inches of rainfall a year; the Chihuahuan Desert averages only about five inches, while the Mojave and the Sonoran receive still less. Even those parched-sounding statistics can be misleading because the rainfall is unreliable, and some years may be wetter than aver-

Rain pours down on Monument Valley, Arizona, one segment at a time; behind it blazing sun and dry air quickly eliminate the moisture and within hours will erase all traces of the storm.

age while others are drier. When rain does come to the desert, it may be in cloudburst quantities that cannot be soaked up by the thirsty land before they run off. Furthermore, much of the rain that does not run off is quickly evaporated, especially in the hot months of summer. Left with but a fraction of the water they receive, deserts support only a sparse population of plants and animals especially adapted to the rigors of their desiccated land.

One of the principal causes of American deserts is rain shadow. If the Cascades and Sierra Nevada were removed, most of the western desert areas probably would cease to exist, for it is these high mountains that drain the moisture from the air that blows in from the Pacific. As that air moves up the western side of the ranges, it cools, expands, and condenses its burden of moisture as rain or snow. Descending the eastern slope toward the deserts, it again compresses and warms; more important, it is now very dry and usually incapable of producing further precipitation. Thus it is no accident of nature that the major American deserts are found on the lee side of the mountain ranges.

T HE GREAT BASIN—so-called not for its shape but because it does not drain to the ocean—is an arid upland of plateaus, fault-block mountains, valleys, and broad dry lakes. On the western edge, precipitation is a sparse five inches, while the eastern edge may receive ten inches a year or more.

The highlight of Great Basin weather is its wintertime snow, precipitated by invasions of cold Canadian air over the Rockies and the slight amount of moisture supplied by Pacific winds slipping through passes and over mountain swales. At times the snow is merely a dusting that quickly disappears: but if the weather is cold and the clouds contain sufficient moisture, the snow may be heavy enough to remain. Desert folklore predicts that snow will lie on the ground a week for every day it lies on the sagebrush (where it is more quickly evaporated or blown away).

In high desert country around Lakeview, Oregon (about 4,800 feet), snow has been known to fall during every month of the year. In *The Oregon Desert*, Reuben Long recalls an unusual Fourth of July snowfall there in the 1890s: It seems that an Irish sheepherder had come to

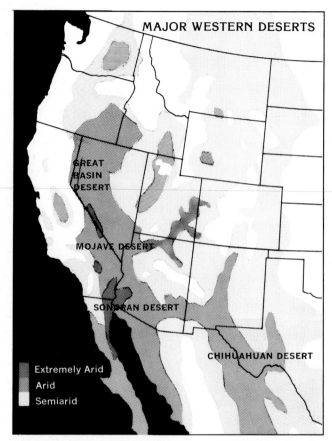

The four major deserts of the West, as defined by the late botanist Forrest Shreve on the basis of climate and plant life. Widely scattered over both arid and semiarid land, and high and low elevations, desert boundaries are often disputed, as is the definition of desert itself.

town for the holiday festivities. After spending the evening in a saloon, he was tossed into his hotel-room bed in a somewhat inebriated state. The next morning, peering out of his window, he saw snow-covered streets and exclaimed, "B'Jaysus, here I've been in town all summer, and I still have money in me pocket!"

The Great Salt Lake Desert covers a hundred square miles of alkali and salt plain within the Great Basin, appearing from a distance like an endless snowfield. Alkali flats are the result of sporadic rain and rapid evaporation in arid regions of the West. In a more humid area, the water that leaches the alkali from the rocks would eventually flow to the sea, but in dry lands what little water flows has no access to the sea, accumulating instead in low basins until it finally evaporates, leaving the alkali

Flash floods can spring out of the mountains without warning—one reason wise hikers never camp in arroyos. Their cold waters may chill the air to its dew point and form surface mist, as here in southern Arizona.

behind. In emigrant days those forced to drink alkali water often died, or at least suffered severe dysentery. The legendary Sweet Betsy from Pike, having crossed the alkali desert, warned "Don't dance me too hard— do you want to know why? / Gol durn ye, I'm chuck full of strong alkali."

When the Donner Party encountered the Great Salt Lake Desert in 1846, their spirits and fortunes reached a new low. Water holes were few and far between, and many of them were encrusted with alkali, fatally poisonous to man and beast. The hostility of the landscape was compounded by empty water casks, an Indian raid on their cattle, and a loneliness that Elizabeth Donner Houghton called "fearful desolation."

In the high desert, storms usually strike in July and August; they are more frequent near the mountains but possible anywhere. Desert thunderstorms are the result of convection: ground-heated air buoyantly rises, expands, and cools, condensing water vapor into clouds and rain. Since the earth is not hot enough for convection to be effective early in the day, most shower activity occurs after noon. Even the heat of the afternoon may not be sufficient to cause the degree of atmospheric instability that results in the vigorous convection required for thunderstorms. When night falls, the puffy cumulus left from the day keep the land warm by reflecting back the heat it radiates, but the tops of clouds cool by radiating their heat, as the land would in their absence. The enhanced temperature difference between the air below the clouds and the cloud tops instigates the lusty churning

147

of the air from which thunderstorms are born. The storms may persist until morning, when the rising sun dries the air but again warms the land.

Few weather spectaculars can match the desert thundershower. Cumulus clouds form above updrafts of hot desert air, gradually multiplying and melding until they seem to fill the sky. Roiling and heaving, the clouds darken and develop anvil tops as they meet high altitude winds. Lightning flashes as the cloud armada advances, challenging the still-blazing sun. Lightning activity increases, striking from cloud to earth to the accompaniment of sharp thunderclaps. As the wind rises, the first drops of rain fall, not vertically but in a curved sheet. Suddenly, in a violent climax, the clouds overhead open and a Niagara of rain descends. But the deluge ends quickly—in minutes it is no more than a light shower. As the storm moves on across the desert, a rainbow may arch over the horizon, signaling the return of the sun.

Dry desert soil can absorb substantial amounts of moisture, but a cloudburst provides too much too fast. Streaming water flushes the ground of loose sand, rocks, and plant material and the arroyos, paths carved by former torrents, suddenly become raging rivers. Perhaps minutes, perhaps an hour after the cloudburst, a flash flood—a wall of mud, sand, and gravel, entangled with debris and uprooted plants—sweeps out of the canyon. Edward Abbey, in *Desert Solitaire*, described a flash flood in southeastern Utah: "It advanced in crescent shape with a sort of forelip about a foot high, streaming in front, making hissing, sucking noises like a giant amoeba, nosing to the right and nosing to the left as if on the spoor of something good to eat."

From time to time when, in the aftermath of a sudden storm, waters of a mountain stream rush down the slopes and over the old alluvium, they continue to the open plain beyond and form a desert lake. Usually it is a shallow, temporary body of water that sinks rapidly into the porous ground and evaporates quickly in the dry desert air, leaving a salt veneer behind.

Much of today's desert was once a land of lakes and rivers. The Mojave, for example, in our era has annual rainfall between 1.3 and 5.0 inches, but it was not always so. At the end of the Ice Age, during the Pluvial period, when precipitation fell generously upon all the warm southwestern lands not covered with glaciers, the Mojave contained many permanent lakes and rivers. The Mo-

RUTH & LOUIS KIRK

Theory has it these rocks are driven by the wind across Devil's Racetrack, Death Valley.

jave, Amargosa, and Owens rivers were united, draining into the Death Valley sink and creating Lake Manly. Today the Amargosa alone flows into Death Valley and then only when its waters are swelled by flash floods or sporadic, heavy winter rains. But evidence of the prehistoric lake remains, with wave-cut terraces and beaches visible at the base of Mormon Point in the Black Mountains east of Death Valley.

The extreme aridity of the Mojave and Sonoran deserts is caused in part by rain shadow and in part by their location at the fringe of the North Pacific high pressure zone, where there is downward-moving air from that high. As air from both sources grows warmer and drier by compression, it dives into the desert. Rarely is there enough moisture remaining in either, and rarely is there enough convective energy, because of the desert's stable air aloft, to form more than a few wispy clouds, leaving these deserts continually parched by the sun.

ENCIRCLED BY MOUNTAIN RANGES, lying too far south to receive much moisture from the mid-latitude westerlies and too far north to receive more than a short spate of intermittent rain from tropical sources, the Sonoran Desert bakes under cloudless skies for months at a time. Temperatures rise sharply as the morning sun moves overhead, then creep down slowly in the evening, in a daily cycle that lasts until rains come and break the monotony for a short while.

Rainfall measures less than fifteen inches annually, falling in two well-defined rainy seasons. Winter rains, starting in November and continuing off and on into March, are related to those that fall in California. They occur during the period when the Pacific High has moved farthest to the south, allowing the passage of rain-producing low pressure areas into and across the southwestern states. When the storm system is extensive, heavy rains may occur over the entire Sonoran region.

Exposed to frequent passage of winter storms, the northwestern part of the Sonoran Desert—including the Central Highlands of Arizona—receives a higher percentage of its annual rainfall during the winter rainy season. The highlands form the northeastern boundary of the desert.

Summer thunderstorms may come to the Sonoran Desert in July, August, or September, when east winds associated with the North Atlantic subtropical high pressure system (the Bermuda High) bring in humid air from the Gulf of Mexico, pushing out air of the Pacific High. South of Tucson, summer rainfall exceeds that of winter, in contrast to the northwestern part of the Sonoran and the Central Highlands of Arizona, where the heavier rains occur during the winter season.

Sonoran rain showers follow the same pattern as those in the high desert. Also common is the "frustrated" thunderstorm, with the usual cumulus cloud buildup, wind, lightning, and blowing sand, but no rain—since all the raindrops evaporate in the hot desert air before reaching the ground.

Rainfall is extremely variable throughout all of the western deserts, but particularly so in the Sonoran.

Yuma, Arizona, for example, normally receives an average of 3.48 inches of rain a year, but on August 15 and 16, 1909, a drenching 4.01 inches fell in only twenty-four hours—a noteworthy downpour in any location but a moment of history for Yuma.

Although snow, like rain, is rare on the low desert floors, it affects the overall weather picture nonetheless. Runoff from melting snow on the mountains surrounding the Sonoran Desert provides a source of irrigation water and also helps to maintain a respectable water level in such perennial rivers as the Colorado.

The winds of the Sonoran Desert, like the rainfall, are controlled by movement of high and low pressure systems. When the Pacific high pressure system is in its summertime position around 40° north latitude, a low pressure system lies slightly to the southeast of the Colorado River delta. Consequently, winds in central Arizona and Sonora come from the south and southeast, circulating counter-clockwise around the low, while in more westerly deserts winds come from the opposite direction, circulating clockwise around the Pacific High. In summer the circulation pattern is altered by local convection of air, and regional patterns blur.

In the desert wind and sand sometimes conspire to create havoc. Sandstorms are not unusual in the Southwest, particularly near Tucson and Phoenix, but one of the more spectacular varieties, the *haboob* (Arabic for "violent wind"), has only recently been recognized in this country. The American haboob is as wild as those around Khartoum, Africa, though not as frequent—two or three a year, as compared to more than twenty in the northern Sudan. The haboob is heralded by a sudden shift in direction and increase in speed of the wind. The air becomes humid, the temperature drops, and a dust cloud arrives moving at speeds as great as forty-five miles an hour. Dust has been known to extend up to heights of eight thousand feet.

The haboob sandstorm of Phoenix springs from downdrafts accompanying thunderstorms that have formed over the Sierra Madre Occidental in northern Mexico. Moving northwest, the thunderclouds align, forming storms. Tongues of cold air from the downdrafts rush ahead of the storms, licking dust from the desert floor into a tumbling cloud. Dust continues to move northwest, individual clouds merging en route until they form one huge cloud which may last several hours. Inside the monster, visibility may be no more than a few hundred yards. In Arizona, where sandstorms have been responsible for several highway deaths, remote-control signs are used to warn motorists of an oncoming haboob.

O F ALL NORTH AMERICAN DESERTS, the Chihuahuan extends farthest south, with most of its expanse lying south of the Mexican border, its southernmost extremity reaching clear to the tip of Baja California. It is a high desert and receives most of its rainfall in summer.

A northern part of the Chihuahuan Desert called the Tularosa Basin lies to the west of Alamogordo, New Mexico, between the Rio Grande and Pecos River. It includes Lincoln Town, center of the famous Lincoln County War, and is referred to locally as "Billy the Kid Country." An interesting feature of the area is White Sands National Monument, which lies on the east side of the San Andreas Mountains and includes more than half of the 400-square-mile dunal area. Along the mountain base is a large alkali flat, the catch basin and evaporating pan for the gypsum-bearing waters which sluice from the mountains. Prevailing southwest winds pick up the white gypsum particles from a southern section of the flat—as they have been doing for centuries past—and deposit them in the dune area like great piles of granulated sugar.

These gleaming dunes of nearly pure gypsum (calcium sulphate) are being constantly sculpted by the wind as it ripples their surface, reshapes their contours, and moves the entire dune area gradually eastward. This shift is evident in the coarse, free-standing pillars of granular gypsum, some fifteen feet high, which remain behind when the dune moves on. They are structurally supported by the roots of a desert shrub called sumac, or squaw bush. Once used by the Indians to make baskets, the sumac now serves only to bind the dunes and, when they move, flag the locations of old dune tops.

Part of the Texas segment of the Chihuahuan Desert lies in an undrained basin north of the Rio Grande, the Diablo Bolson—a region between the Guadalupe and Hueco mountains in which rainfall is less than eight inches a year. Within this basin are large salt flats at the foot of the Guadalupe Mountains, the easternmost extension of the desert that the Spanish conquistadors referred to as the "northern mystery."

Less than ten inches of annual rainfall would not seem to be sufficient to sustain any form of desert life, but surprisingly, numerous varieties of plants not only survive but flourish in all the deserts of the West: creosote bushes, cactus savannas, and agave thickets on the limestone soil of the Chihuahuan Desert; vast forests of giant cacti and evergreen and deciduous shrubs in the Sonoran; low shrubs—creosote and burro bush—and the yucca tree, most typical of the Mojave; sagebrush and shadscale, a low spiny salt bush, on the alkali flats of the Great Basin.

Plants which have adapted to arid conditions are called *xerophytes* (a Greek word meaning "dry plants"). They survive by exploiting rainfall and avoiding heat. For example, most small annuals will sprout only in the rainy season, flower rapidly, and retreat to the seed stage with the return of the dry season. Succulents—plants that store water in their leaves, stems, or roots—continue growth throughout the hottest months and often have extensive lateral roots to soak up surface moisture and long taproots (the mesquite root grows as long as thirty feet) to reach deep into supplies of groundwater. The columnar, fluted stem of the barrel cactus becomes swollen in the rainy season and shrinks gradually, as the plant uses its stored water.

With little shade for protection from the blazing sun, plants must adapt their foliage in various ways. Leaves, when present, have evolved to prevent undue loss of moisture by evaporation. The breathing pores are small and on the underside, often recessed in hair-lined cavities. Some leaves close their breathing pores during the hottest hours of the day; others have a thick leathery skin to conserve water; still others such as the creosote bush and the varnish-leaf acacia, have a protective heat-reflecting, waxy coating. Some plants have hairy stems and leaves, which provide protection from the sun and catch any moisture that wets them. Some turn their leaves, exposing only their edges to the sun; others curl or roll their leaves when the day is hottest, uncurling from late afternoon to early morning.

L IKE THEIR ROOTED NEIGHBORS, desert animals have developed techniques for coping with the arid conditions of their environment. All desert creatures draw moisture from their food. Carnivores, whether mammals, reptiles, or birds, find it in the smaller creatures, including insects, that they consume. They may gain additional water, as rodents and other herbivores do, by feeding on stems, leaves, and cacti. To escape the parching daytime heat, foxes, skunks, wood rats, snakes, and ground squirrels stay in their burrows during the day and are active at night. Even day creatures such as rabbits and most birds conserve energy by resting in shade during the hottest hours.

Physiology plays a major role in adaptation. Birds, for example, are protected from heat and dehydration by their plumage, while the scaly texture and light coloraion of snake skin reflects heat. Snakes are additionally equipped to survive because they lose little water by evaporation and none as urine since waste is excreted in semisolid form. The single greatest marvel of adaptation may be the kangaroo rat, whose metabolism "makes" all the water it needs from the dry seeds it consumes.

Man has not been quite as successful as the kan-

The kangaroo rat is at home in two of the West's hottest places—the Mojave and Sonoran deserts.

garoo rat in adapting to harsh desert conditions, although even before irrigation, refrigeration, and air conditioning, he had found some ways to help ensure his survival.

A person walking for eight hours in the Sonoran Desert during daylight requires about three gallons of water. He may go about two nights or thirty-six miles without water by resting in the shade during the day and traveling only at night. By simply resting, he may hang on for two or three days longer. Because the Great Basin and the Painted Desert in north-central Arizona are cooler than the Sonoran, their rates of dehydration are lower and the survival times extended, possibly doubled.

Unless one is an experienced desert traveler, one should not expect to be able to find a spring-fed stream; they do exist, but usually hidden in canyons, perhaps known only to the animals or a seasoned "desert rat." Clear, lifeless ponds or still streams should be avoided, for the deceptively clear water may contain deadly poisons.

Cottonwood trees are one sign of moisture in the desert. Even if surface water is unavailable, they indicate that there is water below the surface, which the trees have found and tapped.

EARLY EXPLORERS of the Great American Desert, like men of other times and other places, decried the desert as one of nature's most hostile environments. Yet through the ages an impressive variety of plants and animals have found it hospitable enough to call it home. And modern man, spurred by food and living space pressures that make those of a younger America seem insignificant, is taking another look at the desert's possibilities himself. Already his hydroelectric projects and irrigation systems have turned the biblical injunction into reality and made the desert flower. Now bustling cities and air-conditioned suburbs are luring hundreds of thousands of human residents to call the desert home, too.

These achievements are often seen as monuments to human intelligence and ingenuity. And in a sense they are. But other observers are beginning to question where it all may lead. Can nature tolerate all this tampering? If it continues, what will happen to the desert climate? The climate of neighboring regions? Of the world? Will some future generation of westerners never know the experience of desert at all?

CHAPTER 14

PRAIRIE AND PLAINS

The turbulent heart of the continent, where polar, Pacific, and tropical air masses meet ❖ The excesses they produce—arctic cold and torrid heat, floods and droughts, blizzards, hail, tornadoes

IN THE EARLY EIGHTIES, when most of the West was still frontier, a New Yorker waggishly described the plains of Kansas and Oklahoma as having "more rivers and less water, more cows and less milk, where one could see farther and see less than anywhere else in the world." Even today the name "Great Plains" calls up visions of spaces so vast they are reckoned, not by the acre, but by the section; a treeless land as big as the sky, where winds are lusty and the air is dry, grasses are short and tough, and the high-protein wheat—traditional crop of the plains—is flinty and hard. When this book speaks of the plains, this is the country it means: a 300-to-400-mile swath of open country stretching east of the Rocky Mountains from Mexico north into Canada, the largest single belt of semiarid land in North America.

This region is not to be confused with prairie, which lies to the east in the subhumid borderlands of the plains, or with desert, which lies to the west. Bernard DeVoto, in *Across the Wide Missouri*, looked at the prairies and plains designations historically: "To the American pioneer as far west as Illinois and Missouri, the word 'prairie' meant a place without trees but with a soil so rich that planting it might be, as the Big Bear of Arkansas said it was, dangerous. The pioneer followed the Missouri River across the state named for it, and all the way the land was lush and fecund. At the western border of the state the Missouri turned north—and the word 'prairie' began to mean 'desert.' From here on, the river was the boundary between God's country and the Great American Desert."

Clinging to the original meaning of the word, this book will use *prairies* to identify the more humid, long-grass lowlands that lie east of the Great Plains. This region is a transition zone, sharing some features of plains weather but resembling more closely in climate the states that stretch eastward toward the Appalachians.

In a general way, the prairies include Minnesota, Wisconsin, Iowa, Missouri, Illinois, Indiana, and the eastern parts of North and South Dakota, Nebraska, Kansas, and Oklahoma. They are the central lowlands that flank the Mississippi River, extending as far west as the 100th meridian, the 2,000-foot elevation line, or the 20-inch rainfall line, depending on which geographic definition one chooses to use. (See map on page 154.) West of those boundaries lie the plains—generally the western parts of the Dakotas, Nebraska, Kansas, Oklahoma, and Texas, and the eastern parts of Montana, Wyoming, Colorado, and New Mexico, up to the 4,500-foot level of the Rocky Mountains.

Plains and prairie both experience the extremes typical of a midcontinental climate—torrid summers and frigid winters, with springs and falls as brief as they are balmy—and much of the weather in both regions is created by the same large air masses.

Precipitation on the plains varies unpredictably, averaging around fifteen inches per year. In wet years, when parts of the plains become almost subhumid from the excess rainfall, indigenous long grass at the eastern margins, with its moisture-loving long roots, ventures westward, expanding the prairie. (Today, however, long

When first encountered, the rolling, treeless prairie was shunned by settlers, but they soon discovered that the rich soil and ample rainfall brought abundant harvests.

GRANT HEILMAN

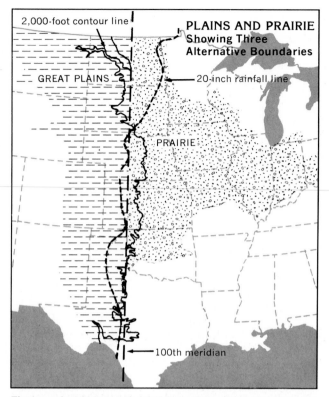

2,000-foot contour line

PLAINS AND PRAIRIE
Showing Three
Alternative Boundaries

GREAT PLAINS

20-inch rainfall line

PRAIRIE

100th meridian

The boundary between the prairies and the Great Plains (where the West begins) has been given alternatively as the 100th meridian, the 2,000-foot contour line, and the 20-inch rainfall line. All three fall close together. Since the 20-inch rainfall line varies from year to year, the one above is based on a 30-year average. West of it, to the foothills of the Rockies, rainfall is insufficient for ordinary farming methods.

grass has been largely replaced by crops.) In very dry years, when the plains become almost arid, short grasses spread eastward, and prairie grasses retreat toward lands with more moisture. For the grasses, it is an existence in flux with the weather.

Nearly all Great Plains rain is born in the meeting of extensive masses of air: from the north, a Canadian air mass that is dry and cool; from the south, a tropical air mass that is usually moist and warm; and from the west, a Pacific air mass that has crossed the Rockies and may be either warm or cold, moist or dry. When any two of these air masses meet, storms may result. The polar and tropical air bodies trigger the fiercest storms, as lighter, warm, moist air from the Gulf rises up and over the heavier, cool, dry polar air. Cooling, either from contact with the cool air or from the buoyant ascent over it, releases moisture, often in violent thunderstorms.

It is along the fronts separating the air masses that storms develop. Where, when, and whether the air masses collide over the plains is at the whim of the global weather machine, thus it is small wonder that plains weather is among the most variable in the country. Since there are no high hills or mountains to break or direct air flow, masses of air sweep across the plains almost unimpeded.

There are four basic weather patterns that affect the plains. The stormiest is the meeting of polar and tropical air, in which, for example, the northern plains might be hit by storms while the southern plains are unscathed or perhaps even in drought. In the second pattern, tropical air sweeps north along the Mississippi Valley, bypassing the plains and sending moisture to the prairies and points east. Alternately, the tropical air may originate, not over the Gulf, where moisture is readily available, but over the dry, dusty plateaus of inland Mexico; when it meets the polar air, there is little precipitation. In a fourth pattern, relatively drier Pacific air meets the polar air, so little or no precipitation results.

Air from three different sources—from the Arctic, the Pacific Ocean, and the Gulf of Mexico—may converge on the plains and spawn some of the most severe weather in the nation.

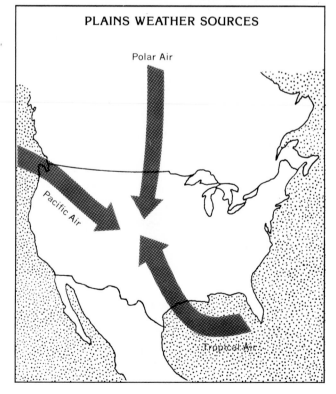

PLAINS WEATHER SOURCES

Polar Air

Pacific Air

Tropical Air

Violent thunderstorms are a hallmark of plains weather. The anvil of this cumulonimbus diffuses as it matures, but roiling new cumulus clouds billow upward to renew the storm's vigor.

As a rule, the farther an air mass travels from its source of moisture, the lighter the precipitation it can produce. This is the reason more rain falls on the southern plains than on the northern. For example, southern Texas averages 25 inches of precipitation annually, while northern Montana averages only 10.

Were it not for the greater amount of sunshine on the southern plains, which increases evaporation, they might have a subhumid climate. To have equivalent available moisture, San Antonio, Texas, would need sixteen inches more precipitation than Williston, Montana. Short grasses that grow within the 14-inch annual rainfall belt in Montana require 17 inches of rain in Colorado and 21 inches in Texas. The belt of shortgrass follows lines of equal precipitation in the northern section of the plains but cuts across them in the south, indicating that, to survive, the grass must have more moisture where the days are long and the sun is hot. Another indication of

the role evaporation plays is the fact that a drought, such as the Dust Bowl era of the thirties, is most keenly experienced in the southern states, such as parts of Kansas, Oklahoma, Colorado, and Texas. Statistics show that during a period of extreme drought the southern plains may have one-third more rainless days than the northern plains. It is fortunate that the region's limited rainfall usually comes between May and July, during the growing season, for if it was concentrated in the winter months, these valuable grazing lands might well be a desert.

Like the topography, average temperatures are fairly level east to west across the plains, rising gradually as one moves westward. But from north to south, temperatures take a mighty leap. The growing season on the southern plains can be two or three months longer than on the northern, and unlike the north, they rarely experience bone-chilling cold.

*A single hailstorm ravaged this Iowa cornfield. Such devastation is a tragic sight
even to the insured farmer; to the uninsured it may mean bankruptcy.*

Perhaps the most dramatic feature of plains weather is its propensity for developing sudden, violent storms: northers, blizzards, tornadoes, cloudbursts, hailstorms. All result from the unfettered flow of air across flat, open expanses. Here, as nowhere else on the continent, there is literally nothing to stop them.

The power of such weather systems might be expected to create erosive havoc upon the landscape, and as history has illustrated, the plains are indeed vulnerable to wind and water. Part of their soil is a fragile, dusty element called loess, deposited during the Ice Ages when rock powdered by glacial action was blown eastward from the Rockies. However, the soil of the plains has long been protected by a cover of shortgrass, whose matted root system, though not deep, is very effective. Nor do the rivers of this region wash it away, for they are usually sluggish, depositing silt from upstream rather than eroding. Thus neither wind nor water has significantly etched

the plains, especially the High Plains. Their surface has changed little since they were newly formed. Only slowly is the erosion that has left the deserts and prairies rolling and gullied beginning to encroach on the plains.

Since Indian times, plains people have coped with the sometimes cruel environment in order to reap the harvests of a rich chestnut-and-brown soil that is the life-blood of the plains. Formed on alluvium cast off by erosion of the Rocky Mountains, it has been enriched by the humus of shallow-rooted seasonal grasses—blue gramma most commonly—and fertilized by great herds of bison.

More than gramma grass once existed on the plains. Paleobiologists are convinced that a boreal spruce forest once covered the northern plains, similar to the taiga existing today in Canada; and that a piny woods once flourished on the southern plains of Texas—the southern outpost of great bison herds. Considerable disagreement exists as to why the trees disappeared from the Great Plains. Some ecologists believe that a decline in rainfall led to the demise of the forests, while others say that continuous grass fires over the years, started either by lightning or by the Indians, destroyed the timber. Whatever the cause, the pioneers were philosophical about the lack of trees:

> There's not a log to make a seat,
>   along the river Platte,
> So when you eat, you've got to stand,
>   or sit down square and flat....
>   —"Crossing the Plains" (folk song)

This absence of trees has had an obvious effect on plains weather. Back east, farmers could count on the trees to blunt the edge of a moving air mass. But on the flat and treeless plains—where the wind blows unimpeded, harder and with more persistence than anywhere else in the interior of the continent—the settler could do little more than plant a line of trees and wait for them to mature and serve as a windbreak. The fearsome winds have become part of the legend and folklore of the West. One of the boats on the Lewis and Clark expedition, while being hauled overland on wheels, was blown along the trail without benefit of sail. Indeed, the unbroken winds and sweeping expanses of the plains are frequently compared to the ocean. Another oft-told tale explains that a sod house was built with a "crowbar hole" in the side to test the outside weather. If a crowbar, shoved through the hole, bent in the wind, the breeze outside was normal; if the bar broke off, "better stay in the house." Plains winds average a persistent ten to twelve miles per hour, except on the Texas Panhandle, where they reach fifteen.

Plainsmen say, "Between Texas and the North Pole, there's nothing but a barbed wire fence—and that's down most of the time." That fence was probably downed by a Texas "blue norther," a cold blast whose severity is magnified by its typical arrival after a period of balmy temperatures. A norther is the cold front of a cyclone, which replaces a wedge of moist, tropical air in the warm sector of the cyclone (cyclones are explained on pages 76-77). If the cyclone is moving fast (usually to the northeast), the front passes quickly. When the polar high be-

hind the front is very cold, as it usually is in winter, the temperature changes can be numbing; and when the pressure differences between the high and low are substantial, again often true in winter, the winds can be furious. Though most notorious in winter, when the air masses have great contrast and polar air advances deep into mild climes, conditions for a norther can occur throughout the year. In the space of two or three hours, temperatures may drop as much as fifty degrees, a hazard to livestock and crops, and a dreaded experience for those exposed to its chilling fury. Lasting only a day or two, northers are followed by warm, pleasant weather as the winds switch to a southerly direction around the passing high.

This lack of natural wind barriers also makes the Midwest's tornadoes a more terrifying hazard. The center of their activity lies over the prairies, focusing on Iowa in summer and near the Gulf Coast in winter. Oklahoma has the greatest frequency of tornadoes, and Iowa, Texas, Kansas, and Nebraska are also visited often by these storms. The collision of hot and cold air masses that gives birth to twisters is most likely to occur during May and June, although the season usually lasts from March through September.

A prairie blizzard has piled undulating drifts on the leeward side of this Iowa snow fence.

GRANT HEILMAN

Another plains fury is the blizzard, a winter storm combining cold, sleet, snow, and high wind. Technically, blizzard snow may be precipitated from clouds or whipped into the air from snow cover left from a previous storm. The Huron, South Dakota, blizzard of January 22, 1952, brought only 4.1 inches of new snow but swirled eight inches of previous snow cover into ten- and fifteen-foot drifts. Major highways were closed for three days; mail service was delayed for five. The low temperatures and drifting snow claimed eight lives, and 2,500 cattle were lost.

While blizzards can often be anticipated during the winter months, a portion of the plains—particularly Wyoming, Colorado, Nebraska, and Kansas—are subjected to sudden, unpredictable hailstorms during the late spring and summer. Although they have been known to kill horses, cattle, and sheep, hailstones wreak most of their destruction on crops. The quirkish selectivity with which these storms level one farmer's field and leave a neighbor's untouched is matched only by tornadoes.

A CONTINUING FEATURE OF PLAINS agriculture has been the specter of drought. Four times since the settlers arrived, long droughts have plagued the region. Two of these—one in the late 1880s and early 1890s, and another in the 1930s—were particularly disastrous because of extraordinary and frequent windstorms that occurred over a period of years. The thirties became known as the Dust Bowl era; farmers fled in desperation as the land they had tilled was transformed into a storm of dust. In one decade more than eighty thousand farmers left Kansas and two-thirds of Nebraska's counties failed to produce a marketable crop for seven years.

The other two major droughts, in the 1910s and the 1950s, were almost as severe, though winds were less destructive in those years. Rainfall was off as much as 50 percent, streams ran at a fraction of their normal run-off, and farm output was sharply decreased because either seeds failed to germinate or the parched seedlings did not survive.

Many meteorologists are predicting that the dry summer of 1974 may herald the beginning of another Great Plains drought cycle. By using dry-farming techniques (developed in 1893), which include strip-cropping, leaving crop residues, and tilling more deeply, farmers may still lose their crops the next time around, but they will keep their soil.

The grassland droughts have occurred with a rhythm set by immense "physical changes in the circulation of air and delivery of moisture," says John R. Borchert, professor of geography at the University of Minnesota. "Intervals between central years of the major droughts of record have averaged slightly more than twenty years. The duration of each major dry period has averaged about a decade."

The first farmers happened to arrive on the plains in a period between major droughts when the rainfall was increasing. Noticing that more rain fell each year, they reached some interesting but misleading conclusions. Writing in the *Commerce of the Prairies* in 1844, a Santa Fe trader observed that New Mexico was becoming wetter and linked this fact with the tilling of the soil. Similarly, in Utah the Mormons attributed the rising level of the Great Salt Lake to their irrigation and cultivation of the desert. Further evidence that rain was increasing came from California and Oregon emigrants who had written in diaries about the rain and mud of the plains, as well as the heat and dust. This optimistic credo—that cosmic law was affected by human activities—was expressed in the maxim, "Rain follows the plow," coined in 1880, just before Eden fell victim to insect invasions, drought, sandstorms, and black blizzards of dust.

During periods between droughts, many soothsayers attempted to convince the populace that the climate was changing and that rain could be coaxed to fall more frequently and more regularly. The region was ripe for the schemes of rainmakers, but in fact the capricious pattern of rainfall on the plains was, and remains, a most enduring weather tendency.

D ROUGHT IS UNDOUBTEDLY the most formidable threat to agricultural well-being. However, floods can wreak far greater catastrophe, because they destroy not only crops and livestock but buildings, personal belongings, and human lives. Writing about the floods in Oklahoma, Will Rogers once said, "When the Arkansas, Red River, Salt Fork, Verdigris, Caney, Cat Creek, Possum Creek, Dog Creek, and Skunk Branch all are up after a rain, we got more seacoast than Australia."

The Missouri River, vital to development of the early

The whims and excesses of plains weather were harsh on homesteaders, and many abandoned their farms.

West, was notorious for its springtime floods. The second longest river in the United States (2,315 miles compared to the Mississippi's 2,348 miles) and the most important waterway of the plains region, the Missouri River rises in the Rocky Mountains of Montana, flows through the heart of the Dakotas, separates Iowa and Nebraska, then splits Missouri into two parts before joining the Mississippi above St. Louis. Millions of tons of soil were washed away when its torrential waters overflowed their banks and created new channels, constantly invading and consuming more rich land as they raged downstream. In contrast, during a dry summer the Mighty Mo ordinarily shrank to a muddy dribble—"too thick to drink, too thin to plow"—its shallow channels blocked by sandbars.

With the completion of six major upstream dams, an assortment of small dams on its tributaries, and 1,500 miles of levees and flood walls—all part of the Pick-Sloan plan approved by Congress in 1944—the Missouri has nearly been tamed. The project was an ambitious one, which made slow progress until 1951, when construction was spurred after one of the most disastrous floods of modern times. Omaha, Kansas City, and a number of smaller river towns were inundated, creating such tremendous damage that President Harry Truman declared the region a disaster area.

By 1974 the dams had been virtually completed, including those at Fort Peck in Montana, Garrison in North Dakota, Oahe and Fort Randall in South Dakota. These upstream dams were built without locks, reducing the navigable limits of the river to the 735 miles from St. Louis to Sioux City, Iowa. The dam at Cavins Point near Sioux City, by storing spring runoff, helps to main-

tain the downstream flow at high enough levels throughout the channel to make navigation safe year round. Although irrigation water is not yet available to most of the Missouri River watershed, other benefits from the project have been electric power generation, conservation, and recreation.

River controls notwithstanding, the danger of floods to many midwestern cities along the banks of the Missouri, the Mississippi, and their tributaries still exists. In late winter or early spring, when snow melt swells downriver channels, midwestern newscasters regularly report the height of an oncoming crest and the prospects for the concerned residents of their particular river town.

THIS DISCUSSION OF WEATHER on the Great Plains—with its account of icy winters and scorching summers, raging winds, sudden storms, and the recurring threat of tornadoes—may seem to paint a bleak picture indeed. Curiously, however, the plains are statistically the most healthful part of the country. Nebraska is an example. In 1949 the western two-thirds of the state was swept by one of the worst blizzards on record; only four years later a May tornado virtually leveled the small town of Hebron. Yet, one section of Nebraska just south of the Platte River has the lowest incidence of heart disease, stroke, and lung cancer in the nation. North Dakotans similarly boast that their dazzling skies and clean air give a man ten more years of life than Los Angeles.

Health is only one reason why, though some natives of the plains and prairies flee to sunnier lands for retirement, many more choose to live out their days in the vigorous climate of their home states. Indeed, many actually prefer the variety, challenge, and excitement of midcontinental weather. Minnesotans, for instance, take pride in their three-month-long deep freeze, celebrating it with the annual St. Paul Winter Carnival.

Theodore Roosevelt, who came to western Dakota in 1884, expressed the sentiments of many plains people when he wrote, "[We] worked under the scorching midsummer sun, when the wide plains shimmered and wavered in the heat. . . . In the soft springtime the stars were glorious in our eyes each night before we fell asleep; and in the winter we rode through blinding blizzards. . . . Ours was the glory of work and the joy of living."

HENRY LANSFORD

A GALLERY OF WESTERN CLIMATES

Nearly every type of climate that occurs in the world's temperate zones can be found somewhere in the American West. This is hardly surprising, for the area covered in this book has a land mass as great as all of Europe outside the Soviet Union. It ranges from subtropical desert at its southern limits to arctic-like tundra on its mountain peaks. And it stretches two thousand miles east from a foggy seacoast to the deep heart of the North American continent.

The following pages sample that great diversity as it sweeps inland from the Pacific in successive swaths that roughly parallel the north-south trend of the great geographical features that affect weather—the Pacific coastline and the major mountain chains. A mere sampling it is, for within each region—coast, Far West valleys, mountains, desert, plains, or prairie—is still more variation, provided by microclimates and seasonal change.

Sea fog is a hallmark of summer along the Big Sur coast in central California; it forms in the chill air above an offshore bank of cold water and flows landward on the wind.

STEVE CROUCH

162

A GALLERY OF WESTERN CLIMATES

Sugar beets (here), lettuce, and other crops thrive in the Salinas Valley of California, favored by the available water, abundant sunlight, and fertile soil shared by many such far western valleys.

OVERLEAF: *Rays of late afternoon sunlight stream between the clouds while over the snowy Tetons cumuli move in from the west, their undersides darkly shadowed.*

BOB CLEMENZ

The wind, usually a minor player in the shaping of the land, has built this fluid, ever-changing dunescape virtually by itself (Coral Pink Sand Dunes State Park near Kanab, Utah).

167

*Ominous yet beautiful, an anvil-topped cumulonimbus may bring
welcome showers—or destruction from hail or tornadoes.*

Part 4
WEATHER IN YOUR LIFE

On the human side of the weather drama may be found the researchers and forecasters, who take its pulse; the early rainmakers and modern weather modifiers, who have hoped to change its ways; the city dwellers who also alter the weather, unknowingly; and all those westerners who enjoy the weather for recreation and outdoor living.

CHAPTER 15

A LOOK AT THE FORECAST

Early forecasters from Aristotle to Franklin ❖ How professionals
predict: balloons, probes, planes, satellites, computers ❖ Why
experts are sometimes wrong ❖ How to be your own weatherman

ONCERN ABOUT THE WEATHER is as old as man. In his desire to understand and predict its vagaries and movements, man incorporated rudimentary weather knowledge into his earliest civilizations. Even while he tried to control the weather through magic, he also prudently sought signs by which it could be predicted. Thus the first weathermen appeared. Clues to coming weather were often sought in signs far removed from the elements—in sacrificial offerings, the habits of insects and animals, the state of vegetation—but the more discerning of prophets went to the sky itself for weather signs. As Elihu tells Job in the Bible, "Out of the south cometh the whirlwind and cold out of the north."

In the first book on weather, entitled *Meteorologica*, Aristotle attempted to explain the origins of weather using scientific reasoning and wrote of his belief that coming weather could be foretold by observing the sky. One of his students, Theophrastus, later compiled all kinds of down-to-earth weather indicators in his *Book of Signs*, which, with Aristotle's explanations, dominated meteorological thought for the next 2,000 years. During that time, if anyone who used the theories of Aristotle failed in a weather prediction, it was thought, not that Aristotle was wrong, but rather that the forecaster was inept.

Scientific studies of weather came of age once there were tools for taking its pulse. Before the beginning of the seventeenth century, there was no way to measure temperature, pressure, humidity, and wind speed. It could be said that the day was hot or cold, but not how hot or how cold. With the advent of weather instruments, new discoveries about the behavior of gases, and understanding of the laws of heat and energy, meteorological science began to advance quickly.

These developments, though momentous achievements, had little effect on the public. They could not provide the kind of weather predictions that could easily be found in almanacs—booklets containing calendars, astronomical happenings, folk wisdoms, and weather admonitions reached by guesswork or the luck of the draw. The *Farmer's Almanac*, first published in 1792 and still available today, contains delightful, if tongue-in-cheek, weather prognostications. An almanac of historical interest was *Poor Richard's Almanack*, published by Benjamin Franklin for twenty-five years. However, Franklin made more lasting contributions to meteorology. In addition to his famous, but risky, experiment that demonstrated lightning to be a form of electricity, he also deduced the previously unknown facts that winds do not necessarily indicate the direction from which a storm is approaching, and that storms may move progressively from one place to another.

In the 1800s, the first synoptic weather maps were drawn—*synoptic* coming from the Greek word for "a seeing together." A synoptic weather map contains weather data collected from many locations but observed at the same time. Once these early weather maps were prepared, they were only of academic interest because the weather on them had long since passed, there being no rapid communication available then. That problem

A computer at the fingertips of the meteorologist will be the heart of the future weather office,
where high-speed data processing and television will aid in forecasting.

171

was solved in 1844 by the nearly instantaneous transmissions of the telegraph. The historic first long-distance telegraph message from Washington to Baltimore, "What hath God wrought?" could prophetically have been answered "Clear and warmer in Baltimore today."

Since so little was known in the mid-1800s about the lives of storms, it was naively thought that forecasting weather with the aid of the telegraph would require little more than sending ahead the news and speed of advancing storms. With the frontier extending over "every part of the southern and western portions of North America," as Joseph Henry, the first secretary of the Smithsonian Institution, wrote in 1845, there could be "a ready means of warning the more northern and eastern observers to be on the watch from the first appearance of an advancing storm." Within two years, Henry, through the cooperation of the then flourishing commercial telegraph companies, had established a network of one hundred fifty weather observers who regularly telegraphed weather data to the Smithsonian. From these observations, Joseph Henry made daily, synoptic weather maps but not forecasts. However, little shrewdness was required to guess that rain was likely in New York if Pittsburgh was stormy.

The first daily weather forecasts based on primitive meteorology rather than quackery were begun on September 22, 1869, in the *Weather Bulletin*, founded by Cleveland Abbe of the Cincinnati Astronomical Observatory and underwritten by the Cincinnati Chamber of Commerce. Less than six months later, the federal government organized a national weather system, spurred on by the need for warning of storms such as those that sank or damaged 1,164 ships on the Great Lakes in 1868 and an even greater number in 1869. On November 8, 1870, the first predictions of the federal government's weather service came from Professor Increase A. Lapham, a man who had encouraged its formation and who became America's first official weather forecaster.

Begun as the Meteorological Division of the United States Army Signal Service, the growth of the "Weather Bureau," as it was popularly known even in those days, was irrepressible. The weather duties of the Signal Service rapidly overshadowed its military responsibilities, prompting a congressional study that culminated in the formation of the United States Weather Bureau as a division of the new Department of Agriculture on July 1,

1891. The Weather Bureau was transferred to the Department of Commerce in 1940 and, in 1970, renamed the United States Weather Service, a branch of the National Oceanic and Atmospheric Administration (NOAA) within the Department of Commerce. (NOAA was preceded from 1965 to 1970 by the Environmental Science Services Administration, or ESSA.)

There were those who were willing to challenge the fledgling weather service in making forecasts. The weekly predictions of Oliver Wiggins, a former frontier scout, were published in the *Denver Republican* alongside the official weather forecast. Wiggins, whose only weather instrument was an old battle wound, was, much to every weatherman's embarrassment, often closer to being correct than the Weather Bureau. The irreverent Mark Twain parodied the weatherman's penchant for overconfident predictions by once forecasting "probably northeast to southwest winds, varying to the southward and westward and eastward, and points between, high and low barometer swapping around from place to place; probable areas of rain, snow, hail, and drought, succeeded or preceded by earthquakes, with thunder and lightning."

For both practical reasons and scientific interest, weather observers have always desired to break tether with the ground and raise their instruments into the weather. In 1749 a Scotsman hung thermometers from individual kites connected in a line and thereby obtained air temperatures at several different altitudes at the same time. Benjamin Franklin's famous kite experiment followed three years later. In 1783, the first balloonist drifted across the French countryside, and irregularly thereafter meteorological instruments went on the flights as well. The Weather Bureau used kites for atmospheric soundings from 1898 to 1933, and one of them reached an altitude of over 23,000 feet.

Rapid improvements in aircraft design during World War I and the Air Commerce Act of 1926 spurred rapid expansion of the Weather Bureau's services, as improved weather reports and forecasts were needed for increasingly longer flights. At first some pilots were skeptical of the Bureau's advice, among them Charles Lindbergh, who, in his early years as a pilot, preferred to appraise the weather for himself as he flew.

The Weather Bureau saw aviation as an efficient method to probe weather aloft. Beginning experimentally

Scientists use instruments borne high by helium-filled balloons for atmospheric research. Most large balloons are launched in the still air of dawn from the National Scientific Balloon Facility near Palestine, Texas.

in 1919, weather planes were by 1931 flying daily over Chicago, Cleveland, Dallas, and Omaha. Pay did not start until a base altitude of 13,500 feet (later 16,500 feet) was attained, and for each flight there was a 10 percent premium for every thousand feet above that. With the advent of the Weather Bureau's use of the radiosonde—a balloon carrying miniature weather-measuring gear and a radio transmitter—around 1940, weather pilots went out of business.

Soundings higher than those accessible by balloon are made by rockets and earth satellites, which now provide worldwide coverage. By night as well as day, TIROS (Television and Infra-Red Observation Satellite), Nimbus, and other weather satellites take television pictures of cloud coverage on the earth; some are available immediately to anyone below the satellite with a picture receiver, while others are recorded for later trans-

mission. The ESSA satellite series has provided pictures from eight hundred miles up, high enough to view nearly 4 million square miles at a glance. The extent of snow and ice cover can also be determined by the interpretation of satellite data. Photographs of the snowpack in western states aid the river and flood forecasting service of the Weather Service.

There are two principal methods by which professionals forecast the weather. The objective approach expresses pressure, temperature, winds, and other properties of the atmosphere in terms of mathematical equations, adds data from weather stations, and solves the equations as accurately as time allows on an electronic computer. In the subjective approach, the professional weatherman pieces together tomorrow's weather from past weather, his practical experience, and a general knowledge of the normal evolution of weather systems.

A Synchronous Meteorological Satellite (SMS-1) of NOAA's newest series. Body facets are solar cells that power cameras behind the oval window.

In the past century, the subjective approach has dominated weather forecasting in the absence of anything better. Models of particular meteorological situations were used to categorize successions of weather changes, and still are. For instance, a belt of rain is usually preceded by a particular sequence of clouds whose bases sink lower with the approaching storm. Before meteorologists accepted the three-dimensional concepts of air masses and fronts, all weather models had to link to a small number of pressure systems—highs, ridges, troughs, lows, and so forth. Thus it was known that from the Mississippi and Missouri valleys to the Atlantic Coast, winter rain accompanied a low barometer, and on the Pacific Coast, precipitation began with a falling barometer. The relationship of low atmospheric pressure and foul weather is today traditionally preserved on every household barometer. It is, however, sometimes mislead-

ing, as in the Rocky Mountains and Great Plains, where precipitation often begins on rising pressure, after a storm center has passed to the south or east.

The forecaster sometimes extrapolates the trends of the past and present into the immediate future on the assumption that there will be consistency in the weather. For example, since the passage of a cold front frequently brings clear weather, the imminent passage of a cold front is likely to bring a "clear" forecast on the assumption that the front will continue on the same course. For short forecasts—up to twelve hours in advance—this method is excellent, averaging 65 percent to 70 percent accuracy, compared to only 80 percent for Weather Service forecasts that take into account many more variables. Extrapolating the present cannot, however, predict new weather systems, which tend to become more numerous and more significant as the span of the forecast period increases.

One way to leap subjectively into the future of weather is to use "analogs," or similar weather situations in the past, and trace what happened to them. The forecaster discerns the major features of the day's weather map and, considering it much as a detective would a fingerprint, searches his files for a "suspect." Once found, he uses its behavior on subsequent days as a guide. A better method is to match weather patterns, past and present, over periods of several days—a full hand of fingerprints. From United States weather maps dating back about seventy-five years, meteorologists have cataloged the frequently observed "weather types" (and a number of subtypes for different seasons), covering periods up to a week; these are routinely used by private forecasters, but not the National Weather Service, for weather forecasting.

For most weathermen, subjective forecasting serves as an adjunct to modern computer-generated forecasts for local weather prediction. The computer handles certain jobs more efficiently than its masters: collecting and analyzing data, drawing weather maps, and making lengthy mathematical calculations. The computer cannot, however, always substitute for the experience of the human forecaster in taking into account the effects of local topography and winds on storm movement and precipitation. By astute "guesstimation" of the behavior of weather systems, subjective weather forecasters can make quite useful general predictions of weather five days in advance.

Numerical, or objective, weather forecasting relies on the computer because it calls for extremely rapid analysis of large quantities of data. The first numerical forecast was attempted by meteorologist Lewis F. Richardson in England in 1922, long before electronic computers had been invented. Richardson worked with equations derived by Leonard Euler, a Swiss mathematician, which described wind velocity, pressure, density, and other atmospheric variables. His computation was for one day, but it took several years to complete and was not only hopelessly out of date, but as a weather forecast, it was a dismal failure as well. However, Richardson's attempt set the stage for modern numerical weather forecasting.

By 1952 meteorologists had a sophisticated enough computer to attempt a forecast before it became too old to use. Designed by John von Neumann and Julian Bigelow, and programmed with a simpler version of the equations used by Richardson, the computer manipulated data from 768 weather stations for forty-eight minutes before it produced the first useful twenty-four-hour numerical forecast.

Though highly intricate, numerical forecasting is now a valuable method, but one that is suited to use only on patterns, such as contour lines of temperature or pressure. It still does not get very close to forecasting practical, tangible, visible "weather" such as cloud cover. What is computed is used to infer the location of, say, moving fronts. Details of rain, snow, hail, frost, fog, sunshine, and cloud types have to be supplied by the human forecaster.

Since it has been estimated that more than 50 trillion computer operations would be needed to make general 100-day forecasts—still a weatherman's dream—prospects for really accurate long-range predictions of local weather by this method are not immediately foreseeable. Forecasts from the near future to about five days are now routinely executed. They are remarkable in that meteorologists can see storms appear in the computer's forecast for two or three days hence that are not on today's weather map. There are, however, few numerical forecasts that cannot be improved by the adept human subjective forecaster. Before it is even remotely possible to do numerical forecasts for such local weather hazards as hail and tornadoes, both faster computers and more detailed weather data are needed.

Weather forecasts may be short term (twenty-four to seventy-two hours), extended (several days to a month),

Even though computers handle many forecasting tasks, they have not supplanted their slower but wiser masters. Here a forecaster applies his skills to a computer-drawn weather map.

NOAA

THE WEATHER MAP

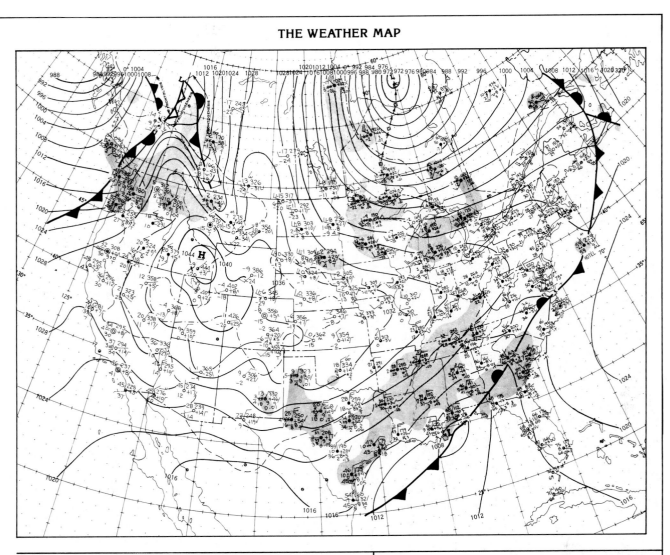

⭕ CLEAR   ◔ 1/4   ◑ 1/2   ◕ 3/4   ● TOTAL OVERCAST   ⊗ SKY OBSCURED

•   RAIN; up to ⦂• for heavy continuous rain.

✳   SNOW

▽   SHOWER

�   THUNDERSTORM

◡•   FREEZING RAIN

≡   FOG

╀   BLOWING SNOW

⤳   SANDSTORM OR DUST STORM

└──•   WIND SPEED (fifteen knots from 270° west)

H   CENTER OF HIGH PRESSURE

L   CENTER OF LOW PRESSURE

▼▼▼   COLD FRONT

●●●   WARM FRONT

▲●▲●   STATIONARY FRONT

▼●▼●   OCCLUDED FRONT

〰   ISOBARS, connecting points of equal pressure

▓▓▓   Area where rain currently is falling

One of the tools of the weather forecaster is the synoptic weather chart, which maps in symbols the weather conditions over a wide area at a given time. The chart shown above was for 7:00 A.M. (EST), Sunday, January 12, 1975. Rain is falling over the northern Northwest states and nearby Canadian provinces as part of an occluded front coming landward from the Pacific. A high-pressure region centered on Pocatello, Idaho, will keep the storm to a path north of the Great Basin. Clockwise winds of the high, as well as a low over Hudson Bay, are sending cold air plunging deep into the Midwest. Dodge City, Kansas, has −15° F. temperatures and clear skies. Wind speed there is 10 knots, or 12 miles, per hour from the southeast, as indicated by the barbed shaft on the map. (A short barb means 5 knots, a long one, as here, 10 knots; often used in combination.)

*By identifying electrical signals from tornadoes,
a "tornado detector" may warn of their approach.*

fluctuations of ocean surface temperature, volcanic activity, and other elements that influence the solar radiation balance of the earth. A long time must pass to verify some of the forecasts, and there have been no startling successes. Climatic forecasting is in the infancy that weather forecasting outgrew more than fifty years ago.

A LMOST ANY OBSERVANT PERSON is capable of making a short-term weather forecast and seeing it come true. Even a casual glance skyward in the morning may be enough to judge the day's weather. Using a few simple weather instruments—thermometer, barometer, weather vane, and hygrometer—the layman can forecast local weather. The keys are to apply a few basic ideas of how weather works and common guides to mid-latitudes weather, and to note weather patterns in the local area. Amateurs can excel in local forecasts, and be more accurate than the regional forecast.

Clouds often foretell future weather by their kind, speed, and direction of motion. Fluffy, globular cumuli dotting the skies mark fair weather, but if they are building taller, a thunderstorm may be in the making. Delicate high cirrus may be the advance messengers of rain (or snow in winter). Cirrus often precede the arrival of a warm front, and if cloud bases lower and thicken to stratus, rain is almost a certainty. Even in otherwise clear skies, the increasing persistence of jet contrails may warn of an approaching warm front. Because cold fronts are steep, their associated clouds can appear as an advancing wall, bearing down with little warning, but passing perhaps within hours.

Together, barometric pressure and wind direction tell a weather story. An individual barometric reading indicates little, but by noting its rate and direction of change (rising, falling, or stationary), one has an indication of the speed of approach and intensity of a weather system. If a high, for example, is moving quickly into an area, the pressure over that area will rise rapidly. However, a very intense high traveling slowly would give the same indication but the barometer would show a greater pressure. The wind tells where the storm is with respect to the amateur forecaster. Again using the example of a high, if the winds are from the north, then, since air circulates clockwise around a high, the high must be to the west. (Winds of a cyclonic storm are more complicated and

and long range (several months and beyond). For its forecasts, the National Weather Service uses a combination of numerical and subjective forecasting techniques. The longer the forecast period, the more general the forecast and the more susceptible it is to error.

One of the most significant difficulties that meteorologists have in weather forecasting is the lack of adequate interpretation of the many influences on weather: the sun, oceans, ice, interactions of weather systems, and many others. Walter Orr Roberts says, "We don't understand why two storm systems that look the same in their early stages of development will suddenly become so different. One will move out across the Great Plains and just drift lazily for days, never increasing in size. Another will start out the same way and suddenly work into a ferocious storm system."

Scientists have made attempts to forecast weather and climate over years, decades, and longer. To do so, they have used a variety of tools, some old and some new, including numerical modeling and such data as the sunspot cycle, the area of the ice and snow cover at high latitudes,

A GUIDE FOR THE AMATEUR FORECASTER		
WEATHER CLUES	**PROBABLE FORECAST**	**EXPLANATION OF FORECAST**
Falling barometer Thickening clouds and lowering cloud bases Winds shifting to south, east, or points between Sudden rise in temperature	STORMY	Approach of a low Warm front is coming The winds shift in advance of a warm front A warm front is passing
Rapidly rising barometer Clouds breaking and bases rising Winds shifting to west, northwest, or points between	FAIR	Approach of a high Clouds not easily maintained because humidity is usually lower behind a cold front High passing to south or southwest of observer
Steady or rising barometer West wind Clear sunset Morning fog breaks early Nights dewy or frosty	CONTINUED FAIR	Persistent high Observer in northern part of high Dry air to west, hence no approaching storm Plenty of sunshine and air too dry to support low clouds by day Clear, dry air of a persistent high allows radiation cooling
Passage of cold front Rising barometer Winds shifting to northwest, north, or points between On Pacific Coast: east or northeast winds in winter	COLDER	Air behind a cold front is cooler than air preceding it Air of the high following a low is usually colder Air from northerly regions is likely to be colder Sign of a Santa Ana wind or stable air foehn
Passage of a warm front Winds shifting to southwest or south Nighttime clouds Chinook arch over mountains	WARMER	Air behind a warm front is warmer than air preceding it Air from southerly regions is likely to be warmer Clouds prevent heat loss by radiation Chinook may be on the way, bringing warmer temperatures

are shown in the diagram on pages 76–77.) Strong winds are a sign that weather systems are intense, while a pronounced and rapid shift in wind direction signals the passage of a front. Without a weather vane, wind direction can be found from cloud motion.

The barometer-wind-weather relationships depend on these meteorological facts: generally highs bring fair weather while lows bring stormy weather; air circulates in a known way around highs and lows; and weather in the United States travels approximately west to east. There are a few general rules, namely that a rising barometer means fair weather, a falling barometer means storms, and a steady barometer means continuing weather. But beware! These rules are often misleading. The table on page 210 is a working reference for interpreting barometric readings.

Relative humidity can be a weather indicator. Steadily increasing relative humidity often accompanies the passage of a front. If humidity is high at dusk, and the sky is clear, radiation cooling may lower air temperature below the dew point, and dew, frost, or fog may form.

Most living things contend with weather as it comes, but man must know about it in advance. Either directly or otherwise, weather affects almost every aspect of his activities. Crop harvesting, airline and ship routing, building construction, and fuel supplies are but a few of the areas where decisions hinge on the weather and the weatherman's ability to forecast it. The engineer choosing whether to ride his motorcycle or his car to work, the family planning a Saturday picnic, or the skier planning his winter holiday, all wonder what the weather will be—today, this weekend, or this winter. As man cannot yet tailor the weather to his wishes, he must learn to accommodate himself to it.

CHAPTER 16

THE NEW URBAN CLIMATE

The unhealthy climate of cities, concocted of too few plants,
too many people, and too much pollution ❖ Heat islands and
dust domes ❖ The insidious element—smog ❖ Industrial pollutants

FOR MOST PEOPLE THE WORD *climate* evokes images of foggy seacoasts, blazing deserts, bleak tundra lands, all the wealth of natural weather zones the earth provides. And indeed these natural variations were the sole ingredients of climate through most of meteorological history. With the appearance of nature's precocious offspring man, however, a new quantity was introduced into the climate equation. From his first discovery of fire, sometime in his infancy as a species, he was able to modify the weather around him in at least a minute way. Later he learned to plow the earth, congregate in cities, build machines and later factories. Each step forward added a little to his influence on the atmosphere in which he lived. But it has been only in the present century that man's capability has become so formidable that he can actually change climate—for better or for worse.

Scientists experimenting with techniques to alter weather for the better have met with some success already and look for more dramatic developments ahead. (These will be examined in chapter 17.) So far, however, man's greatest impact on climate has been unintentional and, in many instances, undesirable. Nowhere is this more evident than in the great industrial cities of today, where he has created a climate zone never before known on the planet.

Central cities can be more than ten degrees (F.) warmer than their surroundings, particularly from the ground up to about three hundred feet. This warm area, referred to as a heat island, exists in most cities, whether they are flat like Minneapolis or hilly like San Francisco.

J. Murray Mitchell, Jr., a meteorologist with NOAA, has shown that the size of the heat island and its temperature differential corresponds to the size of the city, rising as size and density of population increase. On Sundays, when there is the least industrial and commercial activity, some cities show a less pronounced heat island. In contrast, some cities are warmer on Sundays because smog collected during weekdays has dissipated, admitting more sunshine.

In the interior of the city, many factors contribute to the extra warmth. Because cities are composed primarily of steel, concrete, and asphalt, and because these materials conduct heat about three times faster than, say, moist sandy soil, the buildings and streets of a city absorb more heat in less time than open ground does. At the warmest part of the day, the surface temperature of soil may be higher than that of a south-facing concrete wall, but several inches below the surface, the concrete wall will be hotter, and by the end of the day, it will contain more heat than an equal volume of soil. A city's many structures also break the wind, reducing the amount of heat carried away, and increase its gustiness.

Pavement and the walls and roofs of buildings absorb some of the energy they receive, but they reflect much of it to other absorbing surfaces so that almost the entire surface of a city receives and retains heat. By contrast, in woods or fields much of the energy is reflected away, and only a small portion is captured by the tops of trees or other vegetation, which, like soil, cannot hold much heat. There are internal heat sources in a city as well, such as

Cities add heat and chemicals to the air, carry away rainfall, effectively absorb sunlight, and break the wind. Thus it is not surprising that they have measurably altered their climates.

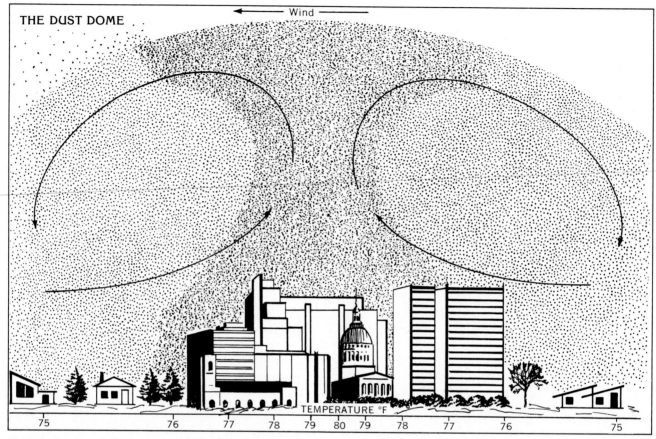

THE DUST DOME

← Wind →

TEMPERATURE °F

75 76 77 78 79 80 79 78 77 76 75

Warmth of a city's heat island, illustrated by the temperature scale at the bottom, causes a "suburb breeze," as air from the outskirts flows into the city to replace warm air rising from its center. These air currents carry dust from the city upward, form-ing a dome that extends to the suburbs. Dust is removed from the dome by winds carrying it off the top. The dust dome and suburb breeze can be detected only when natural winds are light. Strong winds sweep away the dust.

air conditioning in summer (which pumps heat to the outdoors to cool the indoors), heating systems in winter, and all the energy that runs the machines of a city's factories.

Most of a city's surface has been waterproofed. Rainfall is quickly removed by drainpipes, gutters, and sewers, and snow is sucked up by machines and trucked away. This moisture is thus unavailable for evaporation, which would otherwise provide substantial cooling.

A typical weather report may state, "Low tonight 75° in the city, and 65° to 70° in the suburbs," but Helmut E. Landsberg, University of Maryland climatologist, has found that differences in temperature are not the only areas of variation between urban and rural climates. During periods without rain, the relative humidity in the city is less because less water is available for evapora-tion. However, since dust from cities may act as a cloud seeder, rain is about 10 percent heavier in the city, and heavier downwind as well. The differential is greater on drizzly days when not much precipitation occurs over the general area and when updrafts over the warm inner city provide the extra life needed for clouds to form and produce a slight amount of rain. Because of its warmth, a city is apt to have fewer days of snow—about 14 per-cent less than the surrounding countryside—and a longer span between the last freeze in the spring and the first freeze in the fall, adding as much as three or four weeks to the city dweller's gardening season. Furthermore, in the city, with its heating systems, artificial lighting (which is now used for heating in some buildings), in-dustry, and automobiles, there are lower heating bills. Every aspect of climate is changed in the city, to varying degrees. By building his vast metropolises of concrete and steel, and paving every available inch with asphalt and concrete, man has made his influence felt, for better or worse, on the climatic patterns of the land.

THE WORD *smog* was originally coined in 1905 by Harold Des Voeux, a London physician, and his concept persists in the definition still appearing in many standard dictionaries: "A combination of smoke and fog, especially as seen in thickly populated industrial and manufacturing areas." But the physical composition of smog has become far more complex than that definition indicates.

The smog that Dr. Des Voeux observed in London was produced by the combustion of sulfur-containing fuels, such as bituminous coal. Today it has mostly disappeared, as a result of the strict rules for fuel consumption that Londoners imposed upon themselves, including the abandonment of all coal-burning stoves and fireplaces. Most of today's problem-causing smog in the western cities of the United States results from the high-temperature combustion of coal, oil, or gasoline in power plants and internal combustion engines.

Technically, modern smog is considered a special type of air pollution, formed whenever large amounts of nitrogen oxides and hydrocarbons released from automobile exhausts and other sources are coupled with ample sunshine for photochemical reactions. Although the necessary elements to produce smog exist in virtually all cities, with their industry and intense concentration of vehicular exhausts, certain urban areas are more seriously affected because of their topography and weather patterns. Instead of dissipating, the smog accumulates over the city, enveloping it in a poisonous yellowish-brown or gray cloud.

At the Los Angeles International Airport on a weekday in late summer, one can literally become wrapped up in air pollution. At six o'clock in the morning, visibility may be fifteen miles or more, but by nine, after the morning commute, it may be down to two miles or less; air traffic controllers often cannot see from the control tower to the end of the runways, and landings must be watched on closed-circuit television. Starting first as colorless gases, the smog in about two hours' time turns first gray, then yellow, then brown.

Smog is not the plight of Los Angeles alone. In the Valley of the Sun, Phoenix, the landmark Camelback Mountain can fade into a haze that some people have blamed on jet traffic at the airport. There was a time when Seattle residents could tell the weather condition by Mount Rainier: if they couldn't see the mountain, it was raining. Today, when smog is present, the peak cannot be seen even if the sky is cloudless. San Francisco, noted for its delightful ocean breezes blowing east through the Golden Gate, seldom has a smog problem; but Oakland, its neighbor across the bay, blocked in by the Berkeley Hills, can be the recipient of both its own pollutants and San Francisco's. If the air is still, San Francisco itself may be enveloped in smog, and visibility may drop to a few hundred yards.

A dark band of nitrogen dioxide marks the level of a temperature inversion over Boulder.

REACTIONS CREATING PHOTOCHEMICAL SMOG

rx = chemical reaction

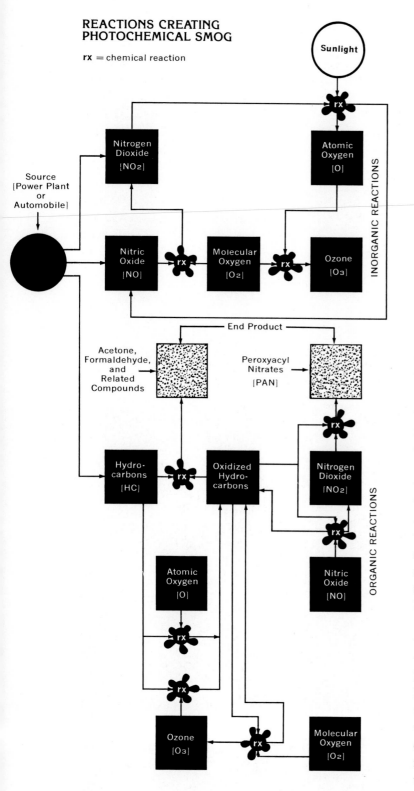

Some of the many paths to the formation of photochemical smog.

Denver, the mile-high city that built part of its reputation on clean air and blue skies, has also fallen victim to the spreading plague of smog. Meteorologist Walter Orr Roberts describes in the *Bulletin of the American Meteorological Society* a drive from NCAR headquarters in Boulder to the Denver airport in 1966. "As I arrived at the edge of Denver I was shocked and affronted by the sight of the city covered over by a thick layer of gray-white smog, so dense as to obscure any view of the mountains to the south, and so overpowering as to make it almost impossible even to see buildings in the center of the city. And as I drove into the smog, it was as offensive to the sense of smell as to the eye. This was the effect of the city on the sky."

As noted, most modern smog is the result of photochemical processes. For example, nitrogen dioxide (brownish in color) breaks up in sunlight into nitric oxide and free oxygen atoms (O), which combine with ordinary oxygen molecules (O_2) to form ozone (O_3). Ozone is a strong oxidant that attacks organic material, including unburned hydrocarbons in automobile exhaust. As a result, more ozone and other oxidation products form. These undesirable contaminants of the atmosphere are eye and respiratory irritants, plant-killing chemicals, and the constituents of haze.

At times, oxides of sulfur may react with fog or water vapor in the air to produce droplets of sulfuric acid, which, because they do not readily evaporate, can form a persistent "pea soup" fog. Various other pollution types can be created, such as the foul-smelling hydrogen sulfide fumes from steel mills, fluorine from aluminum smelters, radioactive radon gas from uranium mines, sulfur oxides from copper smelting, and soot from coal-burning power plants.

Gases are not the only air pollutants. In fact, dust is the most obvious. Air approaching the West Coast from the Pacific is clean and fresh, and visibility is often limited only by the horizon. By the time that same air has reached the Midwest, visibility has been reduced to ten to fifteen miles; and as it leaves the East Coast, the visibility has been reduced to half that or less. This dramatic change results from the addition of particulate matter to the air: dust, soot, ash, "traffic grime"—what the meteorologist calls "turbidity." When air crosses major metropolitan and industrial areas, turbidity may increase twenty-fold. Much of this combination is man-

Contained by surrounding hills, smog in the Los Angeles Basin can go nowhere. Even on this relatively clear day, a view from Mount Wilson shows light smog, with only high ridges escaping the spreading pall.

made, though some is nature's own: wind-blown dust, pollen, and spores.

For all its smog, Los Angeles does not even make the top ten in particulate matter pollution. Of midwestern and western cities, Chicago is number one, followed by Milwaukee, St. Louis, Dallas, and Seattle.

The dust-filled air over a city develops into a dome-shaped mass, since the particles of dust and smoke rise with the air over the warmer central part and settle over the cooler fringes. In recent years, however, this dust hood has become less well defined because of the general dirtiness of the air. The upward motion of air over the central city draws in air from the suburbs, and the column of air that rises over the city descends, upon cooling, over the suburbs. Thus pollutants from in-

dustries in outlying districts are carried into the city, aggravating its already polluted condition.

At night, the dust particles in the upper reaches of the dome become the nuclei on which moisture may condense as fog. Colder than the air above it, the fog forms an inversion, preventing the suspended particles from moving up and out of the system. The top of the fog layer reflects incoming radiation by day and thus retards surface heating, which otherwise would dispel the inversion. One day's collection of solid contaminants is often added to the previous day's, and the pollution continues to worsen. In winter, with shorter days and less sunshine to warm the city naturally, more fuel is burned for heating and, the combustion contributes further to the processes that build up the smog.

DAVID MUENCH

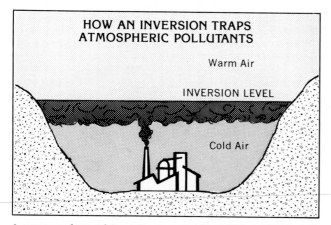

HOW AN INVERSION TRAPS ATMOSPHERIC POLLUTANTS

Warm Air

INVERSION LEVEL

Cold Air

A common form of *inversion* occurs when cold air drains into a valley or basin. An example of very stable air, the inversion prevents upward motion of air and so blocks dispersion of pollutants. Trapped thus beneath the inversion, they become more and more concentrated.

THE AMOUNT OF AIR POLLUTION depends upon how well the air is mixing, or "ventilating." Ventilation is defined in terms of the depth of stable air (which has little vertical mixing) and the wind speed of the surface air. A ventilation study of major cities indicates that New York ranks as one of the "airiest," with Salt Lake City and Los Angeles two of the worst. A city's air pollution problem is determined as much by its ventilation as by the pollutants it produces.

Atmospheric stability (see page 74), or the tendency of air to resist vertical motion, discourages ventilation. It is stability that puts an atmospheric lid over cities and traps their noxious gases. A particularly effective form of stable air is found when an inversion exists.

Along the southwestern coast of the United States, meteorological conditions have established a semipermanent inversion. At Los Angeles, the cool air close to the ground is a result of the ocean breeze flowing in at a very low altitude over the basin. The warm air above is created by the subsidence of air from the semipermanent high pressure area offshore above the subtropical oceans. The Los Angeles smog is seasonal, between June and October, when there is a temperature inversion over the city 80 to 90 percent of the time.

Under the influence of sea breezes, the smoggy air may drift slowly southeast, flowing over the mountain passes of the Santa Anas into the Mojave Desert and beyond, even invading the posh resort of Palm Springs.

According to a meteorologist's letter appearing in the *Los Angeles Times*, a smog trail from Los Angeles has been traced as far east as the western slope of the Rocky Mountains.

METEOROLOGIST L. F. RICHARDSON succinctly described the motion of wafting, moving air in the parody of a verse by Jonathan Swift: "Great whirls have little whirls, that feed on their velocity; / And little whirls have lesser whirls, and so on to viscosity."

Air has a continuous turbulent motion that has been compared to the motion of the sea. And like the sea, the ocean of air may methodically disperse its pollutants. Within minutes, the wind is capable of shifting 90 degrees or more; over several hours it may change 180 degrees; over a month it will shift through 360 degrees many times. In different seasons preferred directional patterns become established, patterns that over the years may remain stable, developing in a particular location a unique wind climate. Frequent fluctuations spread pollution out; the general average wind direction carries it away. The targets vary as the wind gradually turns, giving respite to some regions, but every few days the cycle repeats, over the years creating semipermanent patterns of pollution downwind from factories or cities.

In 1949 an intensive investigation was started to discover why, within fifty miles of an aluminum ore reduction plant near Spokane, ponderosa pine trees were browning and dying. The disease was found to be related to fumes of poisonous fluorine compounds emanated from the aluminum plant. In the 1930s, heavy timber damage resulted from a smelter at Anaconda, Montana. Also many species of trees were damaged in the upper Columbia River watershed of Washington from a copper smelter at Trail, British Columbia. The forest was slow to grow or failed to reproduce its species; the damage progressed as far as forty miles down the Columbia before corrective measures were begun in 1931.

Pollution has severely damaged forests to the north and east of the Los Angeles Basin. The United States Forest Service Range Experimental Station at Berkeley estimated in 1970 that Los Angeles smog was killing more than a million ponderosa pine trees in the San Bernardino National Forest. Lesser injury has been suffered in the Cleveland National Forest in Southern

The Four Corners power plant in New Mexico vents nitrogen and sulfur oxides and ash into still desert air. Once a symbol of brawny industry, the puffing smokestack is now an environmental troublemaker.

California, and near Santa Cruz in Northern California. Within the Los Angeles Basin itself, growing lettuce and spinach profitably is no longer possible; citrus fruit yields have been halved; and flower growers, who must have delicate, unmarred foliage and greens, have been forced to move.

Many plants are so sensitive to the reactive oxidizing gases ozone and peroxyacyl nitrate (PAN), an eye and throat irritant found in smog, that they are proven monitors for detecting these pollutants in the air, showing effects long before human residents do.

In many places pollution has reached proportions that make it a serious hazard to health. What were once ideal town sites are now ideal pollution traps. River valleys, for instance, favorite places for settlement, are also a favorite abode for stable air because of the gravitational flow of cold air into low regions. Donora, Pennsylvania, a town of fourteen thousand located in the extremely narrow Monongahela River valley, was the scene in October 1948 of an air pollution disaster in which twenty people died and several thousand became ill. On a much larger scale, the Great Basin of Utah and Nevada is a huge bowl that contains stagnating air, particularly during the winter months. The San Joaquin Valley in California is another example of an area where polluted air is held by stable air, as evidenced by the persistent surface fogs of the winter season. Denver, located in a broad shallow basin between the slightly higher plains to the east and the Front Range of the Rockies on the west, forms an excellent trap for cool, pollution-prone air.

The delightful sea and land breezes found near the coast or around large lakes sometimes serve a diabolical purpose. They have a diurnal rhythm, with cool, denser sea air blowing toward shore during the heat of the day and a land breeze gently blowing offshore with the coming of nightfall. One of the adverse effects of such a breeze pattern is that pollutants removed from an area during the day may be blown back at night.

Similarly, the diurnal rhythm of mountain and valley winds (see chapter 12) encourages a pollution cycle. In its downhill trek the South Platte River flows through the city of Denver in a somewhat northeasterly direction. In the absence of winds from weather disturbances, a light wind plays along the river valley. At night and into the early morning hours, the air drains downslope. Polluted air is pushed along the river from the city toward the northeast. In the daytime, the winds reverse, blow upslope, draw air from the north or northeast, and carry the already fouled air back across Denver. Thus, it is late afternoon or early evening when heavy pollution besets the central city and northeast suburbs.

Cold, dense nighttime air traveling downslope and converging on an enclosed valley aggravates pollution incidents, for it can promote a ground-level inversion or strengthen a pre-existing inversion formed by radiational cooling.

The Santa Ana winds in Southern California, draining from high inland Nevada plateau regions toward the Pacific Coast, provide excellent ventilation but do not always disperse pollutants harmlessly. As the winds weaken, the air veers toward the northwest and pollutants blown offshore by the Santa Ana are then sometimes blown back to the coast, aided by sea breezes. With the abatement of the Santa Ana wind, a bank of smog offshore spreads out along the coastline, confined by the pervasive inversion of the Pacific High. When blown inland, such a smog bank has afflicted Los Angeles and its whole coastal neighborhood with some of the most severe photochemical smog conditions that they have had to endure.

Sometimes a chinook wind also encourages pollution. The subsiding warm air of the chinook may not always descend to ground level, as can happen east of the Rockies if a cold front from Canada has just passed through. There will be an inversion as the shallow layer of cold air is trapped near the ground below the warm air flowing above, a condition that affects Denver in winter.

Even without a chinook, an outbreak of cold Canadian air in Colorado may lie in a thin layer beneath the warmer air it has displaced. When this occurs, the mountain ranges may be warmer than Denver, and Denverites see their snow-capped mountains through smog-colored glasses.

In CONSTRUCTING CITIES and ejecting such a volume of effluent daily into the air in and around them, man has adversely modified the weather. It is only logical that he should eventually take steps to rectify his error. In Los Angeles, the public was shocked into awareness of man-made pollution when, near the end of World War II, it had its first smog alert. In 1947, the Air

The greatest single polluter of urban air, the automobile, releases a trail of harmful products, worst of which are oxides of nitrogen and hydrocarbons. These vehicles jammed San Francisco during a 1974 transit strike.

Pollution Control District (APCD) was established, one of the most effective such districts in the nation.

The Los Angeles APCD has set emission standards for refineries and power plants, limited the sulfur content of fuels, and specified nonpolluting equipment for use in agricultural and industrial operations. Coal was summarily outlawed, and high-sulfur oil was banned in favor of natural gas and low-sulfur oil. Gasoline loading facilities and petroleum tanks were equipped with special safety devices to prevent the escape of fumes. As part of its pollution control program, the district has eliminated fifty-seven open burning dumps, twelve large municipal incinerators, and over 1½ million domestic burners.

The APCD led the nation in the drive to control vehicle emissions by restricting the olefin content of gasoline. Olefins are the leading organic constituents of photochemical reactions in smog. The State of California has also been a pioneer in setting motor vehicle emission standards, paving the way in 1968 with mandatory crankcase emission controls and subsequently a number of other technical improvements to reduce pollutants in automobile exhaust.

Critics have found fault with the program, some insisting that it is much ado about nothing, but on a smoggy day in the Los Angeles Basin there are understandably those who doubt this. There has been one outstanding gain that outweighs all the shortcomings: it is possible to live in Los Angeles. Smog is decreasing, and officials assert hopefully that it is being abated. New state and federal emission control laws are encouraging signs, too. When the public becomes aroused, miracles can come to pass.

Fortunately, in most of the cities of the West, there are still days when the streets sparkle in clear spring sunshine or pure white snow blankets the rooftops under a rich blue sky. Perhaps as a result of men's concerted efforts to improve urban weather, there will be more such days in the future.

CHAPTER 17

TOMORROW'S WEATHER

Rainmaking ❖ Cloud seeding to control lightning, fog, hail, and storms
❖ The near future: possible drought ❖ The distant future: a possible
return of the Ice Ages ❖ The effects of man, planned and unplanned

THE EARLIEST RECORDS of primitive skywatchers show that they had hoped to control the weather, to change it at will. American Indians blew water from ceremonial pipes in a pump-priming gesture or agitated medicine waters into cloud-like froth, mimicking the action they wished from the heavens. Other rainmakers beat drums and tossed firebrands to encourage thunder and lightning. Frogs were hung from trees in the belief that they fell with the rain. These magic rites were closely associated with religion, and in time religion itself assumed the power.

Though would-be rainmakers turned up from time to time in our country's earlier years, serious scientific attempts at weather modification did not begin until the 1930s. Since then meteorologists have developed an assortment of scientific methods to make rain, curb hail, reduce lightning, dispel fog. Today the probability of coaxing rain from clouds ripe for the harvest is high, but it is still not possible to induce rainfall if moisture is not already present.

Commercial rainmakers claim a number of successes. Since 1955 the Santa Clara Valley Water District in California has engaged in rainmaking, and in these years rainfall has been 10 to 15 percent greater than average. Since 1953 the Pacific Gas and Electric Company has seeded prospective rain clouds in the Sierra Nevada, hoping to increase the water supply for power generators and irrigation; rainfall has increased by about 5 percent. Similarly, the Southern California Edison Company has seeded every year since 1951, and an average of 8 percent more rain has fallen than in earlier years when there was no seeding.

Some meteorologists, however, contest these conclusions as being either not statistically significant or the result of natural causes. Seeding for research purposes has had more mixed results. After almost fourteen years of experimental, randomized cloud seeding near Climax, Colorado, precipitation has increased from 10 to 30 percent. Over the Cascade Range in Washington, a seeding experiment has diverted snowfall from the crest, where it generally falls in abundance, to the edge of the dry plain thirteen miles to the east.

However, some projects have been inconclusive or negative. A Santa Barbara project, to provide water for the municipal water system, seemed at first to indicate that seeding had produced rainfall, but careful analysis by statisticians at the University of California indicated that there was not enough evidence to warrant that conclusion. Project Whitetop in the Midwest showed that less rain actually fell from the clouds which were seeded.

Meteorologists now know that seeding some clouds may not increase rainfall, and that overseeding others can diminish it. Early rainmakers did not recognize this fact, and the variability of many rainmaking tests may be more an indication of the unselective nature of the experiments rather than a basic lack of effectiveness in the method.

The results of other applications of rainmaking are not yet in. During the late 1960s and early 1970s, clouds were seeded over the watershed of the Hungry Horse

This radar antenna, used to help scientists track hail in thunderstorms, is part of a national research project to discover how to lessen hail's destructive power.

Rockets and explosive=carrying balloons made money for their promoters, but never any rain.

Reservoir, a federal power generation project in Montana; over the San Juan Mountains in Colorado to increase the winter snowpack; over the Wichita Mountains to help fill municipal reservoirs of Lawton, Oklahoma; and over the mountains above the San Luis Valley in southern Colorado to help the barley growers. This last venture, privately financed by the Adolph Coors Company of Golden, which bought the valley's barley for malting, backfired when other valley agriculturalists rousingly protested, even though results of the weather modification program were inconclusive.

Weather modification has long been controversial, sometimes bitterly so. Following early attempts, commercial rainmakers expressed overoptimism, tending to exaggerate the evidence favorable to their operations. Many farmers in the semiarid and arid West were gullible and consequently put more money into cloud seeding

than they recovered in profits. Weather makers have been quick to claim credit when the weather behaved as predicted, but whenever challenged by a lawsuit following an outlaw storm, they have hidden behind the lack of scientific proof of causality—thus far successfully. As a safeguard, most weather-modifying companies carry insurance against successful damage claims. One unfortunate coincidence occurred in June 1972, when heavy rainfall and a flood hit western South Dakota, causing $100,000,000 worth of property losses and nearly 250 deaths after cloud seeding near Rapid City. Part of Project Cloud Catcher, sponsored by the Bureau of Reclamation, the seeding project was later said by meteorologists who studied the storm to have had a minimal effect on the disaster area.

Respectability and some acceptance have come as rainmaking has developed as a scientific enterprise, based on logical theories and sound experimentation. Although controls in certain eastern states are still so tight that operation is next to impossible, in the arid West, where weather modification has traditionally found its best reception, regulation has been permissive.

In early 1972 the Colorado legislature passed a weather modification control bill intended to protect the citizen's right to natural weather. There was a good deal of feeling in the state because a number of scientific experiments were under way—pilot projects directed at increasing snowfall in the Rockies and rainfall on the high plains, and a five-year, $15 million experiment on hail in northeastern Colorado's Hail Alley, conducted by the National Center for Atmospheric Research. Weather modifying was not banned; instead, the bill insisted on tight regulation of the weather modifiers, requiring them to seek a permit and justify each operation at a public hearing. The new law also declared weather modification economically beneficial and worthy of state encouragement.

Commercial weather modification projects to date reflect only two reasonably successful activities: cloud seeding and dispersal of cold fog—in which water droplets remain liquid though temperatures are below freezing. It is estimated that fog-clearing operations in the United States cost only 9 percent of alternative fog-incurred operating expenses such as rescheduling or rerouting of planes or closing of airports.

Medford (Oregon), Spokane, Salt Lake City, and Denver have airport problems caused by cold fog, and

The burning flare on this aircraft is releasing billions of tiny silver iodide crystals to seed clouds.
Resembling ice crystals, they stimulate formation of real ice crystals that eventually fall as rain.

they all use fog chasers. The dispersal technique is to drop from one hundred to four hundred pounds of dry ice into the fog deck in a pattern corresponding to the runway. The dry ice initiates the formation of ice crystals in the fog; water droplets turn into snow, which precipitates, usually within an hour, and clears the air. The clearing of the fog is planned to coincide with a series of departures or arrivals, and is successful about 80 percent of the time.

Seeding is, unfortunately, useless against warm fog (above freezing), the variety that afflicts airports at Los Angeles, San Francisco, New York, and Washington. Since fog consists of tiny droplets, formed when air temperature falls below the saturation point of the air (dew point), raising the fog above the dew point evaporates the droplets, and the air clears. The first practical method found to dissipate both cold and warm fog was

A successfully seeded cumulus cloud rises like a
cumulonimbus, and rain may fall within minutes.

igniting fuel oil along the runways at airports, thus warming the air above the dew point. It was used by FIDO ("Fog, Intensive Dispersal Of") in World War II when it was necessary to land planes in any weather, but it is an extravagant proposition by today's standards of efficient energy use. Los Angeles International Airport operated a FIDO type system in the early fifties, but abandoned it when it proved to be expensive and of limited effectiveness. Any thermal method of attacking fog can be used only in still air.

The warm fog dispersal technique equivalent to dry ice seeding is to seed with chemicals that have an affinity for water. The fog collects in large droplets on the particles of chemical and falls as rain. The clearing, though rapid, lasts only until more fog blows into the area, and the chemicals cost considerably more than dry ice. Another method, developed by the Air Force, uses helicopters to disperse fog by mixing it with drier air above the fog layer.

Cloud seeders decided early that they probably could alter the development of hurricanes. When a cloud is seeded, supercooled water is changed to ice, and heat is liberated just as it is when water vapor condenses. Turning this principle to advantage, weather modifiers saw possibilities that the additional heat could disrupt the well-organized wind circulation patterns of the hurricane by intensifying updrafts in selected regions of the storm. In effect, some of the energy to power its circulating winds would be diverted away from the region of highest winds, the rim of the hurricane's eye, and their strength would decrease.

One promising result in moderating the giant storms came from Project Stormfury of the National Oceanic and Atmospheric Administration. It was August 1969, and the hurricane was Debbie. Within hours after seeding of the eye-wall clouds, there was a reduction of maximum wind speed by 31 percent. When seeding was suspended, the storm burgeoned noticeably; after seeding was resumed, maximum wind speeds again dropped, by 15 percent. Rapid shifts in behavior are natural for hurricanes—they have earned feminine names because weathermen find their ways unpredictable—and scientists are quick to acknowledge that overseeding may not have been what took the punch out of Debbie. Thus, in spite of the NOAA's apparent success, a National Academy of Sciences panel considers the procedure still experimental.

Human intervention is not yet able to suppress tornadoes. To destroy a tornado by force would take the power of an atomic bomb. Heat from huge fires or jet engines and the building of artificial hills around cities

NASA

Using rotating cups to generate wind and a cloud of water droplets to make it visible, meteorologist T. Theodore Fujita simulates a tornado in his laboratory. He predicts that in a decade the twister will be controlled.

have been suggested to disrupt tornadoes, but there is little scientific evidence to indicate that they would work. Seeding tornado clouds might alter the flow of warm air and cause the tornado to dissipate, but some researchers argue that it could just as likely feed the storm. Bernard Vonnegut, of the State University of New York at Albany, believes that the power of tornadoes originates in the electrical energy of a thunderstorm and that by interfering with its circuitry through ways such as artificially triggered lightning, a tornado might be aborted.

In the plains region of the West, where crop and property losses inflicted by hail storms reach an estimated $300 million annually, development of hail prevention techniques has high public interest. Older hail-suppression methods, such as the ringing of church bells, the shooting of hail-bearing clouds with cannon or exploding rockets—which are said to produce harmlessly mushy hailstones—and other "weather weapons" have

had little effect. Russian scientists have reported success in identifying clouds that are actively making hailstones, into which they then launch shells that spread silver iodide, a cloud-seeding agent; but other researchers feel that insufficient information has been presented for objective judgment of this method. In this country, the National Hail Research Experiment (NHRE), under the direction of scientists from the National Center for Atmospheric Research (NCAR), is attempting to suppress hail experimentally by selective seeding of clouds from aircraft-launched rockets. Commercial hail-suppressing projects in Hail Alley do not use pinpoint aiming but instead seed generally with silver iodide. The success of these measures is not yet quantitatively convincing.

In the western United States another hazard is lightning, which ignites about ten thousand forest fires a year. Prevention would have significant economic benefits. It may be possible to tame lightning by seeding clouds

Hurricane Gladys, 1968. Towering cumulus clouds, visible in the spiral arms here, release the energy that powers these formidable tropical storms, whose impact is sometimes felt far into Texas.

heavily with silver iodide or dry ice to promote the formation of sharp-pointed ice crystals, which act as lightning rods and drain the cloud of its charge without producing lightning. This has been the theory behind Project Skyfire, the Forest Service's lightning modification program, now more than twenty-five years old. A more recent technique, of interest to researchers from the National Oceanic and Atmospheric Administration (NOAA), is to drop aluminized nylon fibers into the cloud, where they short out the high voltages that would otherwise be generated there. The current that flows through the filaments drains sufficient electricity to prevent the formation of fire-starting stepped leaders of a cloud-to-ground bolt. Heinz Kasemir of NOAA's Atmospheric Physics and Chemistry Laboratory at Boulder says that results of recent efforts to suppress lightning are "not good enough for a statistical analysis, but if you're there and you see the electrical field decay faster than ordinary, you are convinced. I am convinced it works." In tests the seeded storms had 66 percent fewer cloud-to-ground lightning bolts—and presumably that much less ability to kindle forest fires.

THE LATE JOHN VON NEUMANN, the mathematical wizard of early electronic computer technology, once said that control of the weather might be more feasible than prediction. However, with high-speed computing and weather modeling, predictions are becoming increasingly accurate.

Certain ominous, long-range predictions have been made recently by weather watchers without the need of computers. The early 1970s have been plagued with unusual weather. Storms have been moving more slowly than usual, producing floods in some places, droughts in others. Around the globe, there have been storms in areas that normally do not have them, expansion of deserts by drought in others, and less perceptible, long-range changes in temperature and rainfall. During the spring of 1973, Colorado was hit by a heavy blizzard; across the nation tornadoes numbered nearly four hundred; the South had heavy snow, and on the Great Lakes abnormally high waves raised by spring storms washed away highways and beach-side homes. In the middle of August, a summer storm covered wheat fields of western Canada with eight inches of snow; such a

SANDIA LABORATORIES

A modern windmill, potentially useful as a power generator, spins with wind from any direction.

storm as has not been generally known since New England farmers cursed them in the nineteenth century.

Over the last several years, there have been colder winters in the West and relatively warm winters in the East, reversing a trend established over most of the last decade. The poles and the equator are currently having increasingly contrasting temperatures. Jerome Namias, of the Scripps Institution of Oceanography, has explained that the circumpolar jet stream now projects low over the central United States, sweeping cold northern air southward along the jet stream's western boundary, and warm southern air from the Gulf of Mexico northward.

With the jet stream in its current position, a high plains drought has been predicted for the mid-1970s. Normally, cold air from Canada and warm air from the Gulf of Mexico mix and produce rain in the lee of the Rockies. However, high-speed winds in the jet stream

HELIOS ASSOCIATES, TUCSON, ARIZ.

COWET. 72

THE SOLAR ENERGY FARM

Until now, solar energy has been directly used only in the photosynthetic process of green plants. Major fuels come from deposits formed largely by that process. An alternative to these fuels would be direct use of the sun to produce heat and electricity. The idea is at least several decades old, but only now, at a time of energy awareness, has power conversion from solar radiation become a topic of public interest.

The concept of the solar energy farm—a large-scale operation capable of generating large amounts of power (in the megawatt range and higher)—is partly responsible for revitalizing interest in solar power. Proposed about two years ago by the team of Aden and Marjorie Meinel, the solar farm would gather incoming sunshine in the arid Southwest. Because sunlight is particularly abundant in the desert area where Nevada, California, and Arizona meet, and along the Rio Grande valley in Texas and New Mexico, these regions would be well suited to the purposes of an energy farm. Using an area of about fifteen thousand square miles for the collection of solar

energy, the farm would concentrate the heat, use it to boil water or some other fluid, then with the steam operate turbines of an electric power plant. The technology already exists that could do this.

Though energy would be removed from the desert environment for delivery elsewhere, it is believed that the desert ecology would not need to be altered. The average color of the desert would be noticeably darkened by the solar collectors, but this effect would counteract the cooling that would also result as heat was extracted. In the long run, there would be a net increase in heat in the region of the solar farm, but the Meinels say this could be neutralized if areas could be painted white near where power was being removed. They further suggest that heat wasted by the turbines could be used to desalinate seawater and thus usefully preserve the region's thermal balance. The Meinels are sure that solar radiation will be the energy source of the future, perhaps even of the next century, and deserts a great national asset. Solar energy may be an idea whose time has come.

are blowing that mixing point eastward. There have been eight successive dry periods in the recorded history of this region, each separated by twenty to twenty-three years; the cycle is presently due to repeat itself. The 1974 drought in the Midwest may have been the beginning of a new cycle, and if so, past records suggest that it will last from three to eight years.

Besides observing unusual spot weather, meteorologists are looking for long-term trends. Some believe there are signals that a major shift in the weather is now under way. For instance, the average temperature of the Northern Hemisphere has been decreasing since 1940. Also, the equatorial zone has become wetter, in contrast to the arid and semiarid regions, which have been drier than at any time in the first half of the century.

Dr. H. H. Lamb, a leading European climatologist, believes that the recent spate of unconventional weather is an indication of the greatest shift in world climate since the eighteenth century. According to climatologists the duration of global warming is usually about ten thousand years—approximately the length of the earth's present interglacial warm spell. If another ice age is indeed near, it probably will not come quickly. The climate in the year 2000 will not be substantially cooler than it is now. Thousands of years are required for ice sheets to build and the cold climate to achieve maximum development. If the earth slips into a deep freeze again, man will have time to adapt.

IN THE 1950s astronomer Harlow Shapley made the point that life is a force in climatological evolution. The pyramiding technology of man is active in that evolution and may pose a serious climatological threat.

Of the billions of tons of carbon dioxide in the atmosphere, perhaps 15 percent is man-made. Because of the greenhouse effect (discussed on page 73), there is worry that if the percentage increase of carbon dioxide remains at its present rate of about 0.3 percent a year, it will soon reach a level that will have a material effect on world climate by raising temperatures, melting the ice caps, and increasing desert areas. The heavy shroud of carbon dioxide around Venus is partly the reason for its uninhabitably hot 800° F. temperatures. Though it is unlikely that man-made weather pollution could ever make the earth as warm as Venus, there was a suspicious

rise in the average temperature of the earth that coincided with the increasing dependence of society on fossil fuels. Curiously, since 1940 the average temperature of the earth has begun to drop, although certain areas of the globe are still warming.

Any variation of the earth's albedo—the fraction of light reflected back to space from the earth—will result in a temperature change at the earth's surface. The greater the albedo, the less energy will reach the surface to warm the air. It is the thesis of Reid Bryson of the University of Wisconsin that dust from volcanic and other sources has increased the albedo, triggering past cool episodes. However, he has calculated that volcanic activity in this century cannot totally account for the temperature fluctuations that have been observed, and he believes that man's activities are playing an increasingly significant role. Dust is produced in mining, combustion of fuels, construction, mechanized farming, and overgrazing of semiarid pasture. The cooling from the increasing dust veil may be balancing or exceeding the greenhouse effect of excess carbon dioxide from burning of fossil fuels.

Astronomer Donald Menzel also considers it possible that past ice ages were caused by volcanism, but for another reason. The great quantities of dust injected into the air by an active volcano serve as nuclei on which water droplets form, and Menzel estimates that about five hundred thousand tons of such nuclei-forming material would initiate the significant worldwide precipitation that accompanies ice ages.

One theory has it that recent weather changes are a consequence of the expansion of snow and pack ice in the Northern Hemisphere. Being highly reflective, snow and ice can raise the albedo, lower the heat received by the earth, and thus alter the behavior of global air circulation. Of current concern is the raising of albedo by contrails of high-flying jets. A major environmental argument against the proliferation of supersonic transports was that they would have been capable of depositing a persistent thin, but climatically significant, layer of cirrus in the stratosphere.

Among the many factors that may affect the weather are the intensity of the sun's radiation, changes of water to ice or vapor, the amount of dust in the atmosphere, and changes in albedo. Other influences of lesser importance are the electrical conductivity of the atmos-

Contrails of jet aircraft often create "false cirrus" by adding moisture to the cold upper troposphere. Meteorologists are concerned that increasing numbers of jets and their contrails may alter weather.

phere and of the earth's crust, photochemical reactions such as in plants, the earth's radioactivity, and changes in the chemical composition of the atmosphere.

Because of its many governing factors, not all known, weather may prove too unstable and complex either to predict accurately or to control effectively. An equally pessimistic view is that the forces controlling weather compensate each other so well as to preclude any significant effects from man-made influences. However, it is the belief of weather control advocates that to alter the weather, one must only find the right catalyst to trigger the desired change, as the rainmakers have done with their partial successes in cloud seeding.

If man is changing the earth's climate, it is purely by accident, for historically his weather interference has been incidental to other purposes. When vegetation is burned, some of the sun's energy from earlier times is released. So by burning for warmth, electrical power, industry, transportation, and agriculture, man is a thermal element of weather.

Old-timers in Arizona say that with the coming of irrigation canals, the weather has become more humid. Until vastly more acreage is irrigated, however, this humidity will be very local—a matter more of microclimate than of climate. Tests have shown that, a few feet over a 100,000-acre irrigation project near Yuma, humidity is higher than normal, but twelve feet above it, humidity is normal. Smog, however, has more influence. On some days in 1966, the solar radiation reaching Phoenix was reduced by 50 percent owing to air pollution—a cooling effect that might well be a factor in local weather.

By the weight of numbers, human populations have adversely affected the atmosphere without trying. The question remains whether man can do better on purpose. The weather changers are not discouraged. Two decades of cloud seeding belie the lament, variously attributed to Charles Dudley Warner and Mark Twain, "Everybody talks about the weather, but nobody does anything about it."

199

IT'S A GOOD DAY FOR...

Sailing, skiing, fishing, hiking, picnicking, or simply getting a suntan—the choice depends on the season, the region, and your preference of leisure-time activities. But if you live in the West, the odds are that, weatherwise, it **is** a good day for fun. Most parts of the West have less annual precipitation than most parts of the East. And what rain or snow there is tends to be concentrated in the winter months, leaving more days of predictable sunshine each year. In fact, the whole southern half of the West averages more sunlight than any eastern state.

Warm ocean currents keep winters mild along the Pacific Coast, even at latitudes that are freezing and blizzard-bound farther east. Inland, on the deserts of the Southwest, prevailing weather patterns provide sunny, summery days much of the year. Thus in many places golf, tennis, swimming, boating, hiking, and other activities can be enjoyed year-round. So can homelier pleasures like gardening or a family barbecue on the patio. It is no wonder that outdoor living has become a hallmark of the western life-style.

In the balmiest climes of the West, winter sports enthusiasts can have their cake and eat it, too—or rather, have their sun and ski, too—for within a few hours' drive of most western cities are high mountains that stand in the path of winter storms and trap heavy snowpacks on their slopes. Those who live in Pasadena or Phoenix, for example, might even swim and ski on the same day—a good day for almost anything!

Boating—*the exhilarating feel of sun and surf, and the challenge of pitting a seaman's skill against the elements—no wonder so many westerners say, "I'd rather be sailing!"*

ROBERT F. SYMONS

Soaring—*engineless flight that takes inspiration from the circling hawk, for they share the same air currents: "thermals" rising above sun-baked ground and "waves" over hills and mountains.*

Hang-gliding—*the daring young sport that goes soaring one better for ultralight flight. Palisades along the Pacific provide an ideal combination of terrain and updrafts for those with the courage to try their wings.*

ROBERT CAMPBELL

GRANT HEILMAN

Fishing—*on the many lakes, streams, and seashores throughout the West. On an overcast day fish lurk just below the surface. But who cares if they don't bite, when the day is spent on Montana's beautiful Lake McDonald!*

LEE FOSTER FROM FPG

Tanning in the sun—*whether with a lively game of volleyball or relaxing on the sand. On Catalina Island off the Southern California shore, as in much of the West, a tan can be nurtured all winter long.*

Playing at the beach—*the annual sand castle event at Carmel, California, attracts a gallery of all ages armed with picnic baskets and sand shovels; it is usually held in the fog-free days of mid-autumn.*

Skiing—*at one of the many winter sports areas scattered through all the mountains of the West, either the popular downhill variety or cross-country, the object of Yosemite's annual spring races.*

Climbing—*an increasingly popular sport, but not for the timid. On many western peaks, as here on Ingraham Glacier, Mount Rainier, winter mountaineering can be practiced all year long.*

Riding—*mountain trails, like this one at Snowmass in Colorado, invite exploration during the three snow-free months of summer. With horsepower to climb the slopes, a rider can just drink in the scenery and the mountain air.*

Hiking—*in the woods, perhaps in the filtered sunlight and lush green beauty of Washington's Soleduck Valley rainforest; . . .*

208

. . . or in the mountains, as in the Cascades, where backpackers can expect to find occasional snowfields on the higher slopes, even in summer; . . .

. . . or along a seacoast, like this wild, driftwood-strewn beach in Olympic National Park, where a chill wind and restless waves make winter invigorating.

209

APPENDIX

HOW TO READ A BAROMETER				
Wind Direction	**Barometer Reading**	**Rising**	**Steady**	**Falling**
N	30.51–31.00	A	A	F
	30.01–30.50	C	A	F
	29.71–30.00	C	A	H
	29.41–29.70	C	D	H
	29.01–29.40	C	D	E
	28.00–29.00	D	E	H
NE	30.51–31.00	A	A	F
	30.01–30.50	C	A	F
	29.71–30.00	C	A	G
	29.41–29.70	C	H	G
	29.01–29.40	D	H	H
	28.00–29.00	E	H	H
E	30.51–31.00	A	A	F
	30.01–30.50	A	A	F
	29.71–30.00	A	A	G
	29.41–29.70	G	G	G
	29.01–29.40	H	H	H
	28.00–29.00	F	H	H
SE	30.51–31.00	A	B	F
	30.01–30.50	A	A	F
	29.71–30.00	A	A	G
	29.41–29.70	G	G	G
	29.01–29.40	H	H	H
	28.00–29.00	F	H	H
S	30.51–31.00	B	B	F
	30.01–30.50	A	B	F
	29.71–30.00	A	A	G
	29.41–29.70	G	G	H
	29.01–29.40	E	E	H
	28.00–29.00	E	E	H
SW	30.51–31.00	B	B	F
	30.01–30.50	A	B	F
	29.71–30.00	C	A	G
	29.41–29.70	D	E	E
	29.01–29.40	D	E	E
	28.00–29.00	E	E	E
W	30.51–31.00	B	B	B
	30.01–30.50	A	A	F
	29.71–30.00	C	A	G
	29.41–29.70	C	C	E
	29.01–29.40	C	D	E
	28.00–29.00	D	E	E
NW	30.51–31.00	A	A	B
	30.01–30.50	C	A	F
	29.71–30.00	C	A	G
	29.41–29.70	C	C	E
	29.01–29.40	C	D	E
	28.00–29.00	D	E	E

Determine the current prevailing wind direction. Locate in "Barometer Reading" column the present pressure as determined from your barometer, then follow that line across to the column indicating the movement and speed of change on your barometer. Now refer to the code below.

A—Fair weather, not much change in temperature.

B—Fair and warmer.

C—Fair, becoming cooler (colder, in winter).

D—Clearing within 12 hours.

E—Rain, showers, or snow—clearing and becoming colder in 12 hours.

F—Increasing cloudiness followed by rain or snow.

G—Rain, showers, or snow.

H—Rain, showers, or snow, becoming colder.

WIND CHILL CHART

Temperature (°F)

Wind speed (mi/h)	45	40	35	30	25	20	15	10	5	0	−5	−10	−15	−20	−25	−30	−35	−40	−45
4	45	40	35	30	25	20	15	10	5	0	−5	−10	−15	−20	−25	−30	−35	−40	−45
5	43	37	32	27	22	16	11	6	0	−5	−10	−15	−21	−26	−31	−36	−42	−47	−52
10	34	26	22	16	10	3	−3	−9	−15	−22	−27	−34	−40	−46	−52	−58	−64	−71	−77
15	29	23	16	9	2	−5	−11	−18	−25	−31	−38	−45	−51	−58	−65	−72	−78	−85	−92
20	26	19	12	4	−3	−10	−17	−24	−31	−39	−46	−53	−60	−67	−74	−81	−88	−95	−103
25	23	16	8	1	−7	−15	−22	−29	−36	−44	−51	−59	−66	−74	−81	−88	−96	−103	−110
30	21	13	6	−2	−10	−18	−25	−33	−41	−49	−56	−64	−71	−79	−86	−93	−101	−109	−116
35	20	12	4	−4	−12	−20	−27	−35	−43	−52	−58	−67	−74	−82	−89	−97	−105	−113	−120
40	19	11	3	−5	−13	−21	−29	−37	−45	−53	−60	−69	−76	−84	−92	−100	−107	−115	−123
45	18	10	2	−6	−14	−22	−30	−38	−46	−54	−62	−70	−78	−85	−93	−102	−109	−117	−125

When does 25° F. not feel like 25° F.? When there is a wind blowing against the exposed human body. In a wind of twenty miles per hour, that 25° will feel like −3°. This effect is called *wind chill*, the measure of cold one feels regardless of the temperature. Its basis is the understandable fact that body heat is more effectively whisked away by moving air than by still air. Chill increases as temperatures drop and winds get stronger, up to about 45 miles per hour, beyond which there is little increase. Thus at 10° F. increasing the wind from 0 to 5 m.p.h. reduces temperatures by four degrees, but a change in wind speed from 40 to 45 m.p.h. reduces it only one degree.

The wind may not always be naturally caused. For example, someone skiing or riding a snowmobile into the wind, or even cross-wind, may receive quite a chill. If one is moving into the wind, the speed of travel is added to the wind speed; thus if the wind is blowing at ten miles per hour and one's speed is fifteen miles per hour into the wind, the actual air movement against the body is twenty-five miles per hour. At 15° F. this air speed gives a wind chill equivalent to −22° F. (A reading of the chart above will supply other examples.) This is easily cold enough for exposed parts of the body—hands, cheeks, ears—to sustain a painful chilling or even frostbite.

WESTERN WEATHER RECORDS

TEMPERATURE

HIGHEST: 134° F. at Greenland Ranch, Death Valley, California, July 10, 1913.

LOWEST: −70° F. at Rogers Pass, Montana, January 20, 1954.

RAINFALL

HIGHEST AVERAGE ANNUAL RAINFALL: 144.43 inches at Wynoochee Oxbow, Washington.

LOWEST AVERAGE ANNUAL RAINFALL: 1.78 inches in Death Valley, California

RECORD RAINFALL FOR A SINGLE YEAR: 184.56 inches at Wynoochee Oxbow, Washington, 1931.

LONGEST PERIOD WITHOUT RAIN: 993 days at Bagdad, California, from August 18, 1909 to May 6, 1912.

SNOWFALL

HIGHEST AVERAGE ANNUAL SNOWFALL: 575 inches at Paradise Ranger Station, Mount Rainier National Park, Washington.

RECORD SNOWFALL FOR A SINGLE YEAR: 1,027 inches at Paradise Ranger Station, Mount Rainier National Park, Washington, the winter of 1970/71.

RECORD SNOWFALL FOR A SINGLE DAY: 75.8 inches at Silver Lake, Colorado, 1921.

CLIMATE STATISTICS FOR SELECTED WESTERN CITIES

	Avg. Low (°F) Jan.	Avg. High (°F) Jan.	Avg. Low (°F) July	Avg. High (°F) July	Record Low (°F)	Record High (°F)	Annual Precip. (inches)	Season with Most Precipitation	Snowfall (inches)	Rainfree Days	Avg. Wind Speed (miles per hour)	Percentage of Maximum Annual Sunshine
Abilene	33	56	72	94	−9.4	109	23	Sp, Su, F	4	300	13	73
Albuquerque	36	63	73	99	−17	104	11	Su, W	1	307	9	86
Billings	13	33	61	89	−38	105	13	Sp, Su, F	55	271	11	62
Bismarck	0	20	58	86	−43	108	15	W, Sp, Su	39	269	11	59
Boise	20	35	59	91	−23	111	11	F, W, Sp	21	274	9	66
Denver	15	42	57	88	−29	104	15	Sp, Su, F, W	59	278	10	70
Fresno	37	55	63	100	18	111	11	F, W	T	322	6	78
Las Vegas	33	55	76	105	8	116	4	F, W	1	341	9	83
Los Angeles	47	65	63	83	28	110	15	W	T	331	6	73
Mpls.-St. Paul	6	23	63	85	−34	104	25	Sp, Su	43	252	11	56
Oklahoma City	28	46	72	91	1	109	31	Sp, Su, F	9	284	13	67
Omaha	13	32	68	89	−21	114	28	Sp, Su	32	266	11	62
Phoenix	35	65	75	105	17	118	7	W, Su	T	331	6	86
Portland	33	44	56	79	−3	107	37	F, W	8	213	8	45
Rapid City	9	33	59	86	−27	109	17	W, Sp, Su	38	269	11	61
Salt Lake City	17	36	61	92	−30	107	15	Sp, Su, F, W	56	277	8	68
San Diego	45	65	63	77	31	111	10	F, W	T	324	7	67
San Francisco	46	56	53	64	30	101	21	F, W	T	298	9	67
Seattle	37	46	56	75	11	100	34	F, W	8	213	7	45
Spokane	19	31	55	86	−25	108	17	F, W, Sp	54	250	8	58
St. Louis	24	40	67	89	−11	111	35	W, Sp, Su	17	259	10	59
Wichita	22	42	69	92	−12	113	28	Sp, Su	15	282	12	69

WEATHER RADIO BROADCASTS

Two sources of weather information and forecasts exist to broadcast news which, though prepared for marine and aviation purposes, is useful to the outdoorsman. Both broadcast twenty-four hours a day and 365 days a year.

One is VHF (Very High Frequency) radio weather, a service of the National Oceanic and Atmospheric Administration (NOAA). Like FM, VHF is static free. Its transmission range is limited to about forty miles, but sensitive receivers can pick up the signal from perhaps sixty miles away.

This broadcast uses one of two frequencies, depending on location. Most widely used is 162.55 MHz (megahertz), transmitted in the West by Seattle, Portland, Eureka, Sacramento, San Francisco, Los Angeles, San Diego, Salt Lake City, Phoenix, Denver, and Wichita; in the west central states by Minneapolis, Des Moines, Kansas City (Mo.), and St. Louis.

Astoria, Eugene, Monterey, and St. Joseph (Mo.) use the 162.40 MHz frequency. The three-to-five minute broadcasts offer information on weather systems and their motions, radar weather observations, and wind and weather conditions for various points throughout the local area, as well as detailed weather forecasts, updated every two or three hours or as needed.

The second source of radio weather information was created for the aviation industry and offers information similar to that on the VHF band. It is broadcast in the 200 to 400 KHz (kilohertz) frequency band used by aeronautical beacons. Again the range is limited, in this case between fifty and one hundred miles. The stations are closely spaced and can be found on the receiver by simply tuning through the frequency band until the desired station is picked up.

MAJOR WEATHER AGENCIES

With the exception of commercial and military weather forecasters, and specialized state and local agencies (for example, air pollution monitoring), all weather-related activities are managed by the National Oceanic and Atmospheric Administration (NOAA), a branch of the Department of Commerce responsible ''for expanding effective and rational use of ocean resources, for monitoring and predicting conditions in the atmosphere, ocean, and space, and for exploring the feasibility and consequences of environmental modification.'' Within NOAA, the National Weather Service, supported by other NOAA subdivisions, prepares the familiar weather reports. Below are described the National Weather Service and some of its important agencies.

National Meteorological Center (NMC), Washington, D.C.

Receives ship, aircraft, and sounding observation reports from around the world and all available data from weather satellites; prepares short-range forecasts for periods from 24 to 72 hours ahead, intermediate forecasts up to 120 hours, and long-range forecasts for 30-day periods; provides special weather information for other government agencies.

National Severe Storms Forecast Center (NSSFC), Kansas City, Missouri.

Prepares for public and aviation use messages concerning expected local severe storms, called Tornado or Severe Thunderstorm Watches, which are issued when necessary, along with routine summaries twice daily.

National Hurricane Center (NHC), Miami, Florida.

Surveys areas of potential tropical cyclone formation in the Atlantic, Caribbean, and Gulf of Mexico.

Pacific Hurricane Center (PHC).

The Eastern Pacific Hurricane Center (EPHC), San Francisco, and Central Pacific Hurricane Center (CPHC), Honolulu, identify, track, and predict tropical cyclonic storms in regions north of the equator and west from the United States' western coastline to the 180th meridian.

Regional Center for Tropical Meteorology (RCTM), Miami, Florida.

Analyzes and forecasts tropical and subtropical weather patterns, emphasizing development and progress of tropical storms.

Public Weather Service, state and local.

Provides for the public, in cooperation with news media, current general weather information, warnings, and forecasts. Information comes from the National Meteorological Center, the National Hurricane Center, Eastern Pacific and Central Pacific Hurricane Centers, the National Severe Storms Forecast Center, the state forecast offices, and local and zone forecast offices.

Aviation Weather Service, Domestic Program.

Prepares weather reports for use by pilots including airport, regional, and selected-route weather forecasts, winds and temperatures aloft, and warnings of hazardous flying weather. The Aviation Weather Service disseminates information through its weather radio stations, special pilots' telephone weather services, or by direct contact with National Weather Service personnel in airport weather offices.

Marine Weather Service, Coastal and Offshore Waters Program.

Prepares weather reports tailored specifically for commercial and recreational marine interests. Beyond ordinary weather reports, winds, severity of waves, visibility, and sea ice are emphasized. Marine weather is available from weather radio, the coast guard, commercial radio and television in coastal areas, and recorded phone messages in some larger coastal urban areas.

GLOSSARY

altocumulus: clouds of the middle layer, occurring in patches or sheets with a wavy appearance. Individual clouds may be rounded masses, rolls, or parallel bands. Usually their outlines are sharp, resulting from small water droplets in the main part of the cloud. The small droplets allow coronas to occur and shadow the cloud's interior, darkening it. In low temperatures, falling ice crystals may produce a mock sun, or sun dog. Altocumulus clouds are often found with other cloud types. Precipitation may occur as a fine drizzle or light snow.

altostratus: a middle cloud with a sheet or layered appearance. There are water droplets and ice crystals present in the cloud and at its base, giving the underside a feathery appearance, particularly if the precipitation does not reach the ground. Light but continuous rainfall can be expected if precipitation extends to the ground.

anticyclone: the circulation of air around a high pressure center, flowing clockwise in the Northern Hemisphere. *Anticyclone* and *high* are interchangeable terms.

atmosphere: the earth's envelope of air containing several subdivisions all bound to the earth by gravitational attraction.

atmospheric pressure: the weight of the earth's atmosphere—about 14.7 pounds over each square inch at sea level; as meteorologists measure it, 29.92 inches of mercury, or 1,013 millibars.

aurora: light emitted from the upper atmosphere that is visible evidence of an attack on the atmosphere by charged particles ejected by the sun during solar storms.

barometer: an instrument used to measure atmospheric pressure.

blizzard: a strong, cold wind blowing fine, dry snow picked up from the ground. Technically wind speeds in excess of 32 miles per hour, visibility reduced to 500 feet or less by falling or blowing snow, and temperatures of 20° F. or lower.

chinook: American name for a foehn wind that is warm, dry, and usually capable of rapidly melting and evaporating a ground cover of snow.

cirrocumulus: a high cloud that forms a thin, white patch or sheet without shading. It is almost exclusively an ice crystal cloud. Sometimes a corona or iridescence is observed. Cirrocumulus are often associated with cirrus and/or cirrostratus clouds.

cirrostratus: a high cloud that is semi-transparent, either fibrous or smooth, and is seen totally or partly coating the sky. It often produces halos and is generally comprised of ice crystals.

cirrus: a high cloud of delicate wisps or narrow fibrous bands composed almost exclusively of ice crystals. The trails of the ice particles curve irregularly because of wind shear and particle size variations.

climate: characteristic weather conditions for any place or region, measured over a long period of time (usually decades).

cold front: the leading edge of an advancing mass of colder air that is replacing warmer air in its path.

condensation: the process by which a gas changes to liquid or solid form.

condensation level: the height at which rising air becomes saturated and forms clouds.

condensation nucleus: a solid or liquid particle that serves to initiate the condensation of water vapor in the atmosphere.

condensation trail (contrail, vapor trail): a cloudlike trail of water droplets or ice crystals emanating from aircraft flying in cold, clear, humid air.

continental climate: a climate that is characteristic of the interior of a large landmass, having large daily and annual temperature ranges and a generally light or moderate rainfall coming at irregular times.

convection: the vertical motions of warm and cool air masses due to their differing densities.

Coriolis force: an invisible force due to the rotation of the earth that causes any moving substance, such as wind or ocean currents, to veer to the right of a straight line path in the Northern Hemisphere, and to the left in the Southern Hemisphere.

corona: one or more colored rings around the sun or moon when veiled by thin clouds, caused by diffraction of light by large numbers of water drops. Its color is prismatic, ranging from blue inside to red outside, the reverse of colors in the halo. The smaller the corona, the larger the water droplets and the closer any impending storm.

crepuscular rays: alternating light and dark bands which appear to diverge from the rising or setting sun in a fan-like bundle of rays.

cumulonimbus: a large, dense cloud with vertical development. The top often spreads into an anvil; the base is usually dark. Precipitation is frequently heavy and showery; lightning and thunder are common. The upper part is composed of ice crystals; the lower, water droplets. It may also contain hail or snow.

cumulus: a large, individual cloud with sharp outlines, vertical development, dark base, and white sunlit tops; if precipitation occurs, it is showery.

cyclone: the circulation of air around a low pressure center, flowing counterclockwise in the Northern Hemisphere. *Cyclone* and *low* are interchangeable terms.

dew point: the temperature to which air must be cooled in order to reach saturation.

diffraction: the bending of light around small objects.

dispersion: any process that separates light into its component colors.

dust devil: a small but vigorous whirlwind that is visible because of dust and debris picked up from the ground. Usually short-lived, it forms over intensely heated ground in dry regions on hot, calm afternoons when the skies are clear.

equinox: that point in the revolution of the earth—on the first day of spring and the first day of fall—when the sun is directly over the equator.

evaporation: the process by which a liquid changes to gas.

Fahrenheit (F.): a temperature scale having 32° as the melting point of ice and 212° as the boiling point of water.

foehn: a warm, dry wind on the lee side of a mountain resulting from the compression of air on the descending slopes, often augmented by heat from condensation; a chinook.

fog: a stratus cloud at or near the earth's surface, having water droplets so microscopic they are not easily distinguished by the unaided eye.

front: the transition zone between two air masses of different temperature.

halo: any of several forms of atmospheric optical phenomena that produce white or colored rings around the sun or moon from reflection and refraction of light striking ice crystals; associated with cirrostratus clouds.

haze: fine dust or sea salt particles that have dispersed through part of the atmosphere and limit horizontal visibility.

high: an anticyclone, or area with high atmospheric pressure.

humidity, absolute: the weight of water vapor in a given volume of air; usually expressed by meteorologists in grams per cubic meter.

humidity, relative: the ratio of the amount of water in the air to the total amount that the air could hold under saturation conditions.

inversion: a departure from the usual decrease of temperature with increasing altitude.

iridescence: colors exhibited by clouds, due to the diffraction of light around fine water droplets and ice crystals.

jet stream: strong, high-speed winds that are concentrated in a narrow segment of the atmosphere.

lenticular cloud: a lens-shaped wave cloud with a sharp, smooth outline formed in air that is forced to rise over a mountain barrier.

low: a cyclone, or area with low atmospheric pressure.

mackerel sky: a sky that resembles the scales on a mackerel, produced by cirrocumulus or altocumulus clouds.

mares' tails: long wisps of cirrus cloud that are usually thicker at one end than the other.

maritime, or marine, climate: a climate that is characteristic of the sea coast, having narrow daily and annual ranges of temperature and periods of coldest and hottest weather retarded one or two months after each solstice.

Mediterranean climate: a climate that is characterized by hot, dry summers and rainy winters.

mirage: a phenomenon in which light is refracted so that an object appears displaced from its real position and possibly duplicated, either upright or inverted.

nimbostratus: a light to very dark gray cloud of great vertical and horizontal development. It is always accompanied by falling rain, snow, or sleet, which may or may not reach the ground. Nimbostratus does not have a well-defined base as does stratus or the lighter-colored altostratus.

occluded front (occlusion): the front formed when a cold front overtakes a warm front.

rain shadow: a region on the leeward side of a mountain or mountain range where precipitation is markedly less than that on the windward side.

reflection: the deflection of a light ray back into the substance in which it was traveling, caused by the boundary between that substance and another in which the light travels at a different speed.

refraction: the bending of a ray of light as it passes from one material into another in which it travels at a different speed.

Santa Ana: a dry wind blowing from the Great Basin primarily to the Southern California coast, which can occur at any time of the year but is most frequent in winter.

solstice: either of two instants in the year when the sun is farthest north (the beginning of summer) or farthest south (the beginning of winter).

squall line: a narrow band of thunderstorms.

stationary front: a boundary separating two air masses that moves very slowly, if at all.

storm: a disturbance in the normal condition of the atmosphere.

storm track: the path followed by a traveling low.

stratocumulus: a low cloud, usually composed of water droplets, appearing as a patch, sheet, or layer having dark sections. The cloud elements may or may not be merged, but they are usually in orderly groups or wavy undulations; they are large, smooth, and flat-topped. When thin, a corona or iridescence may be seen. Pre-

cipitation rarely occurs.

stratus: a low cloud layer with a fairly uniform base. It is usually composed of small water droplets that may yield drizzle or a light snow.

subsidence: the sinking of air with subsequent warming by compression.

sun dog (mock sun): either of two bright spots that flank the sun at elevation in the sky, and appear 22° or more away from the sun. It is produced by refraction in hexagonal ice crystals that are oriented with long axes vertical. There is coloration, often limited to a reddish hue on the inner part of the phenomena.

sun-drawing-water: a phenomenon similar to crepuscular rays in which bright bands of light are discernible in hazy or dusty air because of scattered openings in a cloud layer.

thermal low: a non-frontal area of low atmospheric pressure formed by intense heating of the earth's surface.

tornado: a whirling column of air with a funnel-shaped cloud descending toward the earths' surface from a cumulonimbus cloud.

virga: streaks of water droplets or ice particles falling from a cloud and evaporating before they reach the earth's surface; frequently trail altocumulus and altostratus clouds but may also be seen below any precipitating cumulus-type cloud.

warm front: the leading edge of an advancing mass of warmer air that is replacing colder air in its path.

waterspout: a tornado formed over water.

wave cloud: clouds formed in the upper parts of waves induced in the air, usually by an obstacle such as a mountain range. They are stationary with respect to the object causing them and typically are lenticular.

weather: the short-term variations of temperature, pressure, wind, moisture, cloudiness, precipitation, and visibility of the atmosphere.

wind chill: the increased cooling of a body due to the motion of air.

SOURCES AND SUGGESTED READING

NOTE: *indicates an introductory work.
†indicates a technical work.

Air Pollution

Air Pollution by Richard Scorer; Pergamon Press, 1968.
Cleaning Our Environment by the Subcommittee on Environmental Improvement; American Chemical Society, Washingon, D.C., 1969.
*Fundamentals of Air Pollution** by Samuel J. Williamson; Addison-Wesley, 1973.
The Unclean Sky: A Meteorologist Looks at Air Pollution by Louis J. Battan; Anchor Books, Doubleday, 1966.

Aviation and Weather

Aviation Weather by William P. Nash and others; Weather Bureau and Federal Aviation Agency, United States Government Printing Office, Washington, D.C., 1965.
A Pilot's Meteorology by Malcolm W. Cagle and C. G. Halpine; Van Nostrand, Reinhold, 1970.
Weather Flying by Robert N. Buck; Macmillan, 1970.

Climate

"The Climate of Cities" by William P. Lowry; **Scientific American**, August 1967.
*Climate and Man's Environment: An Introduction to Applied Climatology** by John E. Oliver; John Wiley, 1973.
*Climates of North America,** World Survey of Climatology, Vol. II, edited by Reid A. Bryson and F. Kenneth Hare; Elsevier Scientific, 1974.
Climates of the United States by John L. Baldwin; United States Government Printing Office, Washington, D.C., 1973.
*The Climates of the United States** by Robert DeCourcy Ward; Ginn, 1925.
*Climate Through the Ages** by C. E. P. Brooks; McGraw-Hill, 1949.
*Climatic Atlas of the United States** by Stephen Sargent Visher; Harvard University Press, 1954.
*General Climatology** by Howard J. Critchfield; Prentice-Hall, 1960.
*An Introduction to Climate** (Fourth Edition) by Glenn T. Trewartha; McGraw-Hill, 1968.

Clouds

Cloud Physics and Cloud Seeding by Louis J. Battan; Anchor Books, Doubleday, 1962.
*Clouds of the World** by Richard Scorer; Stackpole Books, 1972.
International Cloud Atlas (Abridged Atlas) prepared and published by the World Meteorological Organization, Geneva, Switzerland, 1969.
The Science of the Clouds by R. A. R. Tricker; American Elsevier Publishing, 1970.

General Weather Information

*Climate and Weather** by John A. Day and Gilbert L. Sternes; Addison-Wesley, 1970.
†Dynamic Meteorology and Weather Forecasting** by C. L. Godske, T. Bergeron, J. Bjerknes, R. C. Bundgaard; American Meteorological Society, Boston, and Carnegie Institution of Washington, Washington, D.C., 1957.
*Elements of Meteorology** by R. W. Longley; John Wiley, 1970.
*Environmental Geoscience: Interaction Between Natural Systems and Man** by Arthur N. Strahler and Alan H. Strahler; Hamilton, 1973.
Eric Sloane's Weather Library (3 volumes) by Eric Sloane; Meredith Press, 1963.
From Raindrops to Volcanoes: Adventures with Sea Surface Meteorology by Duncan C. Blanchard; Anchor Books, Doubleday, 1967.
†Glossary of Meteorology** edited by Ralph E. Huschke; American Meteorological Society, Boston, 1959.
Hailstorms of the United States by Snowden D. Flora; University of Oklahoma Press, 1956.
Instant Weather Forecasting: A 24 Color Photograph Guide to Weather Forecasting from the Clouds, for Use by Farmers, Fishermen, Yachtsmen, Golfers, Holidaymakers, in fact Anyone to Whom the Weather in the Near Future is of Vital Importance by Alan Watts; Dodd, Mead, 1970.
*Introduction to the Atmosphere** by Herbert Riehl; McGraw-Hill, 1972.
*Introduction to Meteorology** by Franklyn W. Cole; John Wiley, 1970.
*Introduction to Meteorology** (Third Edition) by Sverre Petterssen; McGraw-Hill, 1969.
Jet Streams: How Do They Affect Our Weather? by Elmar R. Reiter; Anchor Books, Doubleday, 1967.
Man and the Winds by E. Aubert de la Rue; Philosophical Library, 1955.
†Numerical Weather Prediction** by George J. Haltiner; John Wiley, 1971.
1,001 Questions Answered About Storms and Other Natural Disasters by Barbara Tufty; Dodd, Mead, 1970.
1,001 Questions Answered About the Weather by Frank H. Forrester; Dodd, Mead, 1957.
Our American Weather by George H. T. Kimble; McGraw-Hill, 1955.
Radar Observes the Weather by Louis J. Battan; Anchor Books, 1962.
*The Restless Atmosphere** by F. K. Hare; Hutchinson University Library, London, 1968.
The Seasons: Life and Its Rhythms by Anthony Smith; Harcourt, Brace, 1970.
The Thunderstorm by Louis J. Battan; New American Library, 1964.
Tornadoes of the United States by Snowden D. Flora; University of Oklahoma Press, 1953.
Traveling Weatherwise in the U.S.A. by Edward Powers and James Witt; Dodd, Mead, 1972.
Watching for the Wind: The Seen and Unseen Influences on Local Weather by James G. Edinger; Anchor Books, Doubleday, 1967.
Weather by Philip D. Thompson, Robert O'Brien, and the Editors of Time-Life Books; Time-Life Books, 1968.
Weather and Health: An Introduction to Biometeorology by Helmut E. Landsberg; Anchor Books, Doubleday, 1969.

Weather Made Clear by Capt. David C. Holmes; Sterling, 1966.

Geography (Regional Climates)

The Cascades: Mountains of the Pacific Northwest edited by Roderick Peattie; Vanguard Press, 1949.

The Changing Mile by James Rodney Hastings and Raymond M. Turner; University of Arizona Press, 1965.

The Climate of Southern California by Harry P. Bailey; University of California Press, 1966.

†**"Climatology of Summer Fogs in the San Francisco Bay Area"** by Clyde Perry Patton; **University of California Publications in Geography**, Vol. X, University of California Press, 1957.

The Great Plains by Walter Prescott Webb; Grosset & Dunlap, 1931.

The Great Plains in Transition by Carl Frederick Kraenzel; University of Oklahoma Press, 1955.

North America: Its Countries and Regions by J. Wreford Watson; Frederick A. Praeger, 1967.

The North American Deserts by Edmund C. Jaeger; Stanford University Press, 1957.

The Pacific Coast Ranges edited by Roderick Peattie; Vanguard Press, 1946.

Patterns on the Land by Robert W. Durrenberger; National Press Books, 1967.

†**"Summer Sea Fogs of the Central California Coast"** by Horace R. Byers; **University of California Publications in Geography,** Vol. III edited by Carl O. Sauer and J. B. Leighly, University of California Press, 1931.

Weather of the San Francisco Bay Region by Harold Gilliam; University of California Press, 1970.

History

A Century of Weather Service by Patrick Hughes; Gordon and Breach, 1970.

Climate, Man, and History by Robert Claiborne; W. W. Norton & Company, 1970.

Early American Hurricanes 1492-1870 by David M. Ludlum; (Vol. 1, History of American Weather), American Meteorological Society, 1963.

Early American Winters I 1604-1820 by David M. Ludlum; (Vol. 2, History of American Weather), American Meteorological Society, 1966.

Early American Winters II 1821-1870 by David M. Ludlum; (Vol. 3, History of American Weather), American Meteorological Society, 1967.

Early American Tornadoes 1586-1870 by David M. Ludlum; (Vol. 4, History of American Weather), American Meteorological Society, 1970.

*****A History of the Theories of Rain** by W. E. Knowles Middleton; Franklin Watts, 1966.

*****Invention of the Meteorological Instruments** by W. E. Knowles Middleton; Johns Hopkins Press, 1969.

Man and the Sun by Jacquetta Hawkes; Random House, 1962.

Meteorologica by Aristotle, English translation by H. D. P. Lee; Harvard University Press, 1952.

Legend and Lore

Myths of the Sun: A Collection of Myths and Legends Concerning the Sun and Its Worship by William Tyler Olcott; Capricorn Books, 1967.

Weather Lore by R. Inwards, edited by E. L. Hawke; reprint by Dover Publications, 1970.

Weather Proverbs and Paradoxes by W. J. Humphreys; Williams and Wilkins, 1923.

Satellite Meteorology

Viewing Weather from Space by E. C. Barrett; Praeger, 1967.

Weather Satellites by Lester F. Hubert and Paul E. Lehr; Blaisdell, 1967.

Snow

Field Guide to Snow Crystals by Edward R. LaChapelle; University of Washington, 1969.

Snow Crystals by W. A. Bentley and W. J. Humphreys; Dover, 1964.

The Wonder of Snow by Corydon Bell; Hill and Wang, 1957.

Weather Modification

Harvesting the Clouds: Advances in Weather Modification by Louis J. Battan; Doubleday, 1969.

*****Inadvertent Climate Modification,** a report of the Study of Man's Impact on Climate; MIT Press, 1971.

†**Weather and Climate Modification** edited by W. N. Hess; John Wiley, 1974.

*****Weather and Climate Modification: Problems and Progress** by the Committee on Atmospheric Sciences; National Academy of Sciences, Washington, D.C., 1973.

The Weather Changers by D. S. Halacy, Jr.; Harper & Row, 1968.

Weather Phenomena

The Flight of the Thunderbolt (Second Edition) by Basil Schonland; The Clarendon Press, Oxford, 1964.

†**Introduction to Meteorological Optics** by R. A. R. Tricker; American Elsevier Publishing, 1970.

Light and Electricity in the Atmosphere by Hal Hellman; Holiday House, 1968.

†**Lightning** by Martin A. Uman; McGraw-Hill, 1969.

The Lightning Book by Peter E. Viemeister; MIT Press, 1972.

*****The Nature of Light and Colour in the Open Air** by M. Minnaert; Dover, 1954.

†**Physical Meteorology** by John C. Johnson; The Massachusetts Institute of Technology and John Wiley, 1954.

†**Physics of the Air** (Third Edition) by W. J. Humphreys; McGraw-Hill, 1940.

Understanding Lightning by Martin A. Uman; Bek Technical Publications, 1971.

Government Publications

(*Write to: United States Government Printing Office, Washington, D.C. 20402.*)

"Climates of the States," describes climates and weather of each state, with a local data summary for each weather station, and a state climatological summary.

"Climatic Guides," local data for some large cities and summary of general climate for their metropolitan areas.

"Climatological Data," a monthly issued for individual states or groups of states; contains daily weather measurements, monthly summaries of temperature and precipitation extremes, and an annual summary.

"Climatological Data, National Summary," a monthly condensation of data for selected United States weather stations; general summary of national weather conditions; summary of severe storm damage; special articles.

"Climatological Substation Summaries," similar to the summary issued in "Local Climatological Data" for various weather stations in each state that do not qualify as full-time weather offices.

"Daily Weather Maps, Weekly Series," a pamphlet containing a surface weather map for each day of the week; also temperature and precipitation charts.

"Local Climatological Data," monthly observational data for approximately 300 cities and towns relating to temperature, dew point, precipitation, pressure, sunshine, wind, sky cover.

"Local Climatological Data with Comparative Data," compiled annually for the same localities as the monthly "Local Climatological Data" publication, but including monthly and yearly summaries of the recorded data. There is a brief description of the local climate and a history of the weather station.

"Monthly Climatic Data for the World," surface and upper air data for a large number of selected worldwide stations.

"Selective Guide to Published Climatic Data Sources," Meteorological Records Documentation, Number 4.11.

"Storm Data," monthly data on the nature of severe storms by state.

"Weekly Weather and Crop Bulletin," weekly summary and charts of weather and its influence on crops; by states.

Periodicals

Weatherwise is the best periodical for the interested layman. Others listed here are of a more technical nature, suitable for the reader with some background in meteorology.

*Bulletin of the American Meteorological Society, American Meteorological Society, Boston; monthly.

†Journal of Applied Meteorology, American Meteorological Society, Boston; bimonthly.

†Journal of the Atmospheric Sciences, American Meteorological Society, Boston; eight issues annually.

Mariners Weather Log, Environmental Data Service, Silver Spring, Maryland; bimonthly.

Monthly Weather Review, United States Government Printing Office, Washington, D.C.; monthly.

Weather, Royal Meteorological Society, Bracknell, England; monthly.

Weatherwise, American Meteorological Society, Boston; bimonthly.

INDEX

Body type: Baskerville and News Gothic by Mackenzie & Harris, Inc., San Francisco, California. Display faces: Windsor, Windsor Outline and Koronna by Atherton's Typography, Inc., Palo Alto, California. Printed by Graphic Arts Center, Portland, Oregon. Bound by Lincoln & Allen Bookbinders, Portland, Oregon.

Designed by Dannelle Lazarus Pfeiffer.